# Good Practice in Safeguarding Adults

# Good Practice in Health, Social Care and Criminal Justice
## Edited by Jacki Pritchard

This series explores topics of current concern to professionals working in social care, health care and the probation service. Contributors are drawn from a wide variety of settings, both in the voluntary and statutory sectors.

*also in the series*

**Good Practice in Child Protection**
**A Manual for Professionals**
*Edited by Hilary Owen and Jacki Pritchard*
ISBN 978 1 85302 205 0

**Good Practice in Supervision**
**Statutory and Voluntary Organisations**
*Edited by Jacki Pritchard*
ISBN 978 1 85302 279 1

**Good Practice in Risk Assessment and Management 1**
*Edited by Jacki Pritchard and Hazel Kemshall*
ISBN 978 1 85302 338 5

**Good Practice in Risk Assessment and Risk Management 2**
**Key Themes for Protection, Rights and Responsibilities**
*Edited by Hazel Kemshall and Jacki Pritchard*
ISBN 978 1 85302 441 2

**Good Practice in Counselling People Who Have Been Abused**
*Edited by Zetta Bear*
ISBN 978 1 85302 424 5

**Good Practice in Working with Violence**
*Edited by Hazel Kemshall and Jacki Pritchard*
ISBN 978 1 85302 641 6

**Good Practice in Working with Victims of Violence**
*Edited by Hazel Kemshall and Jacki Pritchard*
ISBN 978 1 85302 768 0

**Good Practice with Vulnerable Adults**
*Edited by Jacki Pritchard*
ISBN 978 1 85302 982 0

**Good Practice in Adult Mental Health**
*Edited by Tony Ryan and Jacki Pritchard*
ISBN 978 1 84310 217 5

**Good Practice in Brain Injury Case Management**
*by Jackie Parker*
*Foreword by David J. Price*
ISBN 978 1 84310 315 8

Good Practice in Health, Social
Care and Criminal Justice

# GOOD PRACTICE in
# Safeguarding Adults
Working Effectively in Adult Protection

## Edited by **Jacki Pritchard**

Jessica Kingsley Publishers
London and Philadelphia

First published in 2008
by Jessica Kingsley Publishers
116 Pentonville Road
London N1 9JB, UK
and
400 Market Street, Suite 400
Philadelphia, PA 19106, USA

*www.jkp.com*

**Library of Congress Cataloging in Publication Data**
A CIP catalog record for this book is available from the Library of Congress

**British Library Cataloguing in Publication Data**
A CIP catalogue record for this book is available from the British Library

ISBN 978 1 84310 699 9

Printed and bound in Great Britain by
Athenaeum Press, Gateshead, Tyne and Wear

This book is dedicated to Christopher Weston, Priya Biyani and Barbara Salvin. Without their help and support in my working life, I would not have been able to continue working whilst dealing with the aftermath of the flood which occurred in Sheffield on 25 June 2007.

# ACKNOWLEDGEMENTS

First of all I want to thank all my authors who have contributed to this book. They each have huge workloads, a large number of work commitments and are generally over-loaded. I know only too well if you want something doing well ask a busy person because they will get the job done. And so they have and I am extremely grateful to each one of them!

I also feel very privileged that some members of Beyond Existing agreed to work together to contribute a chapter. I know how important it was for them to do this. I am very proud of them all.

I am indebted to Mary Sarjeant, who, through her own professionalism and wisdom, has given me great support and insight, which in turn has helped my own personal and professional development.

As always I want to thank all the victims of abuse whom I meet during the course of my own practice. It is only through them that I know what needs to be written.

# CONTENTS

# INTRODUCTION

## JACKI PRITCHARD

It is seven years since I edited *Good Practice with Vulnerable Adults*, also in this series (Pritchard 2001), and I would like to think that we have made good progress in the field of adult protection work since then. However, I do get very frustrated that we are still moving at what seems to me quite a slow pace; sometimes I hear myself saying the same things I said 20 years ago. Nevertheless, we have moved on and there has been a need for a new volume to follow on from the original book.

Before sitting down to write this Introduction, I went to re-read what I had said in the Introduction to *Good Practice with Vulnerable Adults* and then I asked myself the question: 'How much have we progressed in the last seven years?' There is no doubt that we have moved on and there have been many positive developments but some of my fundamental concerns are still the same. I still do not think we are learning enough from past and current experiences in child protection/safeguarding children work. In all the child abuse inquiries that have been undertaken a recurring finding has been regarding poor communication between agencies. In adult protection work both *No Secrets* (DH and Home Office 2000) and *Safeguarding Adults* (ADSS 2005) emphasise the importance of inter-agency working and working in partnership. We all talk about it every day of our working lives, but do we really communicate or, rather, do we do it effectively enough? In this volume, Deborah Kitson discusses the lessons learnt from inquiries regarding vulnerable adults in residential settings and makes us question whether we have moved on. It is something we need to consider in all aspects of adult protection work.

I have always felt that in the UK as we have moved into specialisms some professionals have become too precious about their own work. Consequently, communication between the practitioners in different specialist fields sometimes does not happen as it should and this can have dangerous repercussions for the vulnerable adults who need to be protected. My own research interests have been focused on the links between child abuse, domestic violence and adult abuse. Therefore, I am delighted that District Judge Marilyn Mornington, along with Jamieson Mornington, agreed to address the issues of domestic violence again, having contributed to the previous volume. Their chapter also addresses two issues which I feel are currently not given enough attention in adult protection work; first, the law[1] and second, honour-based crime (please note that whereas footnotes were used in previous books in the series, this volume uses endnotes, to be found at the end of each chapter).

We need to broaden our perspective when thinking about adult abuse; we should not only be thinking about producing robust policies and procedures in order to promote good practice. We still need to go back regularly and revisit the question 'What is adult abuse?', because certain actions and behaviours are being missed which could constitute abuse. We have got to keep moving on from thinking as we did two decades ago that adult abuse is solely about carers' stress. We now know that the issue is much more complex, but we need to acknowledge that other subject areas need to be considered as well. More attention also needs to be given to using both a criminal justice model and a welfare model; the models can complement each other and do not have to be used exclusively. This was a theme which was introduced in the previous volume and since then there have been developments in both legislation and related guidance (e.g. *Achieving Best Evidence*: Home Office 2002, Criminal Justice System 2007).

At the beginning of my Introduction in *Good Practice with Vulnerable Adults* I discussed the concept of vulnerability and this is very topical now whilst people debate the use of the term 'vulnerable adult' as defined in *No Secrets* (DH and Home Office 2000, pp.8–9). In this volume I wanted to include vulnerable adults who in my opinion have not been given enough attention in adult protection literature: people with brain injuries; older prisoners; and adults within the black and minority ethnic communities.

Research is a necessary requirement to inform us about what should constitute good practice, but in adult protection it is also vital to give victims a voice so that policymakers and practitioners can learn more about their needs and how they can be helped. One of my major concerns is that with all the emphasis on target performance indicators, standards, star ratings, paperwork and debate about correct use of terminology (which are all very necessary) we sometimes lose sight of the people who really matter – the victims of abuse – and what they have to say. They are given a voice in this book which has a recurring theme; that is, the importance of long-term work. Again I feel this is often not addressed properly in many cases because practitioners are usually working under extreme pressures and carrying heavy caseloads, which means that they are doing crisis-intervention work and there is little time for anything else, for example preventative work. If the statutory sector cannot undertake the long-term therapeutic work with victims, then resources must be sought from the voluntary and independent sectors and built into effective and detailed protection plans. The work leading up to this stage in intervention is given attention in a chapter on risk assessment and how it should be undertaken properly in adult protection work.

There are many aspects of adult protection work and not everything can be included in one volume. Therefore, I gave a lot of thought to what I wanted to include – what would be most helpful to practitioners and what is relevant and topical. I then approached people who I know are grounded in good practice and feel passionately about adult protection in the same way that I do. Consequently, the chapters cover a range of topics concerned with policy, practice and guidance development; legislation; abuse in institutions; and the role of the Commission for Social Care Inspection.

The *Good Practice* series is about just that – good practice: something about which I feel passionately. In training courses I run I am constantly reminding practitioners across the disciplines that we must strive to promote good professional practice and each one of us must take responsibility for our own practice. We are living and working in a blame culture. I constantly hear managers and workers venting about 'too much paperwork' and 'not enough time to do the job properly'. Adult protection work is not an 'add-on' to the day job: it is integral to what every worker is doing in their day-to-day practice. Morally and professionally everyone has a duty to protect adults who are being abused and that has to be made a major priority.

Finally, a word about terminology; I think a lot of time and energy can be wasted on debating at length on this. However, I do feel strongly that we need to avoid using jargon which will confuse the service users we are supporting. So when in doubt I tend to ask the service users what they think. In my current research project victims of abuse have said they understand what 'protection' means, but they are confused by the term 'safeguarding'. Most of them also do not have a problem with using both the terms 'victim' and 'survivor'. So, within this book the reader will find all these terms and I have left it up to each author to decide on their own use of terminology.

My hope in editing this book remains the same as in the previous work; that is: 'The chapters will illustrate that effective work can be undertaken to prevent abuse but also that there can be positive outcomes for victims if work is undertaken with them in the long-term' (Pritchard 2001, p.12).

**NOTE**

1   This will be addressed in the *Good Practice* series in a forthcoming volume: Pritchard, J. (ed.) *Good Practice in the Law and Safeguarding Adults: Criminal Justice and Adult Protection.*

# REFERENCES

Association of Directors of Social Services (ADSS) (2005) *Safeguarding Adults: A National Framework of Standards for Good Practice and Outcomes in Adult Protection Work*. London: ADSS.

Criminal Justice System (2007) *Achieving Best Evidence in Criminal Proceedings: Guidance on Interviewing Victims and Witnesses, and Using Special Measures*. London: Criminal Justice System.

Department of Health (DH) and Home Office (2000) *No Secrets: Guidance on Developing and Implementing Multi-Agency Policies and Procedures to Protect Vulnerable Adults from Abuse*. London: DH.

Home Office (2002) *Achieving Best Evidence in Criminal Proceedings: Guidance for Vulnerable or Intimidated Witnesses including Children*. London: Home Office Communication Directorate.

Pritchard, J. (ed.) (2001) *Good Practice with Vulnerable Adults*. London: Jessica Kingsley Publishers.

# CHAPTER 1

# NO SECRETS, SAFEGUARDING ADULTS AND ADULT PROTECTION

## GARY FITZGERALD

### BACKGROUND

Despite the increased attention given to the need to enable protection for vulnerable adults, only one statutory document currently exists within England – *No Secrets* – and this provides a framework within which agencies are required to cooperate (DH and Home Office 2000). Within Wales, the Welsh Assembly produced a similar statutory document at the same time *In Safe Hands* – (SSIW 2000); while Scotland has recently gone further and enacted primary legislation, the Adult Support and Protection (Scotland) Act 2007. In addition, there are a number of other documents, produced by regulators such as the Commission for Social Care Inspection (CSCI) and the Association of Directors of Social Services (ADSS), but these do not have a statutory base and represent either agreements between agencies, such as the CSCI *Safeguarding Adults Protocol* (CSCI, ADSS and ACPO 2007), or good practice guides, such as the ADSS *Safeguarding Adults* document (ADSS 2005).

In the UK, awareness of adult abuse issues really began to be established in the late 1980s, although some limited evidence had begun to emerge as early as the previous decade (Baker 1975; Eastman 1984). Kent County Council produced the first guidance on elder abuse in 1987, and over the next several years other local authorities followed their lead and often mirrored their document. By the turn of the next decade a survey by Hildrew (1991) had established that 11 local authorities had written adult protection guidelines, 26 had functioning drafts and 12 were actively seeking to develop them. It was a slow evolution of understanding that eventually began to include other adults too, including those who had learning disabilities or mental health problems (Brown and Keating 1998). A significant backdrop to this evolution, however, was the struggle by many statutory agencies to appreciate the full extent and complexity of the child abuse scandals and deaths that were emerging from the mid-1970s onward, and this had some impact on their capacity and willingness to address potential abuse within other groups who were also vulnerable.

Not surprisingly, the development of protective systems within adult protection was somewhat haphazard as they inevitably lacked any central coordination, guidance or commitment, but they served to focus attention on what had previously been a neglected area of social policy. In England and Wales, the Department of Health (Social Services Inspectorate) (DH [SSI]) began to publish research documentation regarding abuse. These included *Confronting Elder Abuse* (1992) and *No Longer Afraid* (1993), which gave guidance on elder abuse within people's own homes. Meanwhile, in 1995, the Law Commission consulted on mental capacity issues (Law Commission 1995) and observed that there was widespread consensus on the need to reform emergency protection powers available in cases of suspected abuse. As a consequence, they prepared an outline bill to grant social workers some powers to intervene where they believed an adult may be facing harm or exploitation. It proposed that:

- social services departments should have a duty to investigate allegations of abuse

- magistrates' courts should be authorised to issue entry warrants, temporary protection orders and removal orders in relation to adults experiencing abuse

- a new offence should be created to address obstruction of an officer acting under such a magistrate's order.

This initiative was not, however, supported by successive governments and instead, in 2000, the then Health Minister, John Hutton, launched the *No Secrets* document as governmental guidance, under Section 7 of the Local Authority Social Services Act 1970. As such, while the document did not have the full force of statute, there was a clear expectation that it should be complied with by local authorities unless local circumstances indicated exceptional reasons to justify a variation. This is a key point. The publication of *No Secrets* carried an inherent statement of political will by central government that empowered local authorities and other agencies to act.

### NO SECRETS

Local authorities were given the lead responsibility for coordinating the new procedures outlined within *No Secrets* but Hutton indicated that all agencies were expected to be involved, including general practitioners (GPs) and hospital staff who were perceived as often the first to suspect abuse. As a minimum, *No Secrets* required local authorities to develop multi-agency policies for the protection of vulnerable adults, and to do so in conjunction with a wide variety of agencies including, but not limited to, all commissioners and providers of health and social care services including primary care groups, regulators of such care services and appropriate criminal justice agencies. The challenge facing local authorities was that *No Secrets* carried an expectation that all identified agencies would wish to cooperate in both the development and subsequent implementation of adult protection procedures, but it lacked the necessary powers to compel those agencies to participate. For a significant number of those bodies this new requirement had to compete against increasing financial and work pressures, and against duties that were placed upon them by statute. Consequently, participation in the development of policies varied considerably according to the priorities and commitment of individual agencies or, perhaps more accurately, the priorities and commitment of individuals within those agencies.

A key point of *No Secrets* was that it clearly proposed a significant framework for adult protection, including:

- how to define who may be at risk of abuse, and in what way

- that agencies should consider the merits of establishing a multi-agency management committee – often called an adult protection committee (and latterly, in some parts of the country, a safeguarding adults board)

- that the roles and responsibilities, authority and accountability of each agency should be clarified. It did not specify who should 'run' investigations but indicated that each organisation should have a lead officer with responsibility for protection issues. Additionally, it suggested clear lines of responsibility, from the person alerting the potential abuse to the investigating officer, to the responsibility of the line manager and the adult protection committee

- that there should be joint protocols to govern specific areas of practice such as sharing of information, confidentiality and the conduct of joint interviews. It suggested clear pathways of communication and definitive guidance for all staff about when it is appropriate to break confidence and who should be consulted

- that agencies should have a training strategy for all levels of staff. As well as seeing this within the context of prevention, it envisaged basic awareness training, lead officer investigator training and manager training

- that all staff, service users, carers and other organisations should be aware of the adult protection guidance, policy and procedure for their local area, and know where to go if they had a concern

- that referrals and investigations should be monitored in order to learn from experiences

- that service commissioners, at both national and local level, should ensure that all documents, such as service specifications, invitations to tender and service contracts, fully reflect policies for the protection of vulnerable adults

- that appropriate services should be established for local population needs, including counselling services, refuges and services to support abusers in stopping their abuse

- suggestions on what should be included in procedures for the investigation of individual cases, and how allegations and investigations should be managed. There was no specific description of where referrals should go, other than there should be a place identified and agreed by all partners

- that there should be a procedure for assessment and decision-making, evaluated annually. It also placed a responsibility on all voluntary and independent organisations to devise their own policy and procedure for responding to abuse.

But, while *No Secrets* significantly contributed to the development of an adult protection environment, it suffered from the lack of a legislative framework, and it lacked the necessary powers often needed to ensure effective protection for vulnerable adults. It proposed a general infrastructure and understanding of abuse and of the processes required to coordinate responses, but it failed to address the specifics of what was needed to ensure a consistency of approach. This often meant that local authorities were operating in isolation from each other and this led the Association of Directors of Social Services (ADSS) in 2003 to establish a coordinating central adult protection committee, chaired by a Director of Social Services. A number of regional committees also naturally evolved as part of this process, thus giving adult protection a sense of coordinated direction as well as the opportunity to share knowledge, information and experience.

Coordination however requires the establishment of common under-standings on a variety of factors in order to ensure consistency and a genuine comparison of 'like for like'. For example, to understand why some areas began to have greater referral rates than others as part of the *No Secrets* process required a common starting point; the definition of such referrals needed to be consistent between those areas; and the point at which such contact was being identified as a 'referral' needed to be equally consistent. Effectively, protection interventions needed to be on an equal basis and this required a common interpretation of definitions that was missing from *No Secrets*. The Action on Elder Abuse *Data Monitoring Report* (AEA 2006) adequately demonstrated the variance between local authority areas. While it found that the quality of life and wellbeing of many vulnerable adults was improving as the issue of adult abuse rose up the agenda, and as local authorities and partners tackled abuse in an increasingly systematic and coherent manner, there were questions over the validity of many outcomes for too many adults in vulnerable situations.

Key conclusions from the AEA report highlighted a number of the inherent challenges of *No Secrets* implementation:

- There remained confusion around the roles and responsibilities that organisations, agencies and staff played. Some committees complained of poor attendance and lack of commitment from various agencies at a local level. A number complained that agencies sent inappropriate representatives, unable to either make relevant decisions or to progress them at an appropriate level or speed.

- Very few adult protection referrals were made by members of the general public and this suggested that the issue was still not understood or owned by the wider community. Yet in many ways these were the people who were needed to trigger referrals and alert statutory agencies to abusive situations, as well as having a role in encouraging vulnerable adults to exercise choice, control and autonomy within abusive relationships or family situations.

The nine local authorities who participated in the project had received 639 referrals during the period surveyed and, of those referrals,

- only 0.78 per cent (5) had resulted in a decision to proceed with a criminal prosecution. While there may have been decisions taken outside of the collection period and which subsequently affected this figure, the reality was that the majority of referrals did not result in criminal prosecutions. However, in 7.5 per cent (48) of cases the police had taken some form of action (AEA 2006, p.16)

- paid care workers were identified in 10.2 per cent (65) of cases. Yet disciplinary action was recorded as an outcome in only 1.6 per cent (10) of circumstances and referrals to the Protection of Vulnerable Adults list were only shown in 1.4 per cent (9) of cases (AEA 2006, p.16).

Perhaps more important, the vast majority of outcomes for the adults experiencing abuse were recorded as 'Increased Monitoring' (23.8% (152), and detailed information was not collected on what this actually meant in terms of who was carrying out the monitoring, what the timescale was, and what its purpose was. Of particular concern was the number of outcomes described as 'No Further Action' – 12.5% (80) (AEA 2006, p.15).

What emerged from the project was a picture of adult protection practitioners who felt unable to intervene in abusive situations unless there was significant evidence, preferably supported by a 'competent' witness to compel prosecution. This perception was adequately described by one adult protection coordinator, in response to an AEA questionnaire (AEA 2007), who expressed anxiety at the regular need to rely on the cooperation of an alleged perpetrator to gain access to a potential victim, criticised the inability to legally enter premises without permission, and described a failure to impose sanctions on those who actively obstructed investigations. Overall, the responses to the AEA survey implied a 'silo' approach, whereby the cross-over in terms of experience within other abuse environments (e.g. child protection or domestic violence) was not being recognised, and this was particularly relevant in terms of domestic violence, where many of the strategies were directly transferable into other abusive family situations. Effectively, options in law that were suitable for use within the adult protection arena were being missed because the links were not being made.

## SAFEGUARDING ADULTS

Against this background, in October 2005, ADSS published *Safeguarding Adults*, which it described as a national framework of standards for good practice and outcomes in adult protection work. Its publication caused a degree of confusion as to the status of the document, with some agencies perceiving it as a successor to *No Secrets*, and the Adult Protection Forum in Northern Ireland issuing it widely with departmental approval. In fact, it did not replace *No Secrets* and it had no statutory status. It was intended to describe best practice, define aspirations and propose a set of good practice standards which could be used as an audit tool and guide by all those implementing adult protection work. However, in view of this confusion, it is important to clearly differentiate between the status of *No Secrets* as a statutory document, and that of *Safeguarding Adults* as an industry-based good practice guide.

A key point made very early on within *Safeguarding Adults* was that the terminology used in adult protection was outdated, citing the change of direction in *Fair Access to Care Services* (DH 2002) as an example of the philosophical switch in approach, away from responding to the 'vulnerability' of someone and instead responding to the 'risk posed by abuse and neglect'. CSCI *et al.* accepted this argument in their *Safeguarding Adults Protocol* (2007), stating: 'the Commission supports the reasoning behind this change, which moves away from locating the cause of abuse with the victim and acknowledges that, whilst the statutory framework differs, safeguarding adults work has equal status with safeguarding children' (p.2). Indeed this philosophical argument has now been accepted by the government, and is evidenced in the title of the Safeguarding Vulnerable Groups Act 2006.

It is important, however, to recognise that debates of this type have little impact unless they have a fundamental effect on the quality of life of those to whom the strategies are directed. Age and disability clearly do not by themselves give grounds for abuse and, to that extent, there is no such thing as a 'vulnerable adult'. It is circumstances, environment, opportunity and other people that invariably create vulnerability, thereby creating the potential for abuse. While this is interesting at an academic level it will only be meaningful if it is translated into change 'on the ground', otherwise it becomes no more than navel-gazing and should not get in the way of ensuring safety, security and personal control by adults at risk of abuse. Terminology may have a place in the greater scheme of things, and in certain circumstances can be crucial, but only if it assists in the work and does not hamper or confuse it.

*Safeguarding Adults* proposes eleven standards against which adult protection should measure progress, and these cover:

- partnership working and ownership of the work
- prevention of abuse within the community and care provision
- training
- inter-agency working and consequent roles and responsibilities, and processes
- accessibility, citizenship and the role of service users as key partners.

A concern expressed by adult protection practitioners however was that it placed expectations on some agencies without the consequent authority to enforce or compel participation. On the one hand, this reflected an attempt to address the frustrations experienced by many adult protection committees that key agencies were never, or were rarely, present at the table, but on the other hand it demonstrated the inherent weakness of a system that lacked legislative underpinning. The Minister for Social Care, Ivan Lewis, articulated this aptly in his oral evidence to the Joint Committee on Human Rights in June 2007 when he observed (in relation to human rights) that:

> if you simply exhorted and talked of best practice without legislative underpinning then inevitably public bodies would find ways not to completely implement their obligations, so an element of legislation is, I think, really important. Do we need to legislate to secure every objective and every outcome? No, we most definitely do not. Do I think having an element of this enshrined in law helps? It does. (House of Commons/House of Lords 2007a, p.72)

A second concern worth noting, however, is that *Safeguarding Adults* places great emphasis on the *No Secrets* definition of a vulnerable adult as someone 'who is or may be eligible for community care services'. This gives cause for concern if it is used in conjunction with the Government's guidance as to who may be eligible for community care support in *Fair Access to Care*, i.e. it becomes an exclusive rather than an inclusive approach. *Fair Access to Care* was never intended to be used in an adult protection context and, in this regard, *Safeguarding Adults* required greater clarity. By repeatedly emphasising the community care needs of potential recipients of protection without indicating an appropriate response for those people who do not need external support but want help to stop the abuse, the document runs a grave risk of being misunderstood, and thereby wrongly excluding significant sections of the population.

This approach to definitions had been previously challenged by the House of Commons Health Select Committee Inquiry into elder abuse in 2004, which recommended that

> the *No Secrets* definition of elder abuse should be expanded to include those individuals who do not require community care services, for example older people living in their own homes without the support of health and social care services, and those who can take care of themselves. (House of Commons/Health Committe 2003–4, p.9)

In response, the government sought to clarify the intent of the *No Secrets* definition, by indicating that the reference to 'community care services' was not intended to be exclusive: *No Secrets* relates to abuse or neglect experienced by vulnerable adults no matter their age or living arrangements. It defines a vulnerable adult as 'a person who is or may be in need of community care services by reason of mental or other disability, age or illness; and who is unable to take care of him- or herself, or unable to protect him- or herself against significant harm or exploitation' (DH and Home Office 2000, pp.9–10). This definition is wide and includes individuals in receipt of social care services, those in receipt of other services such as health care, and those who may not be in receipt of care services.

In reality this debate was not so much about community care services or indeed about attempts to exclude people facing abuse from access to protection. Instead, it reflected the complexity of seeking to define and quantify interactions that occur between human beings, e.g. at what point do harsh words regularly exchanged between two individuals become abuse for one of them; at what point does the power relationship become imbalanced in favour of one and to the detriment of another? Clearly there is a need for intelligent intervention that ensures the use of appropriate strategies (e.g. someone facing domestic violence is better served by support under the Domestic Violence, Crime and Victims Act 2004 than through *No Secrets* initiatives) but the key point is that an apparent 'victim' should not have to demonstrate a dependence in order to access adult protection support, any more than would someone facing racial abuse. Equally an apparent 'victim' should get no less support if channelled through *No Secrets* than through alternative legislative routes such as the Domestic Violence Act.

Notwithstanding some of the concerns engendered by the *Safeguarding Adults* document, it remains an aspirational publication that sets a number of reasonable goals which adult protection should aim to achieve. While some local authorities have chosen to adopt it in its entirety, many others have dipped into for those parts that work to their advantage and have chosen to ignore others. This is perhaps the best way forward. In reality, without the enactment of legislation, it is inevitable that agencies and authorities will evolve strategies and policies that accord with their own local needs and histories and will choose to await the inevitable changes that an Act of Parliament must bring.

## LEGISLATION

The development of adult protection systems and processes is at an early stage. The foundations have been laid with the introduction of *No Secrets*, supported by 'industry' initiatives such as *Safeguarding Adults*, but these will not by themselves achieve the societal change needed to effectively challenge and reduce adult abuse. They lack the required duties placed upon key agencies that we see within the child protection field, and therefore will inevitably be limited in their wider impact. They have, however, created the necessary environment that has led to increased focus and attention on adult abuse, and they have contributed toward an impetus for change. The next step must be the introduction of legislation that enshrines the structures of *No Secrets* with many of the concepts of *Safeguarding Adults*.

It is important to note however that legislation by itself cannot deliver the levels of protection and intervention that people would like. Legislation on its own is not the panacea that can guarantee safeguarding in each and every situation. It can only be one option among a range that must include the education of society to alter their perceptions and responses to vulnerability, and that challenges discriminatory practices. In that regard the lessons from 20 years of addressing domestic violence are worthy of note – changing societal attitudes involved a multi-strand approach to the issue that mobilised diverse agencies and governments in a partnership approach over a long period of time. Nothing less will work effectively here either.

In Scotland, the Adult Support and Protection (Scotland) Act 2007 is very similar to *No Secrets*, although it includes circumstances in which the wishes of an adult with capacity may be over-ruled.[1] It:

- establishes a general principle on intervention in an adult's affairs
- defines adults at risk
- specifies a council's duty to make inquiries
- establishes a duty of cooperation among statutory bodies
- confirms how and when investigation visits may be undertaken
- enshrines in law the concept of assessment orders, removal orders against abusers and the protection of a moved person's property
- includes the right to ban abusers from the family home and the duties of the police if banning orders are ignored
- establishes statutory Adult Protection Committees, and defines their membership and procedures
- addresses obstruction and offences by corporate bodies.

A key point is that it has moved the debate away from the concept that adult protection can be achieved through the authority to act (the power) and switched it to a requirement to do so (the duty).

The arguments for legislative change in England are becoming well rehearsed and the Minister for Social Care, Ivan Lewis, indicated at the elder abuse prevalence launch (2007) a willingness to explore this option as part of his intended review of *No Secrets*. What is clear is that current legislation is piecemeal and is often unknown to the key players who are operating on behalf of an abused person. Invariably, adult protection staff express concern at the failure of bodies and individuals to share information – seen as a consistent theme of failure in child protection inquiries – and at the inability in law to access property to assess the needs of a vulnerable adult with capacity, or enter premises to remove people for their own protection. This last point, however, represents a significant area of disagreement within the adult protection field, between those who believe it is necessary at times to over-rule the wishes and decisions of an adult with capacity in their 'best interests', and those who hold the view that such actions would be tantamount to further institutional abuse of an adult who had already suffered an abusive experience. In this regard, the experiences within domestic violence are worth noting as such direct intervention has often had limited success, partly because victims invariably seek 'resolution' of their situation rather than 'prosecution' of the perpetrator.

Significant concern however is often expressed at the inability (and at times unwillingness) of the current criminal justice system to address adult abuse. In part this is explained by the apparent difficulties in establishing the competency of the victim to give evidence, but elsewhere it is argued that there is an inherent prejudice by many judges who feel that special witness measures are not right and who therefore resist their use. Basically, it is suggested that a vulnerable adult has to jump through a number of hurdles to achieve justice: (1) getting *No Secrets* triggered in the first place (whether through failures in regulation, prevarication in care provision, or exclusion through criteria); (2) getting a response from the police that prioritises the crime sufficiently up the agenda to warrant action; (3) getting the Crown Prosecution Service to accept the prosecution; and (4) finding a judge willing to allow special measures. In response to an AEA questionnaire (adult protection legislation consultation, AEA 2007) one practitioner suggested that any protective approaches stopped at the door of the court room and that anyone with a disability – whether physical, mental or age related – faced automatic institutional discrimination; that competency was judged as equal between the perpetrator and the victim and defence solicitors consequently operated without restriction in furtherance of the needs of their clients.

Whatever the arguments about the responsiveness of criminal justice agencies it is clear that there needs to be a relevant duty to act placed upon statutory agencies, a consequent duty to investigate allegations of abuse placed upon adult protection, regulators and care providers alike, and a clear duty of involvement at all levels by relevant agencies. There also needs to be legislative timescales for alerts, investigations and feedback, and the right to demand access to information from independent sector care providers and regulators.

Interventions in adult protection should follow the clear logic of 'positive action' found in domestic violence cases. Where there is evidence of a criminal offence statutory agencies should take positive action against the perpetrator of abuse and failures to take such action should be justified in every case. As inferred previously, it should also be recognised that a criminal prosecution may not always be the preferred or desired outcome of the victim, and that interventions should therefore be measured against the potential impact on that victim. Similar principles can and should be applied in situations of neglect. It should be possible to take positive action against a perpetrator of neglect whilst respecting the autonomy and wishes of the victim. Conversely in some cases it may be necessary, due to the nature of the offence and the remaining risk, to proceed with formal action which is against the expressed wishes of the victim. These are the balances necessary when seeking to address the protection of adults who experience abuse and, to a large degree, this is a good indicator as to why screening/risk assessment processes should only be *tools* in the hands of practitioners. They should not be a replacement for human analysis and intervention.

## THE FUTURE

Fundamentally, the purpose of *No Secrets, Safeguarding Adults* or any new legislation must be to provide balanced and acceptable protection for adults experiencing abuse. Whatever the difficulties that may be inherent in some of the current policies or procedures, there is merit in seeking to use, as far as possible, the range of legislative options that are available.[2] These include (not exclusively):

- Domestic Violence, Crime and Victims Act 2004
- Sexual Offences Act 2003
- Offences Against the Person Act 1861
- Theft and Deception Acts 1968, 1978 and 1996
- Police and Criminal Evidence Act 1970
- Youth Justice and Criminal Evidence Act 1999
- Human Rights Act 1998.

The Joint Committee on Human Rights, while specifically addressing the issue of elder abuse, made a profound statement that would equally apply to abuse in general, whether perpetrated because of age or disability:

> In our view, elder abuse is a serious and severe human rights abuse which is perpetrated on vulnerable older people who often depend on their abusers to provide them with care. Not only is it a betrayal of trust, it would also, in certain circumstances, amount to a criminal offence. (House of Commons/House of Lords 2007a, p.11)

This statement sums up the reality of adult protection and adequately highlights the experiences of those for whom protective systems and processes have been created. In 2000 *No Secrets* stated very clearly the objectives of adult protection. These have not changed and should remain the measurement against which we should judge the success of structures created to enable intervention and support:

> The aim should be to create a framework for action within which all responsible agencies work together to ensure a coherent policy for the protection of vulnerable adults at risk of abuse and a consistent and effective response to any circumstances giving ground for concern or formal complaints or expressions of anxiety. (DH and Home Office 2000, p.6)

It is the victim that matters in this process and, with this in mind, such an objective must surely challenge everyone involved to act to the fullest extent and to seek the tools, wherever they may be, to ensure that we provide that protection and support.

## NOTES

1   For full discussion see K. Mackay, 'Scottish legislative framework for supporting and protecting adults', in J. Pritchard (ed.) *Good Practice in the Law and Safeguarding Adults: Criminal Justice and Adult Protection*. London: Jessica Kingsley Publishers (forthcoming).

2   For further discussion see J. Pritchard (ed.) *Good Practice in the Law and Adult Protection*. London: Jessica Kingsley Publishers (forthcoming).

## REFERENCES

Action on Elder Abuse (AEA) (2006) *Adult Protection Data Collection and Reporting Requirements*. London: AEA.

Action on Elder Abuse (AEA) (2007) *Consultation Paper on the Potential for Adult Protection Legislation in England, Wales and Northern Ireland*. London: AEA.

Association of Directors of Social Services (ADSS) (2005) *Safeguarding Adults*. London: ADSS.

Baker, A. (1975) 'Granny bashing'. *Modern Geriatrics 5*, pp.20–4.

Brown, H. and Keating, F. (1998) 'We're doing it already...' Adult protection in mental health services'. *Journal of Psychiatric and Mental Health Nursing 5*, pp.273–80.

Commission for Social Care Inspection (CSCI), Association of Directors of Social Services (ADSS) and the Association of Chief Police Officers (ACPO) (2007) *Safeguarding Adults Protocol and Guidance*. London: CSCI.

Department of Health (DH) (2002) *Fair Access to Care Services: Guidance on Eligibility Criteria for Adult Social Care*, Circular LAC (2002) 13.

Department of Health (DH) (2004) *The Government's Response to the Recommendations and Conclusions of the Health Select Committee's Inquiry into Elder Abuse*. London: The Stationery Office.

Department of Health (Social Services Inspectorate) (DH (SSI)) (1992) *Confronting Elder Abuse: An SSI London Region Survey*. London: SSI.

Department of Health (Social Services Inspectorate) (DH (SSI)) (1993) *No Longer Afraid: The Safeguard of Older People in Domestic Settings*. London: HMSO.

Department of Health (DH) and Home Office (2000) *No Secrets: Guidance on Developing and Implementing Multi-Agency Policies and Procedures to Protect Vulnerable Adults from Abuse*. London: DH.

Eastman, M. (1984) *Old Age Abuse*. Mitcham: Age Concern.

Hildrew, M. A. (1991) 'New age problem'. *Social Work Today 22*, 49, pp.15–17.

House of Commons Health Committee (2003–4) *Elder Abuse, Volume I: Report Together with Formal Minutes* (HC 111-I). London: HMSO.

House of Commons/House of Lords, Joint Committee on Human Rights (2007a) *The Human Rights of Older People in Health Care, Volume II: Oral and Written Evidence* (HL Paper 156-II) (HC 378-II). London: HMSO.

Law Commission (1995) *Mental Incapacity*. Report Number 231. London: HMSO.

Local Social Services Act 1970. London: HMSO

Social Services Inspectorate Wales (SSIW) (2000) *In Safe Hands* (part of *Protection of Vulnerable Adults in Wales: a Consultation Pack*). Cardiff: National Assembly for Wales, SSIW.

## STATUTES

Adult Support and Protection (Scotland) Act 2007. London: The Stationery Office

Domestic Violence, Crime and Victims Act 2004. London: The Stationery Office

Human Rights Act 1998. London: HMSO

Local Social Services Act 1970. London: HMSO.

Offences Against the Person Act 1861. London: HMSO

Police and Criminal Evidence Act 1970. London: HMSO

Safeguarding Vulnerable Groups Act 2006. London: The Stationery Office

Sexual Offences Act 2003. London: The Stationery Office

Theft Act 1968. London: HMSO

Theft Act 1978. London: HMSO

Theft (Amendment) Act 1996. London: HMSO

Youth Justice and Criminal Evidence Act 1999. London: HMSO

# CHAPTER 2

# 'MILLSTONE TO MAINSTREAM'
## THE DEVELOPMENT OF VULNERABLE ADULT POLICY IN NORTH WALES

**ARWEL WYN OWEN**

## INTRODUCTION

My involvement with the publication of two consequential policy documents on the protection of vulnerable adults in North Wales, over a period of seven years, has given me an insight into the incremental development of vulnerable adult policy. I hope to use that experience to offer some observations on the process of producing and publishing multi-agency guidelines. Alongside this historical analysis I shall propose some thoughts on how vulnerable adult policy can be implemented with some consideration of the subsequent impact of the North Wales policy documentation upon social care practice. The arrangements applied in North Wales do not provide a panacea or necessarily a model policy document but may provide some useful pointers and an outline of potential pitfalls as well as areas of good practice for those involved in adult protection.

## BACKGROUND

In 1998 a DCI within North Wales Police initiated a multi-agency meeting of six local authority areas, the then North Wales Health Authority and three NHS Health Trusts to review our collective response to issues relating to adult protection. This meeting was called following the progress which was made in adopting revised regional child protection documentation and a recognition of the lack of coordination and consistency within vulnerable adult investigations. This led to the formation of the North Wales Adult Protection Forum and subsequent development of policy and procedure across North Wales.

The North Wales Vulnerable Adults Forum incorporates one police force, six local authorities, six local Health Boards and three NHS Health Trusts and serves a population of around 675,000 people over a large geographical area comprising a mix of urban and rural populations.

The North Wales Adult Protection Forum was constituted with the aim of coordinating a multi-agency response to vulnerable adult work and of promoting the provision of consistent, fair and good quality vulnerable adult practice and procedures. It was charged with the responsibility for:

- ensuring that strategic developments, policy initiatives and agreed procedures are actioned

- ensuring that multi-disciplinary partnerships are organised consistently and fairly

- promoting the understanding and status of vulnerable adult abuse policies and procedures throughout North Wales

- ensuring that appropriate training is delivered for all key staff within the partner agencies

- monitoring and evaluating the delivery of services through agreed quality assurance systems

- reviewing and identifying areas of good practice, areas where further guidance is required and to propose improvements and amendments to North Wales Policy Guidance.

Membership at the outset was primarily drawn from the six local authorities (policy officers), NHS Trusts (nurse managers) and police (community protection officers) but was subsequently extended to include representatives from the Care Standards Inspectorate for Wales (CSIW),[1] the voluntary sector, independent care home providers, the Crown Prosecution Service, the Probation Service and the University of North Wales, Bangor.

## POLICY DOCUMENT 2000

The initial meeting was chaired by a DCI from North Wales Police who had shared the concern of others about the lack of synergy and coordination in adult protection and who was mindful of the experience in child protection work following the time of the Waterhouse Report and Recommendations, *Lost in Care* (DH 2000). She had the foresight to highlight vulnerable adult work as underdeveloped and ably led the group in formulating the *North Wales Policies and Procedures for Responding to the Alleged or Confirmed Abuse of Vulnerable Adults* (North Wales Vulnerable Adults Forum 2000). The title of the document alludes to the compromises and the negotiation involved in bringing together so many partners from a range of backgrounds to sign up to a common policy.

At that time vulnerable adults work was viewed by many within and outside social services departments as an added burden and responsibility to be avoided or referred onwards. There was a lack of clarity as to the responsibility for investigation, the involvement of different partners within the adult protection process, and a concern that we could open the floodgates and would inherit responsibility for a plethora of new cases ranging from neighbour disputes to consumer protection.

When the North Wales Vulnerable Adults policy was first published in 2000 it became one of the first cross-boundary multi-agency policy documents to be published in the UK and was formally signed by 14 partners. The document predated the publication of the Social Service Inspectorate All Wales Guidance on the Protection of Vulnerable Adults, *In Safe Hands* (National Assembly for Wales 2000),[2] although the group had been given the advantage of viewing a preliminary proof of the proposed All Wales Guidance before publication.

However, by 2004 the deficiencies and lack of consistency in the original policy document had become increasingly evident and the document had become dated. On reflection the 2000 policy was a collection of individual social services policies, with some common aims and objectives and was an honourable attempt at standardising documentation.

Whilst limited and defective in many areas (and with hindsight inadequate for responding to a number of challenges) it provided an invaluable contribution towards helping to align the responses of local authorities across the region and in promoting understanding of the roles of respective partners. It also supported our initial mantra that it was more important to have everyone on board the ship even if their contribution and experience as sailors was limited. The policy also provided the impetus to support the incremental development of joint procedures and helped expose the differences and inadequacies which existed and which need to be addressed in the new *North Wales Policy and Procedure for the Protection of Vulnerable Adults*, which was launched in October 2005 (North Wales Vulnerable Adults Forum 2005).

## POLICY DOCUMENT 2005

When the decision was made to revise and update the North Wales policy in 2004 the initial document provided the North Wales Group with a confidence and an authority to progress with a more radical approach. Taking that leap of faith would have been more challenging without having the initial document to lead the discussion and to highlight the practical limitations and operational requirements of those involved in implementing adult protection procedures on a day-to-day basis.

Consideration was given to the fact that the revised document would have a number of different readers and that it needed to be both relevant and applicable to a wide range of individuals, from unpaid volunteers to dedicated adult protection coordinators. The level of interest and the depth of knowledge would therefore diverge. Whilst the document aims to encompass all audiences, it is recognised that it would be used primarily as a reference and resource when responding to suspected cases of abuse, and is designed and drafted to reflect the way it is likely to be used. It includes a simple, straightforward summary of the vulnerable adult process in the form of a one-page flow chart which outlines the adult protection process diagrammatically (see Figure 2.1).

The aim is to ensure that people not versed in the policy can identify their responsibility and the salient requirements quickly whilst those who require more detailed information can access that information. The policy was designed as a working policy and includes tools which practitioners could use and develop, supporting thorough assessment, investigation and review of all adult protection referrals.

When completed, the 2005 policy finally amounted to 158 pages and over 36,000 words. It was published bilingually in Welsh and English with an initial print run of 1000 copies. With such a large document the publication costs were significant and this was sponsored by an equal contribution from the partners who each received an allocation of 50 copies. The 2000 policy document was only available in hard copy as the final version had been converted and adapted so much by the printers. This significantly constrained distribution and adaptation, leaving us with a document which could not be updated and which limited ongoing enhancement and work on the follow-on document.

Whilst it was essential to have a hard (paper) copy we were determined to ensure that we had electronic and CD copies too. Most of the partners distributed their allocation fairly quickly and we reached the possibility of having to agree on a reprint. However, it proved more problematic getting all to agree to support an additional outlay for varying quantities and it was unfair for one partner to underwrite the full cost of such a large rerun. Whilst we had initially agreed to sell spare copies of the document to partners and providers we did not want to be limiting distribution of the document only to those willing to pay. We therefore agreed to support the development of a user-friendly version on CD which was then shared more widely with the voluntary sector and other support organisations and which was also posted on Council and Local Health Board websites.

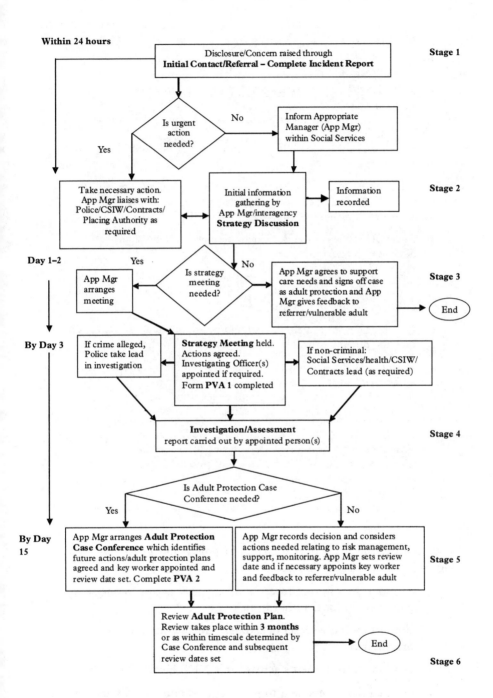

*Figure 2.1 Summary of process for adult protection*
Source: North Wales Vulnerable Adults Forum 2005

## GOOD PRACTICE POINTS

- Consider the visual impact of the document on workplace shelves. Ensure that you use a prominent colour on the file cover. The North Wales document is now colloquially referred to as the purple file. Garish colours tend to attract more attention. In this case it is more important to be noticed than to be loved.

- Ensure that you have electronic copies of the document which are web based and ensure that all partners place copies of the document on their websites.

- Issue CD copies of the document alongside the hard copy to aid distribution and limit costs.

- Give careful consideration as to how the document will be used and ensure it is split into different sections which are relevant to different groups of potential users.

- Consider how the document should be subdivided and reflect on how the document will be used in practice by different partners.

- Ensure that the document is easily understood by different audiences and that individuals can identify clearly their responsibilities and be clear about expectations and what they need to do in particular circumstances.

- Produce a summary confirming responsibility and expectations. This should be clear about channels of communication and whom individuals with concern about potential abuse should contact.

To summarise, the main developments in policy and procedures between 2000 and 2005 were as follows:

- common set of procedures for all agencies and with one set of guidance for local authorities
- support toolkit with set of standard documentation for practitioners
- common arrangements across three NHS Health Trust areas
- detailed risk assessment tools to support and lead discussions reaching to informed decisions

- active involvement of CSIW who check on awareness of the guidance during their formal inspections of care providers.

## APPOINTMENT OF VULNERABLE ADULT COORDINATORS

Prior to the publication of the 2000 policy there were no dedicated vulnerable adult coordinators in North Wales and such posts were a rarity across Wales and the UK. Since its publication there has been an incremental investment in adult protection work and by 2006 all six local authorities within the partnership had appointed vulnerable adults coordinators and included these as core posts on their staffing structures.

The initial appointments were probably supported by a misplaced idea that the appointment of a full-time coordinator would alleviate other staff of the responsibility for vulnerable adults work. Whilst this may have helped gain political and financial support it was important to dispel that misconception and to ensure that the responsibility for vulnerable adults continues to be a shared and collective responsibility.

Although there has been significant progress in the appointment of dedicated adult protection officers there are marked differences in terms and conditions and duties between coordinator posts across the region. Whilst some variance is inevitable and we must acknowledge progress in ensuring that the posts are now embedded within corporate structures, it is important that the post is recognised in its own right and not viewed as an add-on to other duties. There is also a need to ensure an element of alignment in terms of responsibilities in order to reinforce the importance of the post. The challenge is to ensure that it is considered of equal merit with the equivalent role of child protection coordinator.

## ROLE OF VULNERABLE ADULT COORDINATORS

In common with many authorities there has been an ongoing debate in North Wales about the exact role and function of adult protection coordinators, especially whether they should be responsible for chairing strategy meetings or whether they should be acting in a supporting capacity. I do not intend to champion any one case above the other as I believe there are merits in both arguments. One perspective is that allowing the coordinator to take on the responsibility for chairing all strategy meetings will result in the de-skilling of other staff and an abdication of responsibility. Conversely it can be argued that it may be difficult on some occasions for team leaders to be totally subjective when dealing with their peers and there may be benefits in having some autonomy from the service as it also encourages the development of specialist skills and expertise. Within some authorities in North Wales logistical and geographical considerations have dictated or influenced the decision and the consensus has been to refrain from asking the coordinators from chairing most of the strategy meetings.

This debate perhaps amplifies the fact that the adult protection coordinator can be a fairly isolated role and that consideration needs to be given as to how the duties should be supported and covered especially when the coordinator is not available. Whilst coordinators have been appointed in all six authorities the posts are not always full-time dedicated posts. In terms of future progress should the next step be to consider the appointment of a Protection of Vulnerable Adults Team or a network consisting of more than one coordinator or a shared role? With the demise of the generic social worker is there a case for more specialism in adult protection work?

## DATA ANALYSIS

Changes in policy and documentation have been coupled with significant advancements in terms of data collection with a progression in the methods and the statistical returns. Initial reporting was ad-hoc and there were glaring anomalies in the way different authorities recorded and reported data on vulnerable adult cases. This was improved in 2001 with the development of an All Wales paper return which has further evolved with the introduction of the All Wales Database which has helped standardise the reporting mechanism. Returns are now collated by the Social Service Data Unit. Coordinators are required to record information on a common All Wales Database which encourages consistency in recording and leads to systematic collection of data. The database also supports coordinators by confirming thresholds and terminology. A standardisation of documentation has assisted the process and provides proof of how more mature this area has become.

Statistical reviews highlight that there is usually an upsurge in referrals with increased awareness of the procedures. This in my opinion is healthy and it is not necessarily appropriate to equate this with an increase in incidence. It is usually a reflection of what was previously missed as opposed to an increase in prevalence. However, this can sometimes be counterproductive: one local authority was severely chastised in the press following the publication of an annual report recording an increase in figures from previous years. Whilst it was apparent that the employment of a dedicated coordinator, as well as improved awareness and training, was a contributory factor, the headlines did not reflect this and there is a danger that negative reporting can be obstructive to change.

## ALL WALES COORDINATORS' GROUP

Developments in North Wales have also been guided and supported by the All Wales Coordinators' Group which provides a network for adult protection coordinators to consult and share experiences and best practice. Officers have email links and are able to seek guidance and post questions on topical issues. This allows adult protection coordinators to support each other in what can often be an isolated and specialist role.

The All Wales Group was established in 2004 and includes representation from all 22 local authorities in Wales and meets quarterly to promote the sharing of good practice and also the standardisation of some materials across Wales. The value and benefit which coordinators place on the group is reflected in the attendance figures which have consistently been 85 per cent of all the authorities. Recently the group has acknowledged the need to extend the remit of the group to accommodate partners from other services, in particular the Health Trusts, who attend to discuss particular issues. This shows the penetration of vulnerable adult work into the health team and further supports the notion of joint working. The Coordinators' Group feeds the All Wales Advisory Group on Adult Protection which is administered by the National Assembly for Wales Social Services Inspectorate.

## IMPACT OF PROCEDURES ON PRACTICE

Looking back on progress in North Wales, it is evident that the 2005 policy document and vulnerable adult work with the social care sector is now perceived in a very different light and is given significantly more prominence within the social services and the partner organisations. Whilst vulnerable adults will always struggle to gain parity with child protection there is no doubt of its elevation.

What has become apparent is the confidence and the moral authority which policy guidance can give to practitioners and managers involved in investigating cases of suspected abuse. The guidance is now used and viewed as a valuable part of the armoury when responding to cases of suspected abuse and provides a comfort blanket for staff. In many ways the document has empowered staff involved in the process and provides a justification for their actions.

## FUTURE CHALLENGES

There remains an ongoing challenge of ensuring that the policy becomes further embedded into practice along with a need to provide the appropriate apparatus for individuals at all levels across the partner agencies to understand their professional and moral duty to bring suspected cases of abuse, and/or

## GOOD PRACTICE POINTS

### POLICY DEVELOPMENT 1

- Appoint a dedicated vulnerable adult coordinator to provide impetus and direction to vulnerable adult work.

- Ensure that individuals at the highest level within the organisation endorse the aims and objectives as early as possible within the developmental phase. This can provide weight to the work when you encounter objections or reservations and can be used to drive change.

- Get individuals at the highest possible level within the organisation to formally sign the document – Chief Executives as opposed to Directors of Social Services or Health Managers.

- Invite all signatories to attend an official launch and make them fully aware of their individual and collective responsibilities and the reality of adult abuse. (Scare them with actual examples and take a photo to prove their attendance and adherence.)

- Instigate an effective and extensive training programme to support the introduction of the policy. This should be programmed to target different groups of people who work with vulnerable adults or who may encounter vulnerable adults and should not be confined to social care. Remember there are other staff groups (ranging from rent to refuse collectors) who have regular contact with the public and may benefit from awareness training.

inappropriate behaviour, to the attention of others. Although the status of the policy has been significantly elevated and the tools are now more appropriate and purposefully used, there continues to be a need to ensure that the policy penetrates into the internal workings of a wider sphere of social care providers and to raise public awareness that adult abuse does takes place and is wholly unacceptable.

Equally there is a need for dedicated legislation to support the work of partner agencies as we are often obliged to apply a range of fragmented, complicated and sometimes expensive legislative frameworks in our quest to protect vulnerable people and to prevent abuse.

Over the past decade Wales has a reputation for being reasonably well engaged in vulnerable adults work. Perhaps there is an opportunity here for Wales, through the National Assembly, to champion further the cause of vul-

# GOOD PRACTICE POINTS

## POLICY DEVELOPMENT 2

- Ensure that the policy steering group is chaired by a suitably senior person and that the nominated representatives have the time and authority to act on adult protection issues.

- Encourage non-contributors via reference to their peers and if all else fails provide models of good practice from other areas for them to replicate.

- Obtain some specialist endorsement or help – invite external experts to provide a critique and to develop guidance on problematic areas.

- Consult with colleagues from other parts of the country and seek permission to use parts of their documentation and offer to share your document with others.

- Develop a programme of ongoing training which is multi-agency and inclusive and which targets people at different levels within and outside the social care arena. Ensure the inclusion of the voluntary sector, informal carers and direct payment recipients.

- Identify training targets by studying information gleaned from analysis of cases (in North Wales independent residential care staff and mental health were targeted due to low levels of reporting).

- Develop 'Keeping Safe' programmes for service users who may be vulnerable to abuse and/or exploitation. How do vulnerable people know they are being abused if they do not understand what constitutes abuse?

- Ensure that core documents have sufficient prominence (on Anglesey all vulnerable adult forms are printed on red paper; these are easily recognisable and stand out on case file notes).

- Include a reference to the vulnerable adult policy and responsibilities within all contract documentation to ensure that people are clear of expectations and their responsibility to report.

nerable adults and to use the role of Commissioner for Older People to progress the agenda of adult protection in Wales and to influence policy beyond Wales.

## COMMENTARY

With so many partners involved within the Adult Protection Forum there will always be a danger of divergence as both the pace of change and the commitment to progress will vary within different organisations. Attempts have been made to limit this in North Wales and to promote continuity through:

- a regular programme of quarterly Forum meetings with recorded attendance

- a consistency in approach to training and materials. All new materials should be published following approval by the Adult Protection Forum

- a promotion of common information leaflets across all partner agencies and authority areas

- ensuring that vulnerable adult work remains in the public eye and in people's conscience through the adoption of the Adult Protection Charter.

- encouraging the sharing of experiences, both good and bad, to ensure that staff feel empowered and confident to tackle and challenge inappropriate behaviour and standards.

In all cases it is very important to be able to review actions at the end of the adult protection process. This review has in practice focused on the most difficult or complicated cases; however, appraisal of this nature should not be confined to complicated or serious cases as there are often valuable lessons to be extrapolated from the straightforward or simple cases. Such cases can also help forge understanding between partners and can help develop confidence and relationships, which can sometimes be strained in more difficult or challenging circumstances.

Awareness and knowledge of the policy needs to permeate into the organisational culture and be highlighted in all contract and partnership documentation regardless of whether this activity is supported financially. This should include activities supported by voluntary groups which may not be subject to financial support. No organisation should be exempted.

The North Wales Adult Protection Forum has been well supported by the CSIW both as contributors within the Forum but also on a practical level as key drivers and enforcers during the official inspection visits and reports. Inspectors regularly check on the availability and knowledge of the policy document which has helped raise awareness and understanding but also ensured that training events were well supported.

The variance in response times and especially timescales for the completion of investigations remains a challenge in adult protection work. Whilst good relationships have been nurtured with the police, and we are particularly fortunate in the liaisons which have been developed, investigations can be affected by external factors and large-scale investigations can scupper timescales.

We have witnessed an increase in cases and especially in confidence when responding and certain practices are now becoming part of the standard response which was not true at the outset. What is of concern, however, is not how many we identify but how many we miss. There is now more of a shared ownership and responsibility for the process and a clearer osmosis of responsibility at different levels with the partner organisations and with a divergence of responsibilities.

Any Partnership Committee requires the right representation of individuals, who are able to make decisions and who have sufficient interest and responsibility. The group needs to be directed by a clear work plan and to be supported by sub-groups on specific matters. Within North Wales we have adopted the structure shown in Figure 2.2.

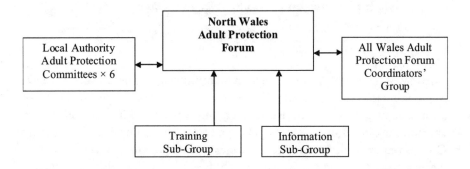

*Figure 2.2 Outline of adult protection groups in North Wales*

In the post-publication period there is a danger of being diverted as so much effort is often invested in the completion of the document. It is important that the momentum is maintained and that enough time is invested in implementing the policy and in creating awareness of the content. We certainly experienced a lull in the Forum's activity. It is therefore important to refocus and to set clear goals. They say that most climbing accidents happen on the way down. Having completed the difficult part of getting the policies approved, there may be a danger of not investing enough effort in implementation. Operationally, it is easy for the Forum to be diverted from a progressive to an overarching supporting role. Establishing a clear focus and goals is helpful and it is often easier to maintain impetus and momentum by driving forward new initiatives.

## GOOD PRACTICE POINTS

ADULT PROTECTION PARTNERSHIPS – FIVE KEY POINTS

- Ensure that the group is chaired by a sufficiently senior representative from one of the main partner organisations: Social Services, Health Trust or Police.

- Consider a fixed tenure for the chair (two years) with the possibility of rotating the post between the partners.

- Ensure that the venues of meetings are rotated between partners. This helps raise awareness and emphasise shared responsibility.

- Invite other parties who may have an interest to participate, e.g. a university or other academic establishment.

- Involve others at key intervals, e.g. the Crown Prosecution Service and Probation Service, and ensure that they are kept informed of progress at a senior level if they do not attend.

The role of the Local Adult Protection Committees is an area which I believe requires review and revisiting. These have an important role but have not always, in my experience, been able consistently to deliver in practice, with an ebb and flow in commitment. Local Area Protection Committee Partnership Groups require a clear mandate and a clear action plan to help chart and lead developments, as their role can be confused or superseded by regional committees.

## MATURITY

Not only have we witnessed a marked change in the way we record, and also what is recorded, but there is now possibly a better understanding of the respective roles of the different partners and what constitutes abuse. Workers are more equipped to identify cases and there is evidence to suggest that referrals are now examined and pursued with more vigour and as a consequence are more likely to progress to prosecution and conviction. In the past many referrals did not progress beyond a strategy discussion or at best a strategy meeting, and a lot of informal information was not systematically recorded and retained. Subsequently, patterns of behaviour which in isolation did not raise suspicion were probably missed. This highlights the contribution of vulnerable adult coordinators in recording and managing information and of their being able to retain centrally details of suspicious events or actions which can highlight inappropriate patterns of behaviour. There is a danger that without a central referral resource cases which could initially be discounted by seemingly plausible explanations will become questionable when considered in the context of other events.

As people become more experienced and familiar with the procedures there is greater clarity of roles and better understanding of the contributions of all partners. It is now easier to distinguish as and when different partners need to be involved where previously everyone was invited to participate even if they had no contribution to make. Equally there is a need to be confident about distinguishing and eliminating behaviours which are deemed unconventional or erratic, as well as having the confidence to eliminate some referrals as not being abuse as there can be a tendency to be over-vigilant.

When we act we must ensure that we do so with best evidence and with due regard to the wishes of individuals. There is a danger that if we act in too much haste (in trying to respond positively) we can inadvertently penalise the individual and may be responsible for increasing their distress. For example, moving an individual from a residential home where there are concerns about the home's ability to manage the care package and placing the person in a nursing home a long distance away from family and friends would restrict the family's ability to maintain contact. In this instance it may be best initially to focus on what can be done to manage the care package in the existing setting.

With the advent of the Mental Capacity Act[3] there is a need to ensure that we use the Act to protect as well as promote the rights of the individual. Experience of financial abuse has shown how calculating and manipulative some determined individuals have been in trying to legitimise their misdemeanours through the falsification and production of supporting testimony. There are in my experience obvious dangers in terms of coercion and the development of faked documents to support abusive actions. We must also focus on the fact that abuse is not always committed by individuals working in isolation and is often committed by family members.

## FUTURE PRIORITIES

Given that the roles of adult protection coordinators are now more established and there is greater understanding of responsibilities, there is a need to consider the impact of coordinators' work on policies and to consider how the procedures are implemented in practice. This will require a review of the policy documentation with specific attention to the experience of implementation. Certain arrangements may appear useful on paper but may be difficult to implement and it is important that policy and practice are correlated and do not become divorced from one another. If a policy is to be successful it must not only guide and assist but also reflect and support staff in their roles and make their work easier rather than more difficult.

Another priority is to ensure a clear ongoing work plan for area and regional adult protection forums. This is often best served with a limited programme of achievable and useful goals. There is possibly a danger in overcomplicating matters by focusing on too many desirable aims, some of which may have a limited impact. In my experience, group dynamics are often characterised by cyclonic periods of creative activity followed by a lull or sometimes, even, inertia. By establishing a clear work plan it is possible to refocus creative energies and to maintain interest.

## CONCLUSION

We are not deluded in suggesting that North Wales has developed a good policy model, but are aware that it has made a contribution in redressing the balance in favour of vulnerable adults in North Wales. The document does not provide definitive answers to all circumstances and there is an ongoing need to revise and update the document to ensure that it remains relevant and reflects best practice. However, I am certain that without the revised procedures and the prominence given to training and supporting staff in the implementation of vulnerable adults policy, a number of cases of adult abuse would have been otherwise missed, tolerated or ignored.

Whilst we have been witness to steady progress in terms of policy development and implementation in North Wales the profile and priority given to adult protection work remains a good ten years behind Children's Services. Despite ample failings within adult protection work across the UK these individuals have not received the same national scrutiny nor elicited the same media attention and there has not been a clamour for developed supporting legislation. It continues to be our aim to ensure that adult protection is accorded the same status as child protection.

Adult abuse deserves to educe the same level of public disgust and stigma as child abuse. Currently when cases receive attention the focus is invariably on the victim as a subject of sympathy or a victim of circumstance. People are not victims of circumstances but of purposeful actions and adult abuse is not an unacceptable indiscretion, but a crime.

The portrayal of victims may elicit our sympathy, but perpetrators rarely elicit our disgust, and until they do, adult abuse will continue to be tolerated as unacceptable behaviour.

## NOTES

1    The English equivalent is the Commission for Social Care Inspection (CSCI).

2   The English equivalent being Department of Health (DH) and Home Office (2000) *No Secrets: Guidance on Developing and Implementing Multi-Agency Policies and Procedures to Protect Vulnerable Adults from Abuse*. London: DH.

3   The timetable for the commencement of the Mental Capacity Act 2005 was slightly different in Wales. Provisions of the Act, namely sections 30–41 in respect of research and independent mental capacity advocates, commenced in Wales from October 2007 as opposed to April 2007 in England. However, the Code of Practice and the criminal offence of ill treatment and wilful neglect was introduced from April 2007 across England and Wales.

## REFERENCES

Department of Health (DH) (2000) *Lost in Care: Report of the Tribunal of Inquiry into the Abuse of Children in Care in the Former County Council Areas of Gwynedd and Clwyd since 1974*. London: DH.

Department of Health (DH) and Home Office (2000) *No Secrets: Guidance on Developing and Implementing Multi-Agency Policies and Procedures to Protect Vulnerable Adults from Abuse*. London: DH.

National Assembly for Wales (2000) *In Safe Hands: Implementing Adult Protection Procedures in Wales*. Cardiff: National Assembly for Wales.

North Wales Vulnerable Adults Forum (2000) *North Wales Policies and Procedures for Responding to the Alleged or Confirmed Abuse of Vulnerable Adults*. North Wales: North Wales Vulnerable Adults Forum.

North Wales Vulnerable Adults Forum (2005) *North Wales Policy and Procedures for the Protection of Vulnerable Adults*. North Wales: North Wales Vulnerable Adults Forum.

## SUGGESTED READING

National Assembly for Wales (2004) *Inspection of Services for the Protection of Vulnerable Adults in Conwy County Borough Council – Social Services Inspectorate for Wales*. Cardiff: National Assembly for Wales.

National Assembly for Wales (2005) *Inspection of Services for the Protection of Vulnerable Adults Summary*. Cardiff: Social Services Inspectorate for Wales.

National Assembly for Wales (New draft 2007) *The Protection of Vulnerable Adults from Financial Abuse: Supplement to 'In Safe Hands' Statutory Guidance*. Cardiff: National Assembly for Wales.

## STATUTE

Mental Capacity Act 2005. London: The Stationery Office.

## ACKNOWLEDGEMENTS

Lorraine Johnson DCI (retired) – North Wales Police Force

T. Gwyn Jones – Chair of North Wales Adult Protection Forum

Gill Lewis – Social Services Inspectorate for Wales

Christopher Phillips – Adult Protection Coordinator, Flintshire County Borough Council

Sian Rammessur – Adult Protection Coordinator, Conwy County Borough Council

Gwyneth Mai Rowlands – Social Worker, Ynys Mon County Council

# CHAPTER 3

# TWO YEARS IN THE LIFE OF AN ADULT PROTECTION COORDINATOR

## PETER SADLER

This chapter will be a reflective piece about what my experience has been like as an Adult Protection Coordinator in a large county. It is important to acknowledge at the outset that job descriptions and actual work roles and responsibilities of Adult Protection/Safeguarding Adults Coordinators around the UK do differ tremendously. I wanted to write this chapter because although my experience will be unique in some ways I hope it will be useful to others who may be thinking of taking on such a role or for those who may be developing funding for such a post in the future.

### BACKGROUND

Lincolnshire County Council Adult Social Care is separated into specialist services: older people; adults with physical disabilities; and adults with learning disabilities. A contract has been agreed with Lincolnshire Partnership Trust where the trust takes responsibility for health and social care services for adults who need to access mental health services.

Within each speciality there are assessment and care management teams; each team has an operational manager in charge. In the older people service the operational manager is called a Practice Manager; in physical and learning disabilities services the operational manager is called a Partnership Manager; and in the Lincolnshire Partnership Trust the operational manager is called a Team Leader. The link to the Lincolnshire multi-agency adult protection policy documents is that the operational managers are known as Liaison Managers.

The Liaison Officer has overall responsibility for coordinating the adult abuse investigations; they have direct supervision responsibility for all County Council-led investigations and have a liaison role in terms of investigations led by other agencies, for example the Commission for Social Care and Inspection and the Lincolnshire Police.

I commenced in the post of Adult Protection Coordinator for Lincolnshire on 2 January 2006. This was a new development and there had not been a post-holder before me. The post is jointly funded by the Police, the Primary Care Trust and Lincolnshire County Council. I was soon to discover when I took up the new post that I was to be managing a process but would have no direct line management for the people who both manage and operate the process. It became apparent that I would be both operational and strategic.

In 2000 when the Department of Health issued the statutory guidance *No Secrets: Guidance on Developing and Implementing Multi-Agency Policies and Procedures to Protect Vulnerable Adults from Abuse* (DH and Home Office 2000), Lincolnshire County Council took lead agency responsibility. Work commenced to develop the multi-agency Adult Protection Committee and this was formed in 2002. I had been a Project Manager in 2001 and was responsible for the development of the first Lincolnshire *Multi-Agency Policy and Procedures* which became operational in November 2003 (Lincolnshire Adult Protection Committee 2003). Prior to this version of the policy Lincolnshire had been developing guidance to support the work around protecting vulnerable adults from abuse from as early as 1996 when a county-wide Adult Abuse Interest Group had been formed, which was made up of practitioners and managers. In 1998 further guidance was issued to assessment and care management teams.

In Lincolnshire the Adult Protection Committee had been established since 2002. Although I had returned to operational duties in 2004 I assisted in the development of a revised policy, which went operational in May 2005 (Lincolnshire Adult Protection Committee 2005). This policy included time scales and a definition of the investigation process.

When I came into the post in 2006, it was the 2005 Lincolnshire *Multi-Agency Policy and Procedures* that was informing the operational work within adult protection. In the previous October the Association of Directors of Social Services (ADSS) had published the national standards framework *Safeguarding Adults*, which identified a range of standards linked to safeguarding/adult protection work. The standards applied to both the strategic and operational aspects of safeguarding adults.

Following a period of induction (four weeks) in which I made contact with the majority of partner organisations, I developed a work plan with my line manager that would focus my work and areas of priority over the next 12 months. The work plan which was designed is shown in Table 3.1.

| Table 3.1 Work plan | |
|---|---|
| **Subject** | **Actions** |
| Adult Protection Committee | <ul><li>Audit attendance of Adult Protection Committee</li><li>Review terms of reference of Adult Protection Committee⋆</li><li>Review membership of the Adult Protection Committee⋆</li><li>To provide clarification of Committee members' responsibilities⋆</li><li>Consider public representation on the Committee⋆</li></ul> |
| Raising awareness strategy | To develop a raising awareness strategy |
| Policy and procedures<br>• Referral<br>• Investigation | <ul><li>To audit the timescale achievements between 1 April and 30 September.</li><li>To produce an audit report for the Directorate Management Team and the Lincolnshire Adult Protection Committee</li><li>To audit the alerts which come through Customer Services.</li><li>To identify and assess cases which have not been considered within Adult Protection Policy and Procedural guidance</li><li>To monitor outcomes from investigation, i.e. case conference outcomes</li><li>To monitor quality of case conferences with reference to minutes, attendance, independent chair, quality of decisions</li><li>To provide advice and support to Liaison Officers and Investigators</li><li>To re-enforce joint working arrangements between partner agencies. With specific reference to the statutory organisations, i.e. Police, Commission for Social Care and Inspection, National Health, Primary Care Trusts, Hospital Trust and Crown Prosecution Service</li></ul> |

| | |
|---|---|
| Multiple investigations care service provider | • To review current Association of Directors of Social Services protocol and integrate into guidance. To review impact |
| Review investigation of adult protection | • Review minute-taking facilities with the Business Support Manager<br>• Prepare and write the Adult Protection Committee Annual Report 2006 to 2007 |
| Review of cross-border investigations | • Check with national guidance and integrate into policy and procedures |
| Communication strategy | • Develop with the Social Services Information Team |
| Training strategy | • Produce terms of reference for Training and Development Sub-Group and review membership<br>• Review training and development strategy including costs<br>• Identify funding arrangements to include pooled resources |
| Review current procedures against best practice (other authorities) and relevant legislation/guidance | • To audit and bring in the Bichard Inquiry recommendations<br>• Mental Capacity Act 2005 – monitoring guidance and ensuring it is integrated into Adult Protection Procedures<br>• Membership of the East Midlands and Eastern Counties Regional Networks for Adult Protection Coordinators |
| Other developments | • Develop with the Criminal Justice Board a support process for vulnerable witnesses<br>• To develop better systems in Lincolnshire for referrals to the Protection of Vulnerable Adults List held by the Department of Health |

Note: * In line with Safeguarding Adults document recommendations.

## AUDIT

The work plan identified a number of key developments on which my new post was to lead. Following discussions with my line manager I felt that there was a need to audit the current position with reference to adult protection. I identified that there were two key areas of strategy and operational services to audit:

1.  The effect of the Adult Protection Committee in terms of its effectiveness in partnership working and strategic lead.

2.  How effective the *Multi-Agency Policy and Procedures for the Protection of Vulnerable Adults in Lincolnshire* (revised 2005) are in terms of impact on operational practice.

I identified that to undertake an audit I needed to have benchmarks against which to audit. I agreed with my line manager and the Adult Protection Committee to use the standards identified in *Safeguarding Adults* (ADSS 2005). The document was intended to set national standards for work undertaken by partner agencies in protection of vulnerable adults from abuse. It was helpful to use the safeguarding framework because there are a range of standards that apply to the strategic direction, role and function of the Adult Protection Committee; there are also standards that apply to the Lincolnshire *Multi-Agency Policy and Procedures.*

Within three months of taking up my post I commissioned an electronic database to be developed and implemented. The process followed in Lincolnshire requires a reporting form (known as the AA1) to be completed at the point the alert is linked to the multi-agency policy. A further form (known as the AA2) is completed when the investigation reaches conclusion at case conference and outcomes are identified. However, the experience of the database indicates that forms are completed inaccurately and not all relevant alerts have been placed within the policy.

During 2006 Lincolnshire County Council moved the process to report alerts to the Customer Services Centre; for the first time just one telephone number was promoted for reporting (a new initiative developed by the county council and partner agencies). Once this development became operational I arranged to be copied in to all alerts of alleged abuse that were sent by the Customer Services Centre to the relevant Liaison Manager. This system helped me identify when alerts were not being placed in policy and procedures and I was able to contact the relevant manager and their line manager to resolve the situation. This audit clearly identified that there were numerous examples of allegations of abuse not being placed into the adult abuse policy and procedures and investigated; these alerts were being dealt with by another process, i.e. assessment and care management (often inappropriately).

*No time frame*

The audit systems also identified that a number of investigations were many months old and that there had been no case conference. In March 2007, it was identified that there were 90 outstanding case conferences that had fallen outside of the policy timescales. Case conferences were not being chaired appropriately and there was evidence of Liaison Managers chairing their own conferences. In November 2006 an Independent Chair rota had been established which was made up of Liaison Managers and their line managers. The main aim in developing the rota was to make it easier for a Liaison Manager to obtain an independent chairperson. *fairness*

The outcome of the audit made both concerning and disappointing reading. It was clear that there was a wide variation of practice across Lincolnshire and a very concerning level of inconsistency and non-compliance of policy and procedural guidance.

## REVIEW OF POLICY AND PROCEDURES

I recommended to the Adult Protection Committee that to achieve a consistency in practice there needed to be a revision of the current policy and procedures which had been implemented in May 2005. Following agreement of this recommendation I set about establishing a working group made up of middle and senior managers from Lincolnshire County Council and Lincolnshire Partnership Trust. On reflection, although this working group was effective in terms of its impact on developing a revised policy, the working group lacked representation from the other key partners, i.e. the other partners from the Health Community, Commission for Social Care Inspection, Police and the Crown Prosecution Service. My view is that if these organisations had been present during the policy development stage there would not have been so many difficulties and challenges when putting the draft revised policy through the decision making process.

*No multi-agency working as driven in* *No jewet*

The development of the final draft policy took over eight months to achieve and a further five months to push through the decision making process of all the relevant organisations. The revised Lincolnshire *Multi-Agency Policy and Procedures* went operational on 1 May 2007 (Lincolnshire Adult Protection Committee 2007). The key differences and improvements in the revised policy were:

- the inclusion of a risk assessment tool and guidance
- an information sharing protocol
- the change of title from Liaison Officer to Liaison Manager, with a detailed description of their key roles and responsibilities
- a description of the process that will be followed following receipt of an allegation of abuse.

## INTERIM GUIDANCE

During the 13 months of development it had become obvious that there was a need for urgent interim guidance and this was issued between 1 April 2006 and September 2007. The process that was encapsulated within the revised policy was designed during this period and the interim guidance gave clarity on the following areas of the process:

- guidance on completion of monitoring forms AA1 and AA2
- the monitoring form in electronic format
- the agenda of the first strategy event
- guidance of the first strategy event
- agenda of a subsequent strategy event
- guidance of a subsequent strategy event
- agenda for a case conference
- guidance for a case conference.

It was also clear that there was a need for interim guidance on other key aspects of the process including:

- a clarification and protocol of when to suspend placements in service providers
- the protocol and interface with the Commission for Social Care Inspection
- guidance on how to give advice on the suspension of and subsequent disciplinary action against paid staff.

## REPORTING ABUSE

The audit carried out between January 2006 and March 2006 identified another key area of concern, which were the difficulties people had in reporting allegations of abuse. At this time there was an expectation that if you wanted to report allegations of abuse you would first need to identify the Liaison Manager within the County Council and Lincolnshire Partnership Trust who would be responsible. The policy and procedural guidance at the time gave a list of telephone contact numbers and local offices; however, there were many examples picked up during the audit period where somebody wanting to place an alert were 'bounced' around a number of offices and individual managers. This was clearly unsafe and another system urgently needed to be put into place. As it happened Lincolnshire County Council were developing a Customer Services Centre with a one-number system. I took advantage of this development and between April 2006 and September 2006 moved the reporting of allegations of abuse to a one-number system so that alerts would be taken by customer service colleagues. By September 2007 90 per cent of alerts were going to the Customer Services Centre.

The strategy adopted to enable this development to happen entailed the following:

- ensuring that the one-number system was advertised: there was a press release and the number was identified in County Council public publications

- the raising awareness leaflets were designed during this period and stated the one-number system (see Appendix 3.1 and further discussion below)

- guidance was issued to all partner agencies asking that they distribute the telephone number through their organisations

- I personally delivered a range of workshops and training events to customer service colleagues to equip them with the skills to take a good referral/alert of alleged abuse

- I established with the Customer Services Centre an electronic system where the alert taken by a customer services advisor was sent to the appropriate Liaison Manager.

On reflection there was a lot of activity in developing the adult protection agenda during 2006. It was during this 12-month period that Lincolnshire County Council and partners established the investigatory process that would link to the revised policy and procedural guidance. There was also key activity in other areas.

## ADULT PROTECTION COMMITTEE

Following the audit carried out between January and March 2006 it became clear that the Adult Protection Committee was *not* meeting its key requirements and objectives. I undertook an audit of attendance over the previous 12-month period and identified that attendance was very low and a number of partner agencies had not attended four meetings in a row. The membership of the Committee is shown below:

- Lincolnshire County Council Community Services Directorate

- Service user representation

- Lincolnshire Primary Care Trust

- United Lincolnshire Hospital Trust

- Commission for Social Care Inspection

- Lincolnshire Police

- Crown Prosecution Service
- National Probation Service Lincolnshire
- Lincolnshire Partnership NHS Trust
- County Domestic Violence Management
- The Pension Service
- Help the Aged (representing the voluntary sector)
- Independent care sector
- District Council Housing Manager Group – represented by South Holland DC
- Lincolnshire County Council member representation
- Supporting People Service
- Multi-Agency Protection Panel
- County Council Legal Services
- Health Care Commission
- Advocacy providers
- Carers' organisations
- Victim Support Services
- Voluntary Service Groups.

From April 2006 I decided that I needed to engage directly with partner agencies to negotiate their ownership and inclusion in the adult protection process. In order to achieve this I developed a strategy to resolve the issues of attendance and objectives. This included:

- meeting with representatives from the key partner agencies to stress the importance of the agenda, the Committee and their organisation inclusion

- presenting a series of workshops to partner agencies to provide information and outline the objectives and functions of the Committee; also to emphasise the importance of partnership working

- ensuring meeting dates and agendas were distributed in good time

- placing a responsibility through the Committee meeting agenda that partner agencies would report their work within the areas of adult protection back to the Committee on a regular basis. This was because I felt that the Adult Protection Committee had become too dependent on my role and the Committee meeting had become a reporting mechanism for my work but there was no interaction regarding partner agencies' responsibilities. I agreed with the Chair of the Committee that we would place an item on the agenda where partners would feed back their progress and work on the adult protection agenda.

To date, this strategy has had a positive effect; the attendance at Committee has increased and the agendas of the Committee have more positive outcomes in that there is interaction and a developing ownership of the overall agenda.

Work is underway to replace the current Adult Protection Committee with a Safeguarding Board for vulnerable adults and the membership of the Board will be at executive officer level within partner organisations. The Board will be represented by the same organisations as on the current adult protection committee with the following additions from:

- Welfare Rights
- Education/community education
- Legal services
- Service users/patients (by accessing citizen panels and groups already established)
- Women's Aid.

It is envisaged that the current Adult Protection Committee will become a permanent working group to support the new Safeguarding Board. The function of the working group will be to implement the strategic decisions of the Safeguarding Board in terms of development plans, budget requirements and implementation of evolving safeguarding practices. There will also be a Training and Development Sub-Group which will drive the training agenda and make recommendations to the Safeguarding Board.

## RAISING AWARENESS STRATEGY

When I came into the post it was clear from comparisons with national research and indices that there was a significant under-reporting of adult abuse in Lincolnshire. From 1 April 2006 a raising awareness strategy was implemented. The key to the strategy was engagement with a range of organisations that interact with vulnerable adults. I was mindful that there were a number of strands to raising awareness, including links to organisations that provide services, assessment and care management services and wider statutory services that included the National Health Service, the Commission for Social Care Inspection, Lincolnshire Police and the Crown Prosecution Service. I sought individuals within the range of services who would promote raising awareness within their organisations. The initial work included developing knowledge of the organisations and, through a process of communication, identifying the relevant individuals.

I was also committed to work with the media, being mindful of the impact the media can have on a campaign but also aware of the historic lack of interest by the media in adult abuse issues. In 2006 I was invited to do a live interview on Radio Lincolnshire and also in the same year I wrote an article in *Lincolnshire County News* (Sadler 2006), a paper distributed by Lincolnshire County Council to all households in Lincolnshire. From feedback and contact it was clear that the involvement of the media had a positive effect on the raising awareness agenda.

In 2007 I started to lead on developing a standard raising awareness training and development pack. The aim was to have a standard pack that all services can use to raise awareness within their organisations. I piloted the pack by presenting the material to eight different residential and nursing homes, four home support services and one day centre service. This was a useful experience in that it showed a very low baseline of understanding the signs and symptoms of abuse from the staff teams I met with and also in some services it highlighted a certain dysfunction within teams including difficulty in communication, negative agendas and lack of leadership. The exercise also highlighted examples of poor supervision and clarity of individual and team responsibility.

I also sought opportunities to link into other initiatives and was able to give presentations at local housing forums for residents of sheltered housing and community safety events across the county where I was talking to older people in the community alongside the police, fire brigade and trading standards. This provided me with the opportunity to reach an audience of potentially vulnerable adults and also engage with friends, neighbours and relatives of individuals who might be abused.

The development of leaflets in order to raise awareness amongst the general public, paid workers and voluntary workers was a crucial task. The Committee produced two leaflets, one specific for paid workers and volunteers and one for the general public, both of which are presented in Appendix 3.1. Another important element of raising awareness was the development of the adult protection/safeguarding pages on the County Council's public internet site (www.lincolnshire.gov.uk).

In terms of impact of such a strategy the one key measurement is the increase in the number of alerts. It is interesting that the number of alerts of alleged abuse during April 2005 to April 2006 was 144 and the number of alerts during April 2006 to April 2007 was 342. This represented an increase in the number of alerts by 137.5 per cent.

It is now clear that the raising awareness strategy has had a significant impact on the paid/service sector where there has been an increase in the number of allegations reported. However, there is ongoing concern that there has not been such an increase in allegations of abuse in the community and people's own homes. This will inform the strategy for the next 12 months.

## COMMUNICATION STRATEGY

It became clear to me during the development period January 2006 to March 2006 that to drive the agenda effectively we would need a communication strategy. The strategy included:

- making contact and developing relationships with colleagues in partner agencies who lead on internal and external communication within their organisations. I was able to tap into this resource to promote the adult protection agenda. I was also able to link the multi-agency policy and other information and annual reports to the internal internet systems of the partner agencies

- ensuring that there was a consistent provision of information by press releases, articles in partner agencies' information sheets and publications. I used this route to stimulate debate and feedback on the development of the revised multi-agency policy, the draft annual reports and the development of the raising awareness strategy. It proved to be a very useful mechanism to stimulate the debate and obtain feedback

- updating the County Council internet site. This proved to be a challenge in that for the site to be effective it needs refreshing on a regular basis or regular readers will cease to access the site.

It has become clear to me how important a communication strategy is to the adult protection agenda and the post of Adult Protection Coordinator. The agenda soon disappears off individuals' and organisations' agendas if you do not ensure that there is a consistent reminder about adult protection and the related current issues.

## TRAINING STRATEGY

It is my view that the lifeblood of quality adult protection work is ongoing training and development. Lincolnshire Adult Protection Committee committed to a training and agenda strategy early on from its inception. A training and development group was formed in 2003 and started to develop a joint agency training and development strategy but failed to deliver the strategy. The key stumbling block was the inability to share budgets and resources. This is an issue that has never been resolved and I see it as being a priority for the proposed Safeguarding Board. If partner organisations are not prepared to share resources we will not move forward on the provision of comprehensive training for all individuals that interact with vulnerable adults. The training and development strategy has a number of key strands.

The expectation is that all partner agencies have a commitment to provide training and development of raising awareness of abuse to its staff. This includes the voluntary sector, independent sector and public services. There are national drivers including the Care Standards Act 2000, but there is still evidence that a number of organisations do not have commitment to training and development. This is an ongoing area of need. It is imperative that all managers across all sectors will receive a higher level of training to enable them to support and to advise. For people who place an alert this is especially linked to issues around whistle-blowing and encouraging individuals to report abuse.

Lincolnshire County Council and Lincolnshire Partnership Trust have developed ongoing specialist training and development for Liaison Managers (operational managers in the two organisations) and Investigation Officers (qualified staff in the two organisations); this training is commissioned externally. The training and development plan includes four days' specialist training for Liaison Managers and three days' specialist training for Investigation Officers. In December 2006 Lincolnshire County Council commissioned a two-day specialist training course for Service Managers who line manage Liaison Managers and their assessment and care management teams. Lincolnshire County Council has also committed its resources to the provision of a series of full-day and half-day conferences since 2002, where the audiences have been selected from the independent, voluntary and statutory organisations.

However, while training and development programmes have been developed and promoted, there is an identified reluctance to take up the training by some managers and practitioners. Through the audit of training it has been identified that a number of managers have repeatedly not turned up for training with no explanation in some cases. The difficulty appears to be that some managers and practitioners do not see adult protection as an integral part of the day-to-day work within their post but rather as an 'add-on' with which they do not wish to engage.

From the work I have undertaken in this area, ongoing discussions with managers and the evaluation of the impact of the strategy, it is clear that there are still significant gaps in the provision of training. The area of most concern is that of raising the awareness of abuse. During the period April to September 2007 a development pack was designed covering raising awareness of abuse, signs and symptoms of abuse and how to report abuse. The first stage of the pilot was completed in September 2007. The pilot period included my delivering the pilot pack across a number of services including residential homes, nursing homes, home support services and day support services. This was invaluable not only to test the effectiveness of the pack but to also have the opportunity as a coordinator to engage with a wide range of service providers.

It was agreed that the next stage of the development is to make a number of amendments to the training and development pack, which have been identified from the first pilot period. It is the intention to copy the pack onto a CD-ROM system which will enable managers to deliver the pack and information through internal workshops and team meetings and also to use in supervision sessions with workers. It is planned to promote easy access to the pack; as well as being available on CD-ROM it will be possible to download it from the County Council website.

An interesting aspect has been raised from this development; that is, a number of managers are expressing concern about their confidence to train. I have raised this issue with the workforce strategy group in Lincolnshire (a group made up of statutory, independent and voluntary sector organisations). It has been agreed by the workforce strategy group that they will build in training-to-train opportunities for managers of services.

## OTHER DEVELOPMENTS

During a very active initial two-year period there were opportunities to explore other key developments that will have an impact on the overall adult protection/safeguarding process. First, there has been the development of a support process for vulnerable witnesses with the Criminal Justice Board. This initiative is still in its infancy. There is clear commitment of the Criminal Justice Board for Lincolnshire to work with the Adult Protection Committee to establish a vulnerable witness profiling service, which will complement the already established vulnerable witness support programmes. This development will enable professionals such as social workers and nurses to develop skills to support vulnerable witnesses through the Criminal Justice System with specific reference to profiling the needs of individuals to enable an effective application for a range of special measures in line with the Home Office guidance *Achieving Best Evidence* (Criminal Justice System 2007).

Second, better systems are being developed in Lincolnshire for referrals to the Protection of Vulnerable Adults List held by the Department of Health. During my initial two years in this post this was a major area of both concern and identified need for development. Within the context of the Care Standards Act 2000 the provision of a Protection of Vulnerable Adults (POVA) List (DH 2006) captures individual perpetrators who during their role of paid worker or volunteer have been found guilty of abuse of vulnerable adults through the process of an adult protection/safeguarding process and disciplinary action taken by the employer against the perpetrator.

The Care Standards Act 2000 identifies that only the employer can refer to the Department of Health to place an employee on the list; or the Commission for Social Care and Inspection if the employer does not. It is clear that confidence needs to be raised to enable more referrals to be made. There is also an ongoing problem with individuals who leave their posts before disciplinary action can be taken. A number of employers do not follow up by taking retrospective disciplinary action and refer to the POVA List. It is important that further work and discussions take place with employers to ensure that they do undertake and complete disciplinary procedures against paid workers who leave their employment while being investigated for alleged abuse of vulnerable adults. I have taken responsibility as Adult Protection Coordinator to become an access point to provide information and advice to organisations and to also act in the capacity of signposting to alternative experts. This has required attending conferences and workshops on the POVA list to ensure that my knowledge is up to date and relevant.

## THE CURRENT POSITION

In June 2007 the Adult Protection Committee decided to change the terminology we used in Lincolnshire from adult protection to safeguarding. The policy, procedural guidance and raising awareness leaflets have been amended to use the safeguarding terminology from 1 October 2007.

It was hoped that when the revised policy went operational on 1 May 2007, supported in the previous few months by interim guidance, there would be a consistent approach to adult protection work across Lincolnshire. However, the reality is that the generic structure expected to deliver a good quality approach to the work does not in fact work effectively. There are many reasons for this including over-stretched operational teams who have difficulties in prioritising and a lack of commitment to the safeguarding work by some workers. In April 2007 I set up two specific audit systems:

- I am copied in to all alerts that come through the Customer Services Centre. I track the alerts and monitor whether or not I receive a reporting form advising that the alert has been placed into policy and procedures. I am able to identify those that are not and follow up with senior managers.

- I track the number of investigations that are falling outside of timescales laid out in the multi-agency policy.

It is clear from these audit systems that in Lincolnshire we have a major difficulty in meeting the timescales and also ensuring all relevant alerts are placed immediately into policy. This has led to a productive open and honest debate with senior managers of the County Council.

The conclusion of the debate was that I presented a business plan to senior managers of the County Council to create and develop a specialist safeguarding team for vulnerable adults. The proposal was that a safeguarding team would consist of three liaison managers, nine investigation officers and one independent chairperson post; with my post (retitled Safeguarding Service Manager) having overall management responsibility (see Figure 3.1).

Communities Directorate

Adult Social Care – Assessment and Care Management

Physical Disabilities and Long-Term Conditions

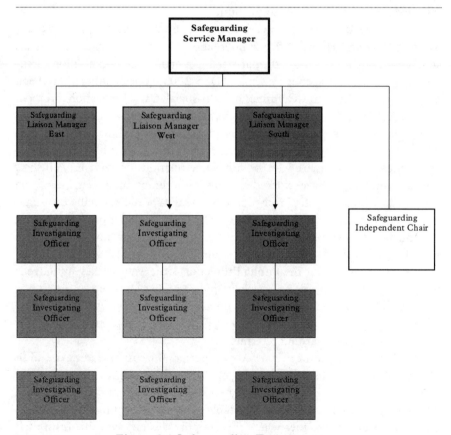

*Figure 3.1 Safeguarding Team structure*

It was proposed that the new team would lead on all aspects of work that falls within the multi-agency policy. The primary aim was to achieve consistency of practice, work within the laid-out timescales and promote good practice in the area of adult protection/safeguarding. The proposal was accepted during July 2007 and very quickly the recruitment process started. Members of the team were appointed during October and the team became operational on 26 November 2007, having had three weeks' induction training, followed by a further two days in December. During the four-week period from the team's inception to Christmas there were 92 alerts.

## A REFLECTIVE CONCLUSION

The first two years in post were a roller coaster of success and disappointments. The agenda that was set when I came into the post was ambitious and I understood when I accepted the position that it would present challenges and test my knowledge and skills to the limit.

One of the key messages in *No Secrets* is about promoting inter-agency working (DH and Home Office 2000, section 3); and in *Safeguarding Adults* standards 1, 2 and 8 focus on the partnership, partnership organisations, joint systems and partner agency systems (ADSS 2005). Locally, there have been ongoing issues with the Commission for Social Care Inspection protocol (CSCI, ADSS and ACPO 2007) which limits their involvement in investigations. This has caused ongoing tension between Liaison Managers, Investigation Officers of the County Council and the Commission. When I commenced in post there was not a positive relationship with Lincolnshire Police. However, I have worked closely with senior management of the Lincolnshire Police Public Protection Unit, which specialises in the investigation of crime against vulnerable adults. This has enabled a positive working relationship to evolve. The Detective Chief Inspector now sits on the Lincolnshire Multi-Agency Committee and I sit on the Multi-Agency Management Committee for the Public Protection Unit Another key initiative is the development of placing a specialist police officer attached to the Public Protection Unit within the County Council Customer Services Centre. There are now two specialist police officers who provide the first point of contact for child and adult safeguarding referrals.

Looking back over the initial two-year period, the cost of leading the adult protection agenda was high on a personal level. Many times I exceeded my contracted working hours, working late into the evening and the weekends. The management of the process inevitably led to me providing direct support to managers and colleagues where this support was not available from their own line managers.

I do believe that in Lincolnshire we travelled a long way in a short time. In the two years from the beginning of 2006 to the end of 2007 the landscape of adult protection/safeguarding work changed significantly. By the end of this period we had in place what I believe to be one of the best multi-agency policy and procedures (which enshrines good practice and process) in the country. All partner agencies have firmly established a process that is easy to understand and easy to follow, accepting the work is very complex within the process. In those two years we laid down positive foundations for the future in terms of raising awareness, training and development, and audit systems. This established a real commitment to partnership working and led to the development of the Safeguarding Board which further enhances this partnership working. It shows the level of commitment when we subsequently presented a half-day conference for 300 delegates across all services in Lincolnshire: the number of people applying to attend far exceeded the number of places available. The conference participation identified the high level of interest and commitment.

However, I am not complacent and there is still a lot of work and development to achieve. We need a stronger working relationship between services and a closer interaction with adults who are vulnerable. There is a need to develop better support and care for victims of abuse; the services currently available are patchy and sometimes difficult to access. The new safeguarding team has been an exciting development and is the start of new improvements and progress that will continue to evolve.

I have often been asked whether I would have accepted this post back in January 2006 if I knew then what I know now. The answer is easy and sincere – a resounding 'Yes'. I am passionate about protecting individuals from abuse and have been privileged to have been able to work with vulnerable adults and make a contribution to the agenda and development of the process and service. I do believe that the post and role of Adult Protection/Safeguarding Coordinator is essential to the development of the work. At times it is a lonely job and not a job that wins you friends and praise; however, I would recommend to anyone interested in this work to apply for such a post if an opportunity arises.

## APPENDIX 3.1: TWO LINCOLNSHIRE AWARENESS LEAFLETS

### How can you help?

Please do not ignore your concerns.
Contact Lincolnshire County Council for advice and assistance.

Telephone Lincolnshire County Council's Customer Service Centre.

Telephone: 01522 782155

All calls will be treated in confidence.

### What will happen next?

What happens next will depend on the wishes of the person at risk and the seriousness of the situation.

In response to your referral, trained staff will carry out a careful and sensitive enquiry.

They will consider the following factors:

- The vulnerability of the individual
- The nature and extent of the alleged abuse
- The length of time it has been occurring
- The impact on the individual
- The use of repeated or increasingly serious acts involving this or other vulnerable adults

Information and advice will be offered so that the person and their family can make an informed choice about any practical help they need or action they wish to take.

If they are unable to make an informed choice, care will be taken to support and protect them.

### The rights of every individual

Every individual has a right to:

- a life free from fear
- be treated with dignity
- have their choices respected and not be forced to do anything against their will

### Lincolnshire Safeguarding Adults

## Helping to protect vulnerable adults from harm

### Introduction

Vulnerable adults are individuals aged 18 and over who rely on other people to help them manage their day-to-day living.

They may be older people, or people with physical disabilities, learning disabilities or chronic mental or physical health problems.

This leaflet aims to help you recognise abuse when it happens and what to do if you are concerned.

*Every day vulnerable adults are physically, psychologically, financially or sexually abused, discriminated against or neglected by others.*

*You can help stop this.*

### What is abuse?

There are many different forms of abuse:

- **Physical abuse**, for example hitting, slapping, pushing, kicking, or other physical harm.
- **Sexual abuse**, including rape and sexual assault or sexual acts to which the vulnerable adult has not consented, could not consent or was pressured into consenting.
- **Psychological abuse**, including emotional abuse, threats of harm, humiliation, blaming, controlling, intimidation, coercion, harassment, or verbal abuse.
- **Financial abuse**, including theft, fraud, exploitation, pressure in connection with wills, property or inheritance or financial transactions, or the misuse or theft of property, possessions or benefits.
- **Neglect**, including ignoring medical or physical care needs, and the withholding of the necessities of life, such as medication, adequate nutrition and heating.
- **Discriminatory abuse**, the exploitation of a person's vulnerability which excludes them from opportunities in society.
  It includes **discrimination** on the basis of race, gender, age, sexuality, disability or religion.

### Who abuses?

Individuals can be at risk from strangers or from people they know.

These may be relatives, friends, neighbours or paid carers.

### Where does abuse happen?

Abuse can happen anywhere. It could be in the person's own home, in a residential or nursing home, in hospital or a public place.

### Warning signs

These are some of the signs which may indicate a vulnerable person is being abused:

- Bruises, pressure marks, broken bones, abrasions and burns can all be indications of physical abuse, neglect or mistreatment.
- Unexplained withdrawal from normal activities, a sudden change in alertness and unusual depression can signify emotional abuse.
- Sudden changes in financial situation may be the result of exploitation.
- Bedsores, poor hygiene and unusual weight loss are indicators of possible neglect.

## What should you do if you discover or suspect abuse?

As an alerter you must always:

- Ensure the immediate safety of the person or people involved. Call the emergency services if necessary.

- Record the information available to you in whatever way available, for example, a note pad or envelope. Keep this record in a safe place.

- Keep any evidence safe; do not dispose of it.

- Report concerns to your Line Manager or Supervisor unless you feel they are involved in which case speak to the next Line Manager.

- If your Line Manager/Supervisor is not available contact Lincolnshire County Council's Customer Service Centre. (See number opposite)

- Be accurate in recording your concerns about alleged abuse or what has been discussed with you.

- Consider the needs of carers: they may also be vulnerable and need support, and may benefit from you reporting your concerns.

- Once your concerns have been passed to your Line Manager they will be referred to a Safeguarding Adults Liaison Officer who will determine whether they need to be formally investigated.

Please do not ignore your concerns. Contact Lincolnshire County Council for advice and assistance.

Telephone Lincolnshire County Council's Customer Service Centre.

Telephone: **01522 782155**

All calls will be treated in confidence.

### The rights of every individual

Every individual has a right to:

- a life free from fear
- be treated with dignity
- have their choices respected and not be forced to do anything against their will

## Lincolnshire Safeguarding Adults

# Helping to protect vulnerable adults from harm

*Information for paid and voluntary workers who support vulnerable adults*

## Introduction

Vulnerable adults are individuals aged 18 and over who rely on other people to help them manage their day-to-day living.

They may be older people, or people with physical disabilities, learning disabilities or chronic mental or physical health problems.

This leaflet aims to help you recognise abuse when it happens and what to do if you are concerned about someone you know.

*Every day vulnerable adults are physically, psychologically, financially or sexually abused, discriminated against or neglected by others.* **You can help stop this.**

## What is abuse?

There are many different forms of abuse:

- **Physical abuse**, for example hitting, slapping, pushing, kicking, or other physical harm.

- **Sexual abuse**, including rape and sexual assault or sexual acts to which the vulnerable adult has not consented, could not consent or was pressured into consenting.

- **Psychological abuse**, including emotional abuse, threats of harm, humiliation, blaming, controlling, intimidation, coercion, harassment, or verbal abuse.

- **Financial abuse**, including theft, fraud, exploitation, pressure in connection with wills, property or inheritance or financial transactions, or the misuse or theft of property, possessions or benefits.

- **Neglect**, including ignoring medical or physical care needs, and the withholding of the necessities of life, such as medication, adequate nutrition and heating.

- **Discriminatory abuse**, the exploitation of a person's vulnerability which excludes them from opportunities in society.

  It includes discrimination on the basis of race, gender, age, sexuality, disability or religion.

## Who abuses?

Individuals can be at risk from strangers or from people they know.

These may be relatives, friends, neighbours or paid carers.

## Where does abuse happen?

Abuse can happen anywhere. It could be in the person's own home, in a residential or nursing home, in hospital or a public place.

# REFERENCES

Association of Directors of Social Services (ADSS). (2005) *Safeguarding Adults: A National Framework of Standards for Good Practice and Outcomes in Adult Protection Work*. London: ADSS.

Blair (2006) www.theyworkforyou.com/debates. Accessed 20 December 1996.

Commission for Social Care Inspection (CSCI), Association of Directors of Social Services (ADSS) and the Association of Chief Police Officers (ACPO) (2007) *Safeguarding Adults Protocol and Guidance*. London: CSCI.

Criminal Justice System (2007) *Achieving Best Evidence in Criminal Proceedings: Guidance on Interviewing Victims and Witnesses, and Using Special Measures*. London: Home Office.

Department of Health (DH) (2006) *Protection of Vulnerable Adults Scheme in England and Wales for Adult Placement Schemes, Domiciliary Care Agencies and Care Homes: A Practical Guide*. London: DH.

Department of Health (DH) and Home Office (2000) *No Secrets: Guidance on Developing and Implementing Multi-Agency Policies and Procedures to Protect Vulnerable Adults from Abuse*. London: DH.

Lincolnshire Adult Protection Committee (2003) *Multi-Agency Policy and Procedures for the Protection of Vulnerable Adults in Lincolnshire*. Lincoln: Lincolnshire Adult Protection Committee.

Lincolnshire Adult Protection Committee (2005) *Multi-Agency Policy and Procedures for the Protection of Vulnerable Adults in Lincolnshire*. Lincoln: Lincolnshire Adult Protection Committee.

Lincolnshire Adult Protection Committee (2007) *Multi-Agency Protection of Vulnerable Adults in Lincolnshire Policy and Procedures*, May. Lincoln: Lincolnshire Adult Protection Committee.

Sadler, P. (2006) 'Developing services to protect vulnerable adults from abuse', *Lincolnshire County News*, August. Lincoln: Lincolnshire County Council.

# STATUTE

Care Standards Act 2000. London: The Stationery Office

# CHAPTER 4

# DOMESTIC VIOLENCE AND HONOUR-BASED CRIME
## JOINED-UP GOVERNANCE AND AN ISLAMIC APPROACH

## JAMIESON M. MORNINGTON AND MARILYN MORNINGTON

### INTRODUCTION

Domestic violence *is* a form of adult abuse but often is not given enough attention in the literature concerned with vulnerable adults and adult protection work. In addition, honour-based violence (HBV) is gradually gaining more recognition but again needs to be addressed in relation to abuse work, as it will affect both adults and children. The aim of this chapter is first to carry out a detailed analysis of the UK Government's policy from 1997 to date in respect of domestic violence (DV). The work will seek to show how factors such as ideology, the shape of the UK's socio-economic environment and the change in attitudes which has taken place globally in respect of the role of the state in preventing violence in the home has resulted in the rising prominence of DV as a significant political issue, and one which the current government has, with varying degrees of success, sought to tackle.

> We have invested an extra £70 million to tackle domestic violence, and on the latest figures that we have, domestic homicides are down, the number of guilty pleas is up significantly, and convictions at court have quadrupled. One of the reasons why that is happening is that there is far greater co-operation across the agencies and a far greater willingness in our court system and among the police to take domestic violence far more seriously. (Blair 2006)

After briefly introducing the key concepts that form the basis of the chapter, we shall look at why there have been significant differences in policy with previous governments, before then going on to analyse a series of policy initiatives observed since 1997. Although DV policy has involved numerous actors, we have chosen to concentrate on the key governmental and non-governmental actors, which we consider to have been most utilised and coordinated in order to produce new policy ideas, and then implement those initiatives effectively. Whilst we acknowledge from the start that the government has not always been successful in achieving its aims, we will argue throughout, that the situation for DV victims and their children is now markedly better now than it was and JUG has proved to be an invaluable component in bringing about improvement.

For the purposes of this chapter, we will make use of the Home Office's definition of DV.

---

### Definition of domestic violence

Any incident of threatening behaviour, violence or abuse between adults who are or have been in a relationship together, or between family members, regardless of gender or sexuality.

(www.crimereduction.homeoffice.gov.uk/dv/dv03a.htm#4, accessed 29 December 2007)

---

Whilst DV clearly affects both genders, it is proven by all respected studies worldwide that women are more likely to be victims, and that the violence they suffer is of a far greater intensity and repetition (World Health Organization 2005), and the analysis will reflect this. In regards to defining JUG, we feel it is important to note that due to the increasing involvement of non-governmental organisations (NGOs) and voluntary organisations in defining and implementing government policy, we therefore acknowledge that the issue is becoming a key example of joined-up governance rather than government. In respect of this work we do not wish to detract from the key issues involved and get tied up in a debate on definitions.

Our second theme is that of the developing UK approach to forced marriage and honour-based crime. We acknowledge them both as forms of domestic violence but that they need a different approach and understanding given their cultural context and that the victims' needs and vulnerabilities may be different. Many (but not all) of the victims of such crimes in the UK are of South Asian origin – victims of their cultural rather than religious backgrounds – their plight ignored and hidden by families and communities by the concept of 'Shame' and by the authorities for fear of accusations of racism. We believe educating victims, families, communities and statutory bodies on the true tenets of Islam (and of other religions) and their interaction with fundamental human rights provides the best way forward to protect and prevent such abuses and to nurture healthy families and societies. We are also looking to learn from countries, such as Pakistan, who have long been tackling such issues and to work in mutually beneficial partnerships with them.

No new DV legislation was brought into effect between 1979 and 2004. The reasons behind this lay not only from the ideological influence, but also due to the economic reality. However, 'The total cost of DV to services (Criminal Justice System, health, social services, housing, civil legal) amounts to £3.1 billion, while the loss to the economy is £2.7 billion. This amounts to over £5.7 billion a year' (Walby 2004, p.1).

The decades pre-1997 produced little in the form of DV-related policy, but the same cannot be said following the election of 1997. There are several factors why the Government has taken up the issue, none more so than the presence of a significant number of female Members of Parliament, with 101 elected into office in 1997, alongside a recognition of how vital it was to appeal to women in order to achieve electoral success. The issue has also tied into many of the core principles of a style of social democratic politics, combining sound economics with an aim to tackle the negative consequences of society: 'The government wanted women to take their place as "economic equals to men" while still supporting them in their accustomed nurturing role. The government's ultimate objective was to encourage as many single parents as possible to enter the labour market' (Fielding 2003, p.200).

As Pollitt (2003) notes, the concept of JUG is not a new one and can be observed to varying degrees in every post-war government. The degree to which significant changes had to be initiated within the DV issue is shown by the statistic that a victim may go to ten different agencies before she eventually gets help and so whilst the Government did not have DV specifically in mind when they promoted the idea of JUG, we would argue that it would be difficult to find another area or issue in which the core objectives of JUG were so desperately required.

## INTER-MINISTERIAL DOMESTIC VIOLENCE GROUP

In 2002, as a result of consultation between District Judge Mornington and the then Chancellor (now Prime Minister) Gordon Brown, the Treasury brought about the revival of the dormant Inter-Ministerial Group on DV. This has become the main engine for bringing about change through JUG. The group is headed by Baroness Scotland (now by Vernon Coaker MP) of the Home Office, and includes senior ministers from, *inter alia*, Health, the Ministry of Justice, the Office of the Deputy Prime Minister, the Department of Housing (now Communities and Local Government (CLG) since May 2006) and the Education Department. The group meets at a ministerial level at least quarterly to coordinate and initiate new DV policy. Senior civil servants supporting the group meet more regularly to carry out the detailed work. Before this group came into being, there was little or no coordination or communication on DV issues between departments and different parts of the country, resulting in a huge waste of resources, lack of a spread of best practice and the response for the victim becoming a 'postcode lottery'. By way of example, at one point there were two separate groups in the Home Office and one in the Ministry of Justice, working on the issues of data protection and the sharing of information in DV cases, without even being aware of each other's existence.

An extremely successful piece of JUG, and which was not without its difficulties for government due to the competing interests of the two major DV charities, was the setting up and funding by government of a national DV helpline (2003), a project run jointly by Women's Aid and Refuge. Another example of the role which JUG has played within the group has been the creation, in 2005, of a joint specialist unit in partnership between the Home Office and the Foreign Office, to create the highly effective Forced Marriage Unit. It is very unlikely that any of the initiatives to be set out below would have taken place without the authority behind the Inter-Ministerial DV group, together with the active support to it of both the Chancellor and PM.

In Table 4.1 is a snapshot of many of the projects which have been brought about since 1997, and although we will not discuss them all within this chapter, we still feel the table provides a valuable picture of how vital JUG has been to the government's policy on DV.

## POLICE AND THE CRIMINAL JUSTICE SYSTEM

Up until 1997, there was no national police policy or training in respect of DV, and little or no acknowledgement of its seriousness as an offence. The only relationship between the police, other government agencies and NGOs was that of mutual distrust, the NGOs being regarded as dangerous feminist lead organisations, hell-bent on destroying the 'family', and the NGOs regarding the Criminal Justice System, and other governmental agencies, as being upholders of a patriarchal society which endangered women and their children. The changes within the police commenced rapidly from 1997 onwards, and were tied up with the alterations in attitudes to hate and race crime. Pockets of excellence developed throughout the UK, in particular in the Metropolitan Police's Hate Crime Unit, which was significantly also responding to the Stephen Lawrence Inquiry (McPherson of Cluny 1999). A London Metropolitan-led project named 'Adhikhar International' in 2000 brought together for the first time in true partnership NGOs, criminal agencies and the judiciary to initiate national policy changes.

The new government had within it female ministers such as Harriet Harman (now Deputy Prime Minister) and Baroness Patricia Scotland QC, Attorney General, who had campaigned for DV victims from a grass roots level throughout their political careers, and were now in a position to provide government support and also seek funding in order to effect change. A further factor was the advent of the Office of the Mayor of London, and the election of then Mayor of London Ken Livingstone, himself a lifelong campaigner on issues of DV. He appointed and funded renowned NGO leaders in the field such as Anni Marjoram to bring about joined-up change within the capital, the good practice of which spread nationwide. By way of example, the Mayor's DV newsletter has, in effect, become the national means of sharing current best practice and information: 'The Mayor published the London Domestic Violence Strategy in November 2001. It is the first citywide strategy to coordinate the work of organisations dealing with the problem of domestic violence' (Livingstone 2002).

Arising directly from the Adhikhar project, the government supported and funded the 'Raising the Standards' inter-governmental initiative (which District Judge Mornington was chairing at the time of writing) from 2000, whereby the governmental agencies and NGOs of England, Wales, Scotland, Northern Ireland, the Channel Islands and the Isle of Man meet regularly to share and develop justice and other policy initiatives throughout the British Isles, with one of the published terms of reference being the 'identifying and sharing what is considered to be best practice in relation to all aspects of dealing with victims and perpetrators of DV including strategies leading to the prevention of future incidents' (DCA 2003, p.2). Adikhar carried out a nationwide 24-hour snapshot of reported DV incidents, providing for the first time a database of the extent of the issue, and discovered, for example, that 'An average of 3% of all calls to the police for assistance are for DV. This equates to over 570,000 each year' (Hall and Wright 2003, p.7).

In the newly proactive climate, the Association of Chief Police Officers (ACPO), under its then lead, ACC Jim Gamble QPM (now head of CEOP), between 2002 and 2006, developed the full partnership of NGOs and government, agreement over national standards and training programmes for all police officers, a policy on the disciplining of police officers who were themselves perpetrators and a protocol between the police and the Civil Courts for the exchange of information on perpetrators. Her Majesty's Inspectorate of Constabulary (HMIC) followed this up with a year-long thematic inspection report on all 43 forces, with the recommendations being continually monitored. The Crime Prosecution Service (CPS) in conjunction with ACPO and other agencies developed a national proactive policy on the prosecution of DV offences, with specialist training for all prosecutors and 43 specialist officers. Partnership between the then heads of ACPO and the CPS was the foundation of the Domestic Violence, Crime and Victims Act 2004, which was personally initiated by the Prime Minister and taken forward by Harriet Harman, through which the government consulted nationally, including the Lord Chancellor's multi-agency DV Advisory Board. As a good example of

*Table 4.1 Overview of Crime Reduction Programme Domestic Violence Projects*

| Project | Initiatives/area | Research/monitoring body | Aims/objectives |
|---|---|---|---|
| Criminal and Civil Justice | • Intimidated witness support service (Brighton)<br>• 'Standing Together': making the law work for women<br>• Coordinated Community Responses | Criminal Policy Research Unit, South Bank University, London | • To decrease police and Crown Prosecution Service discontinuance levels and increase the number of individuals prosecuted and convicted<br>• Increase the number of initial reports and decrease repeat victimisations<br>• Raising awareness and training of police and magistrates |
| Protection and intervention | • Use of cameras and development of a multi-agency database (Thurrock)<br>• Alarm systems (Wales) | Criminal Policy Research Unit, South Bank University, London | • To reduce repeat victimisations and the fear of reporting<br>• Enable women to stay in their homes and provide an improved and more integrated service to those experiencing violence |
| Black and minority ethnic (BME) communities | • Reducing DV Project (Birmingham)<br>• Victim Advocacy and Safety Counselling (Tower Hamlets)<br>• DV Advocacy Service (Croydon) | University of East London | • To raise awareness in Asian and other BME communities<br>• Reduce levels of violence and repeat victimisation<br>• Increase efficiency and protection through use of culturally sensitive services |

| Category | Projects | Institution | Aims |
|---|---|---|---|
| Health | • Early Intervention Project (North Devon)<br>• Enhanced Evidence Gathering Scheme (Salford)<br>• DV Programme (Birmingham)<br>• Primary Care Project (Wakefield) | Faculty of Health and Social Care, South Bank University, London | • To reduce repeat victimisations<br>• Improve Partnership Working<br>• Raise awareness amongst health professionals<br>• Encourage safe disclosures in health settings, improve access to support<br>• Improve training and awareness, recording and monitoring<br>• Developing information sharing protocols |
| Multi-service | • 'Staying Put' (Bradford)<br>• Safety Net (Camden)<br>• Multi-agency DV Project (Cheshire)<br>• Sunflower Centre (Northampton)<br>• Tools for Practitioners (Suffolk) | School for Policy Studies, University of Bristol | • To increase initial reporting<br>• Reduce repeat victimisation<br>• Increase women's self-esteem<br>• Develop multi-agency working<br>• Increase women's safety through screening<br>• Helplines and legal support |
| Education and awareness | • Violence Against Women Project (Bridgend)<br>• NSPCC Patchwork Initiative (North Yorkshire)<br>• STAR Project (Southampton)<br>• Respect Initiative (Thurrock) | Canterbury Christ Church University College | • Raise awareness<br>• Change attitudes<br>• Educate children and professionals and challenge existing attitudes through curriculum delivery, media campaigns, drama and websites |

*Summarised from Hester and Westmorland (2005, pp.22–3).*

JUG in action, in every case where police are called to an incident of DV, regardless of the outcome, if children are present in the home, a report is automatically made to social services.

Judicial training, non-existent pre-1997 at all levels in this area, has been and continues to be expanded and improved. In December 2006, the Family Justice Council (of which, District Judge Mornington is a member together with Chairing its Domestic Violence Steering Group), in response to Lord Justice Wall's report (March 2006) into the Women's Aid investigation into a growing number of deaths during contact, made far-reaching proposals for change within the Family Justice System, including enhanced multi-agency awareness training for all participants in the system. In 2008 the President of the Family Division will issue a new Practice Direction giving firm direction to the courts in hearing cases of residence and contact where domestic violence is an issue – this will enormously enhance the safety of children and their primary carers. A national programme for training in DV awareness for all 100,000-plus lay magistrates is being rolled out nationwide by 43 nationally trained specialist advisors.

As part of the 2004 DV Act, multi-agency homicide reviews including voluntary organisations, the police and social services, and previously piloted by the Metropolitan Police, will be expanded nationwide to investigate and learn from the causes of the current grim statistic that: 'Two women are dying each week and one man almost every other week' (Hall and Wright 2003, p.6).

The partnership between the Ministry of Justice, Home Office, CPS, Probation Service, Judiciary and NGOs has led to the creation of nationwide multi-agency specialist DV Criminal Courts and the first integrated DV Court located in Croydon (based on the New York model and developed under advisement of the New York Court System), by which the same Judge deals with all aspects of a case, civil, family and criminal, operating a joined-up 'one-stop shop'. Since 2007 the Government has funded a national network of Victim Advocates who will support the victim throughout the court process and be his/her liaison with housing, health, education, counselling and all aspects of the court process. This support system is expected to lead to a dramatic reduction in retraction of victim's statements, and vastly increase the rate of successful prosecutions, in stark contrast to the situation when 'Studies demonstrated the reluctance of both the police and the CPS to pursue the prosecution process in cases of domestic assault due to an unwillingness to "interfere" between husband and wife' (Barron 1990, p.28).

In 2006, in the Family Justice System, the Family Justice Council (FJC) DV steering group initiated a national multi-agency training programme on DV risk assessment and awareness, for all 43 local Family Justice Councils. It works in close partnership with ACPO, other government agencies and NGOs, offering advice to ministers in order to enhance the response of the family system to DV. They distribute, in conjunction with the Ministry of Justice, a quarterly newsletter to the local justice councils and by their website, including all the latest news and information. In 20C7 we completed the development of a DVD,[1] which is distributed nationwide to prepare and explain to victims the court process of injunctive relief and to act as a training tool of best practice for practitioners and judiciary at all levels. This is funded and developed as a partnership between the FJC, Ministry of Justice and the Family Law Bar Association and is particularly aimed to assist victims from ethnic minorities. It shows real judges, courts and women's aid workers in action – with the voices of real survivors being heard.

## HEALTH

Prior to 1997, apart from a small number of isolated initiatives, there was no response within the health service to DV despite the fact that 'The cost to the NHS for DV related physical injuries is around £1.2 billion a year. Whilst the estimated cost of cases related to mental health is an additional £176 million' (Walby 2004, p.1). Indeed Ann Keen MP (now Minister of Health) told District Judge Mornington of how, when she was a senior nurse at a London teaching hospital and requested the development of a DV policy for the hospital, she was threatened with disciplinary action if she persisted. The Government have now appointed a national DV advisor to the NHS, and in 2006 published a series of early intervention training guidelines to be distributed and supported nationally. In 2004 DV was added to the curriculum for the training of all medical students and the Nurses Union Community and District Nursing Association in conjunction with the DCA and APCO have developed national best practice guidance for health workers on the specialist DV issue of elder abuse (CDNA 2003). Through the 'Raising the Standards' initiative and the work of the national health advisor, Christine Mann, a national screening programme for all pregnant women has been brought into effect throughout the British Isles. Table 4.2 shows how important the role of health workers is in identifying possible DV cases.

Despite the full cooperation of nurses, psychiatrists and A&E staff, all bodies locally and nationally continue to experience difficulties in engaging General Practitioners in the multi-agency response to tackling DV. This is particularly important as GPs are often on the front line and the first point of contact for the majority of people seeking assistance: 'Normalising victimisation through failing to respond to the disclosures of DV, either because of an acceptance that this is normal within a relationship, or that violence is the outcome of non-compliance with patriarchy' (Williamson 2000, p.184).

The National Health Service through its specialist advisor has, however, been at the forefront of the particular current interest of the Inter-Ministerial

| Table 4.2 Domestic Violence Incidents Identified | | | |
|---|---|---|---|
| | DV cases identified | | |
| Agency | Year 1 | Year 2 | Total across years 1 and 2 |
| Health Visitors | 12 (11% of those screened) | 24 (38% of those screened) | 36 (20% of those screened) |
| Social Care Services: Immediate Needs Team | 11 | 34 | 45 |

*Source: Hester and Westmorland (2005, p.33).*

Group in developing a corporate and work-place response to DV, with policies to assist employers to respond to staff who are victims. In the case of the health service, research carried out by the Corporate Alliance and the several Health Trusts has disclosed that:

> Employees are themselves subject to domestic violence and so cost the service in terms of increased sickness absence, lost productivity and medical and psychiatric care. By raising awareness of the issue and implementing supportive policies, the National Health Service will be helping to reduce the number of DV cases and the costs to the service. (NHS 2006)

## HOUSING/EDUCATION

Government sponsored research, having disclosed the effects of DV on childhood development and education and the necessity for early intervention, led to the then PM himself initiating a Cabinet Office/DFES initiative taking the form of a 'soap' opera DVD to be shown in schools with a full teaching support package. It is called *Watch Over Me* (developed by MissDorothy.com, December 2004) and deals, amongst other issues, with DV and forced marriage. It has still proven difficult, due to pressures of the national curriculum and inevitable costs, to have *Watch Over Me* utilised nationally, and for DV awareness to become part of every school's personal development programme. This is still an area in which a great deal of work is still required.

One of the most staggering statistics we came across during research was that, '40% of all homeless women stated that DV was a contributor to their homelessness...and DV was found to be the single most quoted reason for becoming homeless' (Hall and Wright 2003, p.7). Large amounts of government investment have also been made in partnership with the women's organisations to upgrade existing refuge provision to provide en-suite accommodation, with the ability also to accommodate families with disabilities.

A growing number of refuge places are now funded through the CLG department, including the recent 'Safe Room' initiative (2006); however, there continues to be a long-running disagreement between the Government and the entirety of the women's associations over the funding of refuge places of those who constitute probably the most vulnerable group of DV victims, namely immigrant women who have not yet obtained the right to remain in the UK and therefore have no recourse to public funds.

## DV POLICY DEALING WITH BLACK AND MINORITY ETHNIC (BME) COMMUNITIES

In recent years we in the UK have made the connection between forced marriage, honour crime and domestic violence and have reached out into BME communities where these practices take place and commenced a process of bringing perpetrators to justice, supporting victims and, most importantly, through education in all its forms, sought to change hearts and minds. Forced marriage is a form of domestic violence and an abuse of human rights. Victims can suffer many forms of physical and emotional damage including being held unlawfully captive, assaulted and repeatedly raped. On the issue of violence Islam directs people in the Qur'an as follows:

> O ye who believe! Stand out firmly for justice, as witnesses to Allah, even against yourselves, your parents, or your kin, whether it is against rich or poor, for Allah can protect both. Follow not the lusts (of your hearts), lest you swerve, and if you distort or decline to do justice, verily Allah is well-acquainted with all that you do. (Sura an Nisa 4:135)

In 2000, following an extensive consultation, the Working Group on Forced Marriage published *A Choice by Right* (Working Group on Forced Marriage 2000). The Government has since produced guidelines for the police, social services, education and health professionals on tackling forced marriage. We have also commissioned international guidance for lawyers.

---

### Definition of honour-based violence

It is a collection of practices, which are used to control behaviour within families to protect perceived cultural and religious beliefs and/or honour. Such violence can occur when perpetrators perceive that a relative has shamed the family and/or community by breaking their honour code... [it] can be distinguished from other forms of violence, as it is often committed with some degree of approval and/or collusion from family and/or community menbers. (ACPO 2007)

---

The UK Government sponsored a series of six nationwide multi-agency conferences, which District Judge Mornington chaired, between 2003 and 2004, on the issues affecting victims from the Asian community, with a government minister speaking at each. The strength of a joined-up response has been of particular value in this area, due to the sensitivity and barriers created by cultural, religious and race issues. ACPO has set up a specialist 'honour'-based violence working group, which is developing a coordinated national police response and sponsoring research into this increasingly recognised form of DV. The Government, again through the Inter-Ministerial Group, is using its now established procedures for multi-agency engagement in seeking to develop an effective response, in particular utilising the auspices of the Women's National Commission, to consult and engage with otherwise hard to reach Asian women's organisations. Specialist BME refuges and out-reach services are being set up nationally and in conjunction with Derby University/Karma Nirvana have developed a government sponsored mentoring scheme for victims of forced marriage. The British Council and the Foreign and Commonwealth Office have undertaken an extensive three-year programme to tackle honour crime in Sindh – including a world conference, education and media programmes.

Forced marriage is not solely a 'Muslim' or 'South Asian' problem. The Forced Marriage Unit[2] (FMU) has dealt with cases from East Asia, Africa, the Middle East and Europe. Freely given consent is a prerequisite of Christian, Jewish, Hindu, Muslim and Sikh marriages. It also affects both young women and young men – around 15 per cent of the cases the FMU deals with involve males.

## WHAT HELP IS THERE AVAILABLE FOR PEOPLE AT RISK OF FORCED MARRIAGE?

If anyone fears they may be forced into marriage overseas, or knows someone else who may be, the FMU can help. As well as giving advice, caseworkers can also take practical steps to intervene if they are asked to do so. For example, they can liaise with other authorities for young people in the UK to be made a ward of court and their passports confiscated to prevent them being taken and married overseas – 15 per cent male; 30 per cent minors (3 a week from Islamabad alone). If the young person has already been taken overseas, FCO consular staff can work with the local police and judiciary to try to help those at risk, and, in extreme cases, can mount a 'rescue mission' to rescue and repatriate victims. Over the last four years, the Government has helped almost 1000 cases of forced marriage and has rescued and repatriated around 200 young people from overseas – 15 per cent male; 30 per cent minors (3 a week from Islamabad alone). However, many more cases are not reported and others are dealt with by other agencies.

The minimum age for marriage entry clearance has been raised from 16 to 18; the Government is currently consulting in raising this age to 21. This is to give those who face forced marriage extra time in which to mature and resist familial pressure to enter a marriage that they do not want. In support of this an extra *entry clearance officer* has been established in Islamabad. This officer will help these reluctant spouses, as well as assisting those who have been abandoned in Pakistan by their partners, and who have a right to return to the UK. This increases the ability to support victims and stop further abuse in the wake of forced marriage.

The FMU also undertakes a great deal of publicity, outreach and awareness-raising work to target communities. They speak at around 75 events each year across the UK. They also work closely with the media and have appeared in everything from *Eastern Eye* to 'Dear Deidre' in the *Sun*. They have funded www.dorothy.com to provide a range of videos and online resources particularly aimed at young people. They also acknowledge the work the community themselves are undertaking on this issue. For instance, a range of youth, women's and race groups have been campaigning on this issue for many years, and it is usually women's groups who organise awareness-raising events to which we are invited. Faith groups, too, are playing a role – for example, there has been a conference of Imams in Tower Hamlets, the Sikh community in Walsall has held events, and the Muslim Parliament is very active.

The Home Office has also provided funding for a National Forced Marriage Steering Group bringing together partners from the voluntary sector, statutory agencies and central government.

On 26 January 2005 the Home Office and Foreign and Commonwealth Office launched a new joint Forced Marriage Unit. The new unit is a one-stop shop to undertake policy, projects and give practical advice to people at risk of being forced into marriage. The Unit works closely with a wide range of community groups, women's groups and NGOs in combating forced marriage.

The UK police initiatives have been led by the Metropolitan Police. New and innovative ways of analysing, understanding, investigating and preventing honour-based violence have been developed. The work has informed police training and best practice nationally, particularly with regard to risk assessment and risk management. One conclusion has been that there is no typical case of honour-based violence. Honour killings are 'atypical' and they fall within the 'umbrella' of honour crime and HBV. Many of these crimes are interlinked – being drivers for one another:

- domestic violence
- forced marriage
- acid attacks
- dowry-related crime
- bride price
- female genital mutilation
- honour rape
- customs like 'swara'
- female infanticide
- blood feuds.

Victims are often subject to psychological pressures that can lead to mental breakdown, self-harm and even suicide.

We are not judging cultures: we are judging murderers and those that shield them from justice. Most countries have signed up to human rights conventions and there has been a great deal of research and international cooperation on these issues and yet up to now we seem powerless to effect change. We now understand the misguided concept of 'honour' and that crime committed in its name is based in feudalism, lack of education and denial of the fundamental human rights of women. We acknowledge that it is forbidden by all of the major religions and in particular Islam. We believe that change will only come when there is determined, assertive, consistent action by governments, faith leaders, judiciary, police, the media and educationalists.

## GOOD PRACTICE POINTS

- Governments need to enact legislation that outlaws all forms of honour crime. They need to make funds available (with international help if needed) for training of professionals, education in schools, media campaigns, protection of potential victims and support of NGOs.

- Faith leaders are needed to educate their communities to understand that such crimes are abhorrent to God and all religions. The Qur'an forbids any equation where the product is violence or abuse: 'Let there be a community (or Ummah) among you, advocating what is good, demanding what is right, and eradicating what is wrong. These are indeed the successful' (3:104).

- Police need to develop and enforce best practice and training so that they protect the victims and not the perpetrators. Police in the UK have been at the forefront of seeking to outlaw forced marriage. The Qu'ran states: 'Indeed if any do help and defend themselves after a wrong [done] to them, against such [them] there is no blame. The blame is only against those who oppress by wrongdoing and insolently transgress beyond bounds through the land, defying right and justice, for which there will be a penalty grievous' (42:41/42).

- The judiciary must be well trained to understand the causes and effects of honour-based crime. They have a clear and heavy duty to protect the oppressed without fear or favour. Not only must they ensure that laws are enforced but also put in place measures so that the courts are safe places which victims can access without suffering further at the hands of their oppressors. Our judiciary have been at the forefront of developing innovative ways of using the civil law to prevent forced marriage and protect its victims and have been major supporters of the new proposed legislation.

## CONCLUSION

The Government's record on tackling DV through the use of JUG has been successful to a degree; however, as with other policy initiatives, there have been significant problems. As with other projects utilising JUG, there have been the usual difficulties associated with adopting a more holistic approach to governance, namely issues of accountability, the institutionalising of new structures, a lack of clear communication of aims and objectives by central government, and a scarcity of funding. One has to recognise that in some areas political rhetoric and 'sound bites' have not been backed up with adequate resources.

A report on the Government's record in this area entitled *Making the Grade* (Women's National Commission 2005) identified key failings, including an inadequate response in some regions of the UK due to a lack of effective police training, and a severe lack of response by some social services due to a lack of understanding and resources. The report identifies that in almost every area a more integrated and coordinated approach would bring about huge benefits:

> Attempts at inter-departmental working and partnerships are evident, but are duplicated across DV, sexual offending, prostitution and trafficking. The Home Office could really take the lead in co-ordinating cross-departmental work and it is disappointing to see it is still not reaching its full potential in all areas in this regard. (Women's National Commission 2005, p.27)

Whilst there have indeed been clear problems, we believe, however, that the situation for DV victims is significantly better now than it was before 1997, and that JUG has played an invaluable role within the achievements and changes which have been brought about since 1997. There is of course a lot of work still to be done, but the Government has identified and attempted to tackle an issue which lies at the core of many of society's problems through a circle of violence, the extent to which is still being discovered. A process has started which will eventually lead to the long-term reduction in the number of people within the UK who are victims of DV. We have no doubt at all that any future UK government of any persuasion would continue the improvements that have been made – public opinion would not allow otherwise.

Funding and the lack of it is a constant difficulty for those wishing to bring about improvements for victims of DV and child abuse in the affluent First World. NGOs are swamped and under-resourced and receive only short-term funding, making it very difficult for them to plan ahead. Many women continue to be turned away from refuges due to lack of space. These problems are magnified a thousandfold in developing nations. However, many of the advances we have outlined above have come about due to changing attitudes and methods of practice and by inspired leadership from a very small number of men and women of good will and insight. Much can be achieved on small budgets, particularly if there is cooperation between agencies, countries and regions in seeking to find solutions suitable for different cultures and circum- stances and if we in the privileged first world stand alongside our brothers and sisters offering our support, encouragement, advances and, wherever possible, finances.

## NOTES

1   The DVD is free; tel: 0870 241 4680 or email: homeoffice@prolog.uk.com, quoting reference DVL-DVD.

2   The Forced Marriage Unit can be contacted by telephone on 020 7008 0151 or by e-mail at fmu@fco.gov.uk.

## REFERENCES

Association of Chief Police Officers (ACPO) (2007) [Draft] *Honour Based Violence Strategy.* London: Association of Chief Police Officers and Metropolitan Police Service.

Barron, J. (1990) *Not Worth the Paper...? The Effectiveness of Legal Protection for Women and Children Experiencing Domestic Violence.* Bristol: Women's Aid Federation.

Blair, T. (2006) House of Commons Debates: 6 December 2006 at www.theyworkforyou.com/ debates/?id=2006-12-06c295.8&s=cricket (accessed on 30 June 2008).

Community and District Nursing Association (CDNA) (2003) *Responding to Elder Abuse.* London: CDNA.

Department for Constitutional Affairs (DCA) (2003) *Domestic Violence, No Hiding Place for Culprits*, at http://nds.coi.gov.uk/content/detail.asp?ReleaseID=46409&NewsAreaID=2 (accessed on 30 June 2008).

Fielding, S. (2003) *The Labour Party*. Hampshire: Palgrave Macmillan.

Hall, T. and Wright, S. (2003) *Making it Count: A Practical Guide to Collecting and Managing Domestic Violence Data*. London: NACRO.

Hester, M. and Westmorland, N. (2005) *Tackling Domestic Violence: Effective Interventions and Approaches*. Home Office Research Study 290, February. London: Home Office Research, Development and Statistics Directorate.

Livingstone, K. (2002) 'Digital domestic violence resource used by 5000 in first 25 days'. Press realease at www.london.gov.uk/view_press_release.jsp?releaseid=1046 (accessed 30 June 2008).

McPherson of Cluny, W. (1999) *The Stephen Lawrence Inquiry*. London: The Stationery Office.

National Health Service (NHS) (2006) www.nhsemployers.org/practice/practice-222.cfm, accessed on 29 December 2007.

Pollitt, C. (2003) 'Joined-up government: a survey'. *Political Studies Review 1*, 1, pp.34–49.

Walby, S. (2004) *The Cost of Domestic Violence*. London: The Department of Trade and Industry and Women and Equality Unit.

Wall, Nicholas Lord Justice (2006) *A Report to the President of the Family Division on the Publication by the Women's Aid Federation of England Entitled 'Twenty-Nine Child Homicides: Lessons Still to be Learnt on Domestic Violence and Child Protection' with Particular Reference to the Five Cases in Which There was Judicial Involvement*. London: Royal Courts of Justice.

Williamson, E. (2000) *Domestic Violence and Health*. Bristol: The Policy Press.

Women's National Commission (2005) *Making the Grade: An Independent Analysis of Government Initiatives on Violence Against Women*. London: Women's National Commission.

Working Group on Forced Marriage (2000) *A Choice by Right*. London: Home Office.

World Health Organization (WHO) (2005) *Women's Health and Domestic Violence against Women*. London: WHO and London School of Hygiene and Tropical Medicine.

## STATUTE

Domestic Violence, Crime and Victims Act 2004. London: The Stationery Office.

## RESOURCES

*Watch Over Me* DVD (December 2004)

For more information see www.missdorothy.com (accessed 23 April 2008).

*Domestic Violence* DVD (2007)

For a copy call 0870 241 4680 or e-mail: homeoffice@prolog.uk.com quoting ref DVL-DVD.

## USEFUL CONTACTS

### Forced Marriage Unit

London

Telephone: 020 7008 0151

e-mail: fmu@fco.gov.uk

### Henna Foundation (Wales)

Telephone: 02920 496920

### Karma Nirvana Refuge

Derby

Telephone: 01332 604098

**National Domestic Violence Help Line**
Telephone: 0808 2000 247

**Women's Aid Federation of England**
Head Office
PO Box 391
Bristol
BS99 7WS
England
Telephone: 0117 944 44 11 (general enquiries only)
Website: www.womensaid.org.uk

# CHAPTER 5

# ELDER ABUSE AND BLACK AND MINORITY ETHNIC COMMUNITIES
## LESSONS FOR GOOD PRACTICE

## ALISON BOWES, GHIZALA AVAN AND SHERRY BIEN MACINTOSH

### INTRODUCTION

There is little information, guidance or understanding of issues of elder abuse in black and minority ethnic (BME) communities. The research record is limited, and service delivery suffers from the same limitations as other services for BME communities. O'Keeffe *et al.'s (2007) prevalence study saw particular difficulties in addressing the issue in BME communities.*

This chapter draws on research conducted at the University of Stirling, funded by the Big Lottery Fund and conducted in partnership with Age Concern Scotland. The aim of the research was to identify the impact of cultural diversity on understandings of elder abuse, and to explore the implications of diverse understandings for the provision of services to older people and their carers in an ethnically diverse society. Through exploring the views and experiences of key stakeholders, the objective was to identify good practice lessons for delivering appropriate support to individuals, families and communities on elder abuse issues. The data consist of 28 interviews with exemplary service providers, who were identified through their reputation for carrying out recognised good work in this area; 58 interviews with members of BME communities in four categories – South Asian, Chinese, African Caribbean and European (see Table 5.1); and a series of focus groups involving 51 community members in seven groups and four service providers in one group which explored the 'fit' or lack of it between what the services are doing and the understandings and experiences of the communities (Bowes, Avan and Macintosh 2008).

## Table 5.1 Community members interviewed

| Ethnic category | Gender | | Generation | | Age category | | | | Carstairs score* | | |
|---|---|---|---|---|---|---|---|---|---|---|---|
| | Male | Female | Older | Middle | <50 | 50–59 | 60–69 | 70+ | 1–2 | 3–5 | 6–7 |
| South Asian (Bangladeshi, Indian, Pakistani) | 8 | 10 | 12 | 6 | 5 | 3 | 8 | 2 | 7 | 6 | 4 |
| Chinese | 5 | 7 | 8 | 4 | 2 | 2 | 1 | 7 | 3 | 7 | 2 |
| African Caribbean | 4 | 7 | 7 | 4 | 1 | 3 | 1 | 6 | 0 | 6 | 4 |
| White European | 5 | 12 | 12 | 5 | 2 | 3 | 0 | 12 | 8 | 7 | 2 |
| TOTAL | 22 | 36 | 39 | 19 | 10 | 11 | 10 | 27 | 18 | 26 | 12 |

Note: * Carstairs scores are an index of deprivation – 1 denoting affluent, 7 the most deprived areas. This variable had two 'unknown' participants.

There are good reasons to expect that experience of elder abuse will vary for BME groups. First, the literature suggests that abusive behaviour may be difficult for vulnerable communities to discuss (cf. Samad and Eade 2003) and our experience in the research bears this out. Our work was conducted in collaboration with the Black and Minority Ethnic Elders Group (BMEEG), who provided important discussion and advice from the outset. They were unanimously agreed that we should use the term 'mistreatment' rather than 'abuse', because it was more readily translatable into minority languages as well as being a more acceptable term. Their views reinforced suggestions in previous research (e.g. Biggs, Phillipson and Kingston 1995) and emphasised the need for careful use of language.

Second, there is plenty of evidence that, cross-culturally, beliefs and practices concerning the care of older people vary (e.g. Harper 2006 provides a comprehensive overview) and that some ways of caring for older people are valued more highly than others – for example, in many cultures, there is a strong ideology of family care and decision-making, whereas in others, there is an emphasis on independence for the older person, on their freedom to make their own decisions and on a larger role for services from outside the family. If ideals about the treatment of older people vary, it would be surprising if views about mistreatment did not also vary (and see Kosberg *et al.* 2003).

Third, the context in which BME communities live has to be brought into the picture. The research literature identifies general difficulties experienced by professionals in tackling elder abuse, and these must be compounded where they represent services which have repeatedly been found lacking in their responses to ethnic diversity (Butt and Mirza 1996; Bowes and Dar 2000). It is also well established that many people from black and minority ethnic communities frequently experience additional exclusion through racism, which may compound the effects of ageism in the case of older people from these communities. There is increasing evidence that stigmatised minority ethnicity and lower social class in combination have particularly negative exclusionary consequences (for example, see Nazroo 2001).

Service providers are accustomed to hearing that services do not respond well to ethnic diversity, and this finding has been repeated many times. In our research, we wanted to move on from repetition towards a focus on how services can respond, and to identify some useful practice lessons which tune into the experiences of both BME communities and service providers who have achieved some success in this area. From the outset, however, it is important to note that the issue has received very little specific attention and that it proved difficult to identify specific good practice. We have come to the view that in reality, service providers can build on existing good practice in both services for elder abuse and effective practice with BME communities, but that they need to recognise that elder abuse is an issue for BME communities of particular sensitivity and difficulty. In the end, good practice with BME communities may offer some lessons for general good practice. The chapter will not offer a recipe for addressing elder abuse in BME communities – rather, we will raise some questions that service providers need to consider and identify some potential relevant actions.

## UNDERSTANDINGS AND EXPERIENCES

This section looks at what people from BME communities said about the mistreatment of older people. Everyone was interviewed in the language of their choice, with interpreters being used in a handful of cases where the research team did not have the necessary linguistic skills. Respondents (see Table 5.1) were identified through snowballing to fill quotas for each ethnic category. Within the categories (South Asian, Chinese, African Caribbean and European), we aimed to interview people from a range of backgrounds (ethnic, socio-economic, religious) and to include two-thirds of self-identified older people and one third of people from the 'middle' (aka 'sandwich') generation, who had both older people and children in their families. The sample included 36 women and 22 men. Whilst the research was focused on ethnic diversity, it was important to see how this interacted with other dimensions of difference, so in analysis we examined systematically the impact of socio-economic group, gender, education, generation and religion.

### Understanding mistreatment

The participants spoke about mistreatment on several levels, contextually and society wide, within families and interpersonally. Overall, their descriptions and understandings of mistreatment emphasised the complexity of the relationships involved, and the embeddedness of good and bad treatment (as they saw it) of older people within the wider contexts of BME older people's lives.

The starting point was that 36 people (62%) felt that older people are not generally treated well in today's society. They referred to a wide range of issues, including general lack of respect, disdain for the life experience of older people, limitations of systems of care and support and pensions. The factors they cited were often related to the system of service provision or features of society generally, and sometimes cultural. The cultural issues were most usually related to societal change, and the idea that in the past, older people were more cared for, younger people had more time, and the experience of age commanded greater respect.

> The thing that amazes me about ageism is the way that we treat people who have survived long enough to get old, you know, and this awareness that just like they're a different species or a different planet and that younger people are not going to get old themselves. It's almost like there's no connection. (2206 African Caribbean[1])

In my opinion in this country the older people are not treated well... The main point is the children... The children are not brought up to and educated to honour and to have esteem... If you are not respecting your elders, you cannot expect to be respected by your children. (3254 Polish)

Middle generation respondents were more likely to refer to cultural changes ('lack of culture' or 'lack of religion') than were older people. Muslims were more likely to say that mistreatment was due to religion – sometimes, this referred to the failure of people to live up to their religious values of respecting older people, and in a few cases, it referred to older people being more conspicuous in the street due to their skin colour or dress and therefore more vulnerable to public attack.

There were many references to the general lack of power of older people, seen to be excluded from decision making, to lack economic power and to experience physical weakness, making it difficult for people to exercise choice. People felt ignored, and that their views were discounted. We asked whether respondents felt older people could make choices in their lives – more than half (31 people; 53%) felt that they generally could not, and positive answers were frequently qualified with phrases such as 'as long as they have their health' or 'it depends on their financial position' or 'if you are blessed with a good mind'. There were several respondents who clearly felt themselves to be without power, relating this to their economic position, their age, and their labour market position:

I feel I don't have any value, as I am not wealthy. (2210 Bangladeshi)

For one so old [over 70], what more is there to ask? (3233 Chinese)

---

## CASE STUDY 5.1[2]

Mr A lives with his daughter and her family in a house which he has passed on to his son-in-law. He has a state pension, and gives nearly all of this to his daughter for his keep. His daughter works very hard – she has three teenage children and works full time outside the home. Mr A likes to go out to a local social club three lunchtimes a week and meet with his friends, read newspapers and enjoy their conversation. Increasingly, he finds it difficult to get on and off the bus, and fell and broke his arm recently. His daughter does not want him to take the bus, and he is spending more time in the house. His health is deteriorating, as he does not get out much. Mr A complains that he is being kept at home, that he has no money, and that his daughter is not helping him as she should. He feels he is not being treated well, and that his family has no respect for him.

To illustrate the way that cultural and other factors interacted, it is useful to refer to a particular issue that emerged for the Chinese respondents, that of gambling. This respondent linked it with other causes of mistreatment:

> Racism, institutional racism in society, mental health or health problems…general problems, lack of support from family or extended family, disability, or living in isolation. Another thing is you know, talk about, you talk about economic hardship or even gambling families you know, that's another thing you know. (3244 Chinese)

And this one began by identifying it as a cultural issue that could cause problems:

> There will be some who spend their money gambling and do not give them [their spouses] money to spend and these can cause clashes. Yes, I have heard of such things. A lot of people gamble and some Chinese, a lot of them love to gamble. (3241 Chinese)

This respondent however went on to relate a history of abuse from racists, including court appearances which had resulted from his own attempts to fight back physically. Although people cited gambling as a potential source of problems, it would be incorrect to see it in isolation from other issues, and particularly to cite it as a single cause of mistreatment.

When speaking about the nature of mistreatment, generally the middle generation respondents were more likely to name types of mistreatment in accordance with the lists used by professionals than were the older people. Men were more likely to refer to racism, physical abuse and gaps in services than women. Those who lived in families (as compared with those who lived alone) were more likely to mention psychological abuse, as were those with more education. No South Asians or Europeans identified sexual abuse as a potential type of abuse.

Mistreatment was also strongly identified as occurring within families. Here, the generational changes were echoed, as people looked back to a past in which younger generations had cared for older ones, and noted that the additional factor of migration meant the historic extended family networks were no longer available. Many stories were told of the difficulties faced by families, including economic pressures, lack of support and carer burden – all these were seen as potentially promoting mistreatment of older people.

> Sometimes it's circumstantial, neglect. The carer gets exhausted; they leave the older person at home. Older people slow down and are very needy and people [carers] get tired and frustrated. Also mistreatment happens because

of lack of respect and knowledge of old age. If an older person is disabled they are more likely to be mistreated. (2205 Bangladeshi)

You can get for instance…granny bashing where you get…an elderly person staying where there's three generations in the one house or four and it's just a straw that breaks the camel's back… I don't think there's any particular reason. I would say stress, stress and pressures…they always say that a good daughter is the one that bashes; the bad daughter walks away from the mother, do you know what I mean, it becomes too much. (2224 Jewish)

These quotations also indicate the identification of attributes of the individual as promoting mistreatment, such as becoming dependent, being unable to contribute to the family, or not being mentally strong.

## CASE STUDY 5.2

Mrs C lives in a 'granny flat' attached to her son's house. She has dementia, and is finding it increasingly difficult to look after herself. Recently, she has developed continence problems, and her son will not allow her into the rest of the house, because his wife says she is dirty. During the day, her family go out to work, and leave her locked in the flat. They bring her food regularly, but spend less and less time with her, as they find her 'difficult'. Mrs C is very unhappy, especially as she is seeing less of her grandchildren and having more and more difficulty coping with everyday life.

Overall, therefore, mistreatment was seen very much as arising out of circumstances, and not necessarily to be the prerogative of 'bad' individuals. It was seen as part of the continuum of behaviour towards older people, rather than a clearly identifiable distinctive activity and could take a range of forms. There was a clear message that mistreatment could occur without intent, and an understanding of how it might develop from community and family dynamics. Outside the family, mistreatment could come from strangers in the street, from unresponsive services and, occasionally, from care staff – though these were rarely discussed, most likely because of the rather limited experience of formal services among our participants.

## CASE STUDY 5.3

Mr D lives alone in a small flat in a tower block. He is less steady on his feet than he once was, but enjoys going out to meet with his friends at the lunch club nearby. Recently, he has been troubled by groups of local youths hanging about at the entrance to the block, who shout and laugh at him as he passes by. As a younger man, he had always stood up for himself against racist abuse, and had been in trouble several times for doing so. Now he feels this would be too risky. He always checks whether the youths are around now, and if they are there, he phones his friends and tells them he is not feeling well and will not be at the club.

---

### Disclosing mistreatment

Five (and a suspected sixth) respondents disclosed that they had been victims of extreme mistreatment, including violence and psychological and financial abuse. They had lived with this mistreatment for many years, two women throughout violent marriages. Compared with the incidence of elder abuse identified in the prevalence study (O'Keeffe *et al.* 2007), this is a high rate of abuse. However, unlike that study, our interviews permitted people to define abuse for themselves, and our view is there are reasons to suggest that rates of abuse may be somewhat higher than those identified by O'Keeffe *et al.* and that much abuse remains hidden. First, we did not directly ask our respondents about their own experiences of abuse, and the disclosures were spontaneous. Second, there was much talk of the shame of disclosure, suggesting people would be extremely reluctant to do so. Third, as we will discuss later, people's reactions to abuse would make it more likely not to be disclosed and finally, there is the difficulty of leaving an abusive situation, which is only partly related to the availability of services, as we will discuss below. We would not suggest necessarily that the higher levels of abuse are particular to BME communities, but that it is likely that hidden abuse is widespread.

---

### CASE STUDY 5.4

Mrs B lives with her husband who has severe arthritis and cares for him. She is getting older, and having increasing difficulty helping him with tasks like bathing and dressing. She pays a local woman to come in twice a week to help with the bath. Recently, the woman has been doing bits of shopping for Mrs B, who is worried that prices seem to be going up quickly, and there never seems to be much change from the shopping expeditions. The couple are living on a basic state pension, and have trouble making ends meet. One day, Mrs B, chatting with a friend, hears the story of a local couple who employed a helper who started to steal money from them. The next day, she dismisses the helper, deeply embarrassed that she has been taken in by her.

---

### Reacting to mistreatment

We were interested in how people would react to experiences of mistreatment. When asked, 'If an older person is being mistreated, what will they do?', 67 per cent replied 'nothing'. When asked, 'If an older person from a BME group is being mistreated, what will they do?', the percentage answering 'nothing' increased to 79 per cent. Service support was seen as a possibility by very few respondents (five people). Various explanations were suggested for this reaction, including weakness or a lack of confidence, echoing the views we outlined earlier about the treatment of older people in society generally. Others suggested that the older person would keep quiet in case the abuse worsened, emphasising dependence and vulnerability. Others identified that the older person might have nowhere else to go. It was particularly emphasised that the family, whilst mistreating the older person, might also be their only source of support, and that an older person would not want to bring shame on their family. People spoke of feelings for one's family and sympathy for their situation. There are strong parallels here with the domestic violence literature, which also suggests that getting away from an abusive situation is especially difficult in situations of social exclusion (e.g. Harvie 1991). Two of our cases of disclosure involved women who had experienced marriage-long violence – one woman, widowed, expressed experiencing contentment for the first time.

There was, nevertheless, evidence of mutual support within communities. When asked, 32 respondents reported that they had 'come across' an older person experiencing mistreatment. They related that family and friends had supported the older person, but 14 of them spoke of support from service providers. Specific organisations mentioned were mostly (ten) specialist BME voluntary sector organisations. Three people mentioned help from the local social work department and one explained that they had helped with a financial difficulty through approaching statutory pension providers.

Only seven people felt that the needs of the person they had helped had been fully met – 11 said that some had been met and two, that needs had not been met at all. Where needs had not been met, explanations focused on the lack of knowledge of the older people (eight), concerns that others might find out about the mistreatment (three) and belief that nothing could be done. Half (16) of those whom respondents had 'come across' were said still to be in the same situation.

## The role of services

More than half (32) said that they were aware of services for older people experiencing mistreatment. Six people mentioned Age Concern – this may have reflected their knowledge that the research involved Age Concern Scotland. However, other voluntary sector organisations were listed, including community-based groups for BME older people, some specialist services and statutory bodies including the social work department (mentioned by seven people) and the police (three mentions). However, it was clear that these services were mentioned because of knowledge of their general activities, not necessarily because they were thought to have any specific expertise in supporting older people experiencing mistreatment.

Seventeen people felt that existing services were meeting people's needs, with 22 saying that they were not, and 19 unsure. There was clear doubt here. Several accounts were given of services which had proved helpful, but these were frequently qualified with comments such as 'they do their best' followed by identification of shortcomings such as uncompleted work, and continuing need.

Where people felt that services were not meeting people's needs, we asked what improvements they felt were needed. Those most frequently mentioned were raised awareness (21), training of community members (15), more bilingual support (12) and staff training (10). The emphasis on greater awareness and knowledge was marked, and middle generation respondents were more likely to emphasise this.

Elaborating on their suggestions for further services, many respondents highlighted what they saw as general issues with service provision for people from BME groups. So, for example, they spoke about insecure funding of community-based groups and failures in mainstream services to provide interpreting and/or bilingual staff. Others considered aspects of the place of older people in society and the need for them to be valued and respected. They spoke of the need for older people to have better knowledge of places to go for help, safe places to go and get it, and the possibility of phoning a helpline, but the potential stigma attached to one dedicated to 'elder abuse' specifically.

Only one person knew of work done by existing services with perpetrators of mistreatment – they thought perhaps the social work department might be doing something. We asked what work could be done with perpetrators. There was a strand of punitivism in the answers – for example, a short sharp spell in prison was suggested – but this was not the main response. More typically, there was recognition of pressures faced by family carers and their need for support to prevent a situation of mistreatment arising. 'Mistreatment occurs because carers are stretched to breaking point' (2220 Jewish).

## SERVICE RESPONSES

We now turn to the experiences of services which have attempted work in this area, and highlight some of the issues they have faced. The 28 service providers interviewed for the research (and four who took part in a focus group) were recommended and recognised by others as offering particularly good services for older people from BME communities. Initially, we searched for providers with experience of services relating specifically to elder abuse, but these were so few that we broadened our search to include more general services for older BME people and generic elder abuse/adult protection services. With few exceptions, we found that services for BME older people had limited knowledge of adult protection issues, and adult protection services, with limited exceptions, had paid scant attention to issues for BME communities. There were clear gaps in mutual potential learning. The organisations included in the study were located throughout the UK, in England (12), Northern Ireland (2), Scotland (9) and Wales (2), with three more having a UK-wide remit, with pockets of identifiable good practice widely dispersed. They included statutory and voluntary organisations, and their activities are summarised in Table 5.2.

---

### Key points from the interviews

- People from BME communities have clear views about elder abuse, and specific experience of it.

- They analyse mistreatment of older people as resulting from issues in families and communities.

- Cultural factors have some influence on people's views, but we did not identify systematic, culturally based differences in views and experiences – other variations, including generational and gender differences, were also important.

- Much mistreatment of older people remains hidden, and there are difficulties in acting when mistreatment is experienced.

- Services are not seen as playing a large role in supporting people experiencing mistreatment.

- There is a perceived need for awareness raising and for services to implement basic measures such as staff training and language support.

| Table 5.2 Remits of organisations interviewed | |
|---|---|
| *Activity* | *Mentioned by (n=28)* |
| Counselling and support | 15 |
| Befriending and volunteering | 12 |
| Campaigning/awareness raising | 15 |
| Offering refuge space | 2 |
| Telephone help-line | 7 |
| Day centre services | 7 |
| Research | 9 |
| Working at strategy level | 18 |
| Community development | 11 |
| Residential care | 5 |
| Training | 8 |

*Note: All potential activities mentioned by each organisation were recorded.*

By including voluntary sector service providers, many of which were grounded in local BME communities, our work goes beyond other attempts to identify good practice, such as PAVA (2004), which includes examples from social services and police forces in England. As the comments from the community interviews suggested, where people do seek out service support, the BME voluntary sector is often the first port of call. Yet there are serious questions about how effectively such groups can address mistreatment issues, and how integrated they are into adult protection networks.

### Recognising mistreatment

Most of our respondents (23 of 28) recognised that mistreatment of older people occurs in BME communities. They were quick to identify the issue as a particularly sensitive one, and to emphasise the need to tread carefully, build up trust and so on before it could be addressed. Organisations with a specific adult protection remit readily defined mistreatment of older people as occurring where there were breaches of trust. These organisations also identified a characteristic list of types of abuse – physical, psychological, financial, sexual and neglect – with occasional suggestions that the list could also include racism and institutional (or service) abuse. This 'accepted' way of framing abuse was much less characteristic of the BME voluntary sector respondents, who nevertheless spoke eloquently about mistreatment in the communities with which they worked. These groups tended to frame their discussions around particular issues they had faced, notably issues of neglect or intergenerational issues in families, and their views were clearly more in tune with those of the BME community respondents, seeing issues in a holistic manner. These rather different ways of discussing mistreatment of older people expose one of the key difficulties identified in our research, and suggest that to develop good practice, there is a real need for the expertise of adult protection teams and the grounded knowledge and experience of BME service providers to be brought together. There was little evidence that the adult protection/elder abuse experts had engaged effectively with BME communities, and the organisations with good knowledge of local BME communities often had difficulties moving beyond the specifics of individual examples. Both kinds of organisation tended to focus on interpersonal relationships, however, and in this respect, the community interviews showed a wider analysis of the issue, focusing as they did on structural issues such as ageism and racism.

---

### Service issue 1[3]

'Older BME people don't come here – we have never had a case. It isn't an issue for us.'

- Why is that?

    ○ Is it because older BME people don't experience mistreatment?
    ○ Is it because your service only focuses on young families?
    ○ Is it because your service is 'white' or monocultural?

- What changes could you make to open your service to BME older people?

- Do you have access to interpreters? How confident in them are you?

- Do you have links with the local BME community?

---

Service provision for BME older people, families and communities experiencing abuse is patchy, limited and rarely has specific focus on or skills in addressing mistreatment of older people. All the non-BME service providers interviewed were involved in monitoring ethnicity of their clients, but most felt their effectiveness in reaching BME clients was a 'work in progress', and that further efforts were needed – two said their organisations had no strategy for engagement with BME communities. The BME providers generally offered wide-ranging services for older people, including day-centre facilities, lunch clubs, support with benefits, health advocacy and so on, and mistreatment of older people was, for many, an additional issue for already over-stretched resources. A significant number of these groups expressed reluctance to address the issue specifically, often on the grounds that they would not know of local sources of help to which clients could be referred. Whilst in most cases local adult protection agency groupings existed, local BME groups were not necessarily aware of these, and expressed little faith in mainstream services.

---

### Service issue 2

'I worry too often about those occasions where somebody stumbles on abuse and then says, "Oh, he's in his seventies, or she's in her eighties – couldn't possibly be happening", and walks away. And that could be the one and only time that that older person has a chance to escape from what's happening to them, because people don't want to believe that older people can be abused.'

- Have you walked away?

- How does ageism affect your practice?

- Can you provide a 'safe place' for an older BME person to speak about abuse?

- How can you maintain confidentiality in such a case?

---

**Good practice?**

Service providers were asked to identify what they saw as good practice. In some respects their answers were disappointing, in that they rarely focused specifically on good practice in work on elder abuse with BME communities, but it was nevertheless possible to identify several key pointers.

First, good relationships with local BME communities were clearly important. Many locally based BME groups clearly had these, identifying trusting relationships with local communities and popularity as sources of local support. There were some examples of mainstream services working with local BME groups, some in long-established relationships. In other cases, local authorities, which were only beginning their work on BME issues, as was the case in some of the more rural areas in particular, saw these groups as key allies. In general, mainstream providers focused on joined-up services, such as health services working with community services, or local partnerships where the police service could link in with other services.

Conversely, however, there were many examples of BME groups working alone, isolated and unaware of wider activity and having little engagement with mainstream services. Other BME groups were clearly under pressure, facing huge demand to which they were unable to respond. Thus, limits to collaboration emerged. Furthermore, new organisations were likely to see collaboration as something for the future, suggesting that they did not perhaps see a need to learn from the experiences of others from the outset. Some respondents mentioned examples of organisations with which they would not collaborate for their failure to engage effectively with BME communities.

In connection with partnerships, referrals emerged as an issue. Respondents discussed the difficulties and advantages of referrals. In some cases, older people did not wish to be referred on, even though it was clear that they needed help. In other cases, organisations hesitated to refer as they were not confident that other agencies could provide appropriate services. Their caution applied both to mainstream services which were not diversity responsive, and voluntary sector organisations which did not have the capacity or remit to tackle issues of elder abuse.

Second, basic aspects of cross-cultural working emerged as essential. Having bilingual workers and being culturally sensitive were seen as fundamental by BME service providers, who stressed their community grounding, often that they had started as very local voluntary groups and developed into service providers with local authority contracts. These groups also highlighted gender factors – that in some BME communities, men and women needed to be involved separately, particularly in Muslim communities where men-only or women-only events were often preferred. Others identified other particular cultural factors, such as a Chinese group commenting on the preferred diet of Chinese older people, and a Polish group identifying the culture of older Polish people as differing from that of modern Polish migrants. Non-BME groups did not generally raise these kinds of issues, but rather spoke of the perceived strengths of their more general practice. A small number of them recognised that BME people were often 'disconnected' (as one person put it) with services, unable to seek help and not knowing where to find it. Some non-BME providers commented that their practice was inherently orientated towards diversity – but went on to speak about the continuing need to build relationships with local BME communities.

---

### Service issue 3

'Sometimes you realise in the middle of things that this person is being abused.'

- How do you respond to disclosure of abuse?
- Have you considered what words to use?
- Do you have anything to offer someone like this?
- What do you think would happen to an older BME person who left an abusive situation?
- Is there anywhere locally you would feel confident making a referral?

---

Non-BME groups referred to the importance of quick access to interpreting services, but shortcomings in interpreting services were regularly identified, as well as examples of bad practice. Fifteen respondents used professional interpreting services, with others using family members (five) or staff in-house or elsewhere who 'happened' to know a language (20), and four referring to volunteers. Only one organisation spoke about difficulties with client confidentiality in relation to interpreters.

Third, a number of information and knowledge issues emerged. Both national and some local organisations valued the ability to influence wider debates. Being connected to networks of people on the ground was important for this, so that they could be involved in discussing issues and identifying where service development was needed. Influence at community level was needed to raise awareness of issues and thus empower local people, using a proactive approach. Activity might not necessarily focus specifically on elder abuse or other sensitive topics such as domestic violence, but events such as health seminars could bring people in, and begin to get more difficult topics discussed – one group, for example, promoted a 'citizenship approach' aimed at the more general empowerment of older people; others referred to volunteers who worked with them bringing grassroots experience; one organisation had used interactive theatre to raise awareness. One provider emphasised that elder abuse 'needs to become everybody's business'.

A small minority of service providers saw links between and possibilities for mutual learning about elder abuse and other forms of abuse. One organisation wanted to see elder abuse as high on public agendas and in service practice as child abuse. Another had taken part in discussions about the parallels between domestic violence and adult protection issues.

**Problems for service providers**

A number of key problems emerged. First, there were clear resource issues, especially for the BME voluntary sector, including lack of funding; making multiple funding applications; projects sometimes coming to abrupt ends to the detriment of work done and client relationships built up; lack of training; lack of confidence to develop work on sensitive issues; and in the mainstream services, concern that BME groups were not using services. Respondents identified few BME people coming through adult protection services, which they perceived as geared towards the majority, thus excluding minorities. BME providers pointed out that standardised procedures underestimate the difficulties faced by some BME clients – for example, a Bangladeshi woman who wanted to move away from her family took a long time to tell them so, and in the meantime, the offer of a flat was withdrawn; and people such as some South Asian women, who are used to having others make decisions for them, have difficulties with services which require quick decisions by users.

Second, whilst many organisations reported that some training had been received, there was little evidence that BME issues and elder abuse had been brought together. Statutory providers spoke about anti-racism training or cultural awareness training; some had received training on elder abuse recognition and response, but still felt that frontline staff needed more awareness. Two organisations saw a need to produce training materials suitable for non-specialists, so that elder abuse as an issue could be a concern for everyone. The training received by the BME providers was especially patchy, with only one organisation specifically referring to training on elder abuse.

---

### Important issues raised from interviews with service providers

- Responses to elder abuse in BME communities are limited, even among this group of service providers with reputations for doing well.

- Nevertheless, key elements of good practice are emerging. These include:

  ○ the need to build good relationships with and among BME communities and all service provider sectors

  ○ the need to pay attention to good practice such as cultural sensitivity and awareness and effective language support where needed

- the need to invest in raising awareness and knowledge not simply of elder abuse itself (as we have seen the communities know about this already), but of available support services
- the need to question 'one size fits all' approaches
- improvements in training, involving discussion of elder abuse and BME issues.

- These are not new issues – there is scope for learning from other service delivery, including work on domestic violence.

- There are clear gaps in that the community interviews suggested that service provision was simply not tuned into their real experiences – this raises key questions about how well service providers have engaged with BME issues, despite many of their best efforts.

## NOTES

1   Respondents are identified by number and by the ethnicity of their choice.

2   The case studies are based on our research findings, but do not represent real individuals.

3   The service issues emerged directly from our research findings.

## REFERENCES

Biggs, S., Phillipson, C. and Kingston, P. (1995) *Elder Abuse in Perspective*. Buckingham: Open University Press.

Bowes, A. M. and Dar, N. S. (2000) *Family Support and Community Care: A Study of South Asian Older People*. Edinburgh: Central Research Unit, Scottish Executive.

Bowes, A., Avan, G. and Macintosh, S. B. (2008) *They Put Up With It – What Else Can They Do? Mistreatment of Black and Minority Ethnic Older People and the Service Response*. Edinburgh: Age Concern Scotland.

Butt, J. and Mirza, K. (1996) *Social Care and Black Communities*. London: Race Equality Unit.

Harper, S. (2006) *Ageing Societies*. London: Hodder Education.

Harvie, L. (1991) 'Sexual violence and the voluntary sector: Asian women and wife abuse', in A. and D. Sim (eds) *Demands and Constraints: Ethnic Minorities and Social Services in Scotland*. Edinburgh: Scottish Council for Voluntary Organisations.

Kosberg, J. I., Lowenstein, A., Garcia, J. L. and Biggs, S. (2003) 'Study of elder abuse within diverse cultures'. *Journal of Elder Abuse and Neglect 15*, 3–4, pp.71–89.

Nazroo, J. Y. (2001) *Ethnicity, Class and Health*. London: Policy Studies Institute.

O'Keeffe, M., Hills, A., Doyle, M., McCreadie, C. *et al.* (2007) *UK Study of Abuse and Neglect of Older People: Prevalence Survey Report*. London: Comic Relief and the Department of Health.

Practitioner Alliance Against Abuse of Vulnerable Adults (PAVA) (2004) *The PAVA Project: Practice Directory*. Tiverton: PAVA. (www.pavauk.org.uk/docs/57103_PAVA_Directory.pdf)

Samad, Y. and Eade, J. (2003) *Community Perceptions of Forced Marriage*. www.fco.gov.uk/Files/kfile/clureport.pdf (accessed on 14 February 2008).

# CHAPTER 6

# THE ROLE OF THE COMMISSION FOR SOCIAL CARE INSPECTION

## ADRIAN HUGHES

### BACKGROUND

This chapter will discuss the role of the Commission for Social Care Inspection (CSCI) in safeguarding vulnerable adults in regulated care settings. It will provide information about the legal context in which the Commission operates and how this differs from its predecessor bodies. The chapter will also describe what practitioners can expect from the Commission when safeguarding issues are raised in regulated care services. The Commission has agreed with other key agencies its role in relation to safeguarding adults who use regulated service and have produced a protocol (CSCI, ADSS and ACPO 2007).[1]

The Commission for Social Care Inspection (the Commission) was launched in April 2004 as the single, independent inspectorate for all social care services in England. It was established by the Health and Social Care (Community Health and Standards) Act 2003. The establishment of the Commission brings together the inspection, regulation and review of all social care services into one organisation. This results in a more effective organisation, which has an independent overview of the complete social care industry including the commissioning, purchasing and delivery of services. The Commission has a broader remit than its predecessors had.

The government has plans in place for the Commission to be abolished and replaced by a new health and social care regulator. The new body is to be known as the Care Quality Commission and should be operational by April 2009. In the meantime the Commission will continue to regulate social care services for adults to ensure that people who use services are free from risk of harm and abuse.

Before looking in detail at the role of the Commission in safeguarding adults it is important to set out the range of services which are regulated as this has changed since the introduction of the Care Standards Act 2000. The previous legislation, the Registered Homes Act 1984, placed a duty on local authorities and health authorities to register care homes and nursing homes. The new legislation now requires those providing domiciliary care agencies, nurses agencies and adult placement schemes as well as care homes to be registered. The Commission is *not* involved in the regulation of the emerging self-directed care options available to adults such as direct payments, supported living or individual budgets.

## LEGAL ROLE OF THE COMMISSION IN ADULT SAFEGUARDING

The Commission's specific responsibilities and duties are set out in the Care Standards Act 2000 and the Health and Social Care (Community Health and Standards) Act 2003. These Acts provide the legal framework and strengthen the position that the role of the Commission is primarily as a regulator, focusing much more on the providers of services and safeguarding users of services as a result of the action which can be taken against them. This is not intended to distance the Commission from the safeguarding role but rather reinforces the notion that the providers of care services, the local authority and National Health Service (NHS) commissioners and contractors, play the most significant role in safeguarding adults. It is self-evident that as the body which registers and licenses those who provide care services then it also has the power to remove the licence to operate.

## GOOD PRACTICE POINT

Visit the CSCI website (www.csci.org.uk/professional), download the Adult Safeguarding Protocol and use it to ensure that the local CSCI office, social services and providers are adhering to it.

## REGISTRATION

Before any care agency or establishment is able to provide a service the person, persons or organisation intending to run it must be registered with the Commission. In short, this means they are licensed to operate a care service in line with the conditions attached to the certificate of registration. The process is designed to ensure that only those who are fit to be registered are licensed. In addition, work is undertaken to check on the suitability of the premises for care homes, and that policies and procedures are in place to quality assure the delivery of good quality outcomes and people who use the services are free from harm or risk of abuse. The legislation places the onus on the person, partners in a partnership and a representative of an organisation to prove their fitness. This is demonstrated by references, checks on financial security, criminal records bureau disclosures and an interview with officers of the Commission. In addition if a manager is appointed they too have to be registered. The focus on managers is about assessing their ability to manage a care service and considers their understanding of good practice in care.

The Commission can propose to refuse registration of an owner or manager and if so the applicant has the right to make representation and appeal to the Care Standards Tribunal (CST). It is possible for the CST to determine that an applicant whose registration the Commission has proposed to refuse registration is subsequently registered following a successful appeal.

## GOOD PRACTICE POINT

Visit the Care Standards Tribunal at www.carestandardstribunal. gov.uk where all decisions of the tribunal are listed. Decisions provide a good source of information about what is considered acceptable and what is not.

Once registered, the provider, together with the manager, can start to operate the service in accordance with the certificate of registration. Certificates in respect of care homes are more detailed than those for nurses and domiciliary care agencies or adult placement schemes. These will usually include the total number of people who can live in the home together with service user category. These conditions are important to ensure that the service only accommodates people with needs which can be met and whose needs are compatible.

### POST REGISTRATION

Once registered the expectation is that the service will operate in line with the Act, regulations, national minimum standards (NMS) and good practice guidelines. The Act and the regulations are fairly light with explicit references to safeguarding. Implicit in the standards is the obligation that providers of services will create an environment and culture which minimises risk and protects people who use services from harm.

National minimum standards are specific to different types of services and have been published by the Department of Health.

## GOOD PRACTICE POINT

Visit the CSCI website and download the national minimum standards for each regulated service type:

- Care Homes for Older People
- Care Homes for Adults (18–65)
- Domiciliary Care
- Nurses Agencies
- Adult Placement Schemes.

The standards are not legally enforceable but the Commission will take them into account in determining whether a service is delivering good outcomes. The standards have been criticised as too input based with little emphasis on outcomes. In the Department of Health publication *Modernising Adult Social Care – What's Working* (DH 2007), it is recognised that the NMS have established a minimum baseline across the social care market; Challis *et al.* (2004) are quoted as saying 'users can now expect, at the very least, a minimum "quality" of care no matter where they live and no matter what type of organisation provides their services' – as one respondent put it: 'It's sad to say, but compulsion works' (DH 2007, p.42). Plans are in place to update the NMS in line with the outcomes set out in the White Paper *Our Health, Our Care, Our Say* (DH 2006), but not until the new regulatory framework is in place.

### USING THE NATIONAL MINIMUM STANDARDS TO CREATE A SAFE ENVIRONMENT

The national minimum standards all broadly cover the same areas, although the wording and emphasis may be slightly different. The standards are concerned with creating a safe environment and culture based on premises, staffing and policies and procedures to deliver safe care.

There is insufficient space in this chapter to cover all sets of national minimum standards and show how they should be used, so only those for care homes for older people (DH 2002) will be explored. The standards are divided into seven key areas:

1. Choice of Home (Standards 1–6)

2. Health and Personal Care (Standards 7–11)

3. Daily Life and Social Activities (Standards 12–15)

4. Complaints and Protection (Standards 16–18)

5. Environment (Standards 19–26)

6. Staffing (Standards 27–30)

7. Management and Administration (Standards 31–38).

Abuse is referred to five times within the 38 standards and only twice with reference to adults in the relevant regulations (Care Homes Regulations 2001), so how can these be used by providers to ensure safety?

### Choice of home

The 'choice of home' standards are intended to ensure that a service can meet the needs of prospective users. As indicated before, the service will be licensed to accommodate specific care needs and therefore it is vital that before admission the provider of the service and the person to receive the care understand what is required and can be delivered. The admission of a user with particular care needs which challenge the service may result in providers not being geared to respond. In such cases the risk of harm through ignorance because staff do not know the person, or abuse or harm from other users, is heightened. The use of trial visits and good assessments are prerequisites in getting to know the person and should increase the chances of 'right person, right place'.

### GOOD PRACTICE POINT

Having a vacancy is not enough – support the person to test out if the service will meet specific needs. Encourage users to have trial periods. If the service does not provide trial periods ask 'Why not?'

### Health and personal care

'Health and personal care' standards are vital in ensuring that those who use services are supported as individuals. These standards support providers to pay attention to aspects of daily life, which can mean the difference between good practice and abusive regimes. If staff do not understand how to support people in some of the most intimate aspects of care, how can privacy and dignity be maintained? The fear and anxiety of an older person being bathed or washed by a young care worker can be daunting in itself. It can become psychological abuse if the caregiver is unable to attend to dignity issues. Consider the needs of an older person who has always been able to care for himself or herself now being reliant on others for some of the most intimate care. If the culture in the home does not make it clear 'that which is explicit and that which is not' the caregiver may, whilst supporting the person to have a bath, leave the door open, chat to a work colleague about unrelated matters or make comments about the user. These standards are about setting the tone, reminding carers of the rules and reinforcing the importance of dignity, privacy and respect and the impact on the person when attention is not given to this.

Care plans are a vital tool not only to ensure that the individual receives the care they require to maintain or improve their health and wellbeing, but are also vital to minimise the occurrence of abuse. Good care plans will set out in detail the needs of the individual and how the person likes them to be met or likes to be supported; the care plan should not be a 'one size fits all'. In setting out needs in this way, the likelihood of abuse by neglect or ignorance is reduced. Care plans should also guide caregivers in their response to any challenges to the service from the person. Care homes are increasingly responding to a broader range of complex needs and people are supported to live in the community for longer. On admission to the care setting there is increased risk that the person the user once was is now only seen as someone who needs care. This depersonalisation may mean that we do not get to know the person and what is important to them or why they may challenge. The care plan, along with specific training for all staff, should set out person-centred and personalised responses to all aspects of care. If the individual is someone who lashes out during episodes of care, or refuses medication or care, what are the agreed plans to respond? If the intended response is not explicit staff may resort to what they would deem to be appropriate, such as restraining the person, holding onto hands in an attempt to calm the person, and force feeding or disguising medication.

## GOOD PRACTICE POINT

Ensure that care plans are detailed and support staff to respond to all aspects of care including challenging behaviours. If these are not included ask the manager to consider what action s/he is taking to provide safe care, free from harm and the risk of abuse.

## Daily life and social activities

Life should not stop simply because the person now requires an increased level of support and personal care. Standards around daily life and social activities are in place to set the scene to permit people to maintain a lifestyle of their choosing. The NMS remind us that 'the fact that individuals have reached a later stage of life does not mean that their social, cultural, recreational and occupational characteristics, which have taken a lifetime to emerge, suddenly disappear' (DH 2002, p.13). For example, the provision of meals in care settings can become more focused on price, convenience and ease of preparation, with those who will eat the food being forgotten. Prior to living in the care home the individual will have had their own routine and preferences and used food in a variety of ways in addition to the dietary or nutritional value. Failure to pay specific attention to this and maintaining the lifestyle of the person is likely to have an impact. What scope is there for Mrs Jones to give her grandson juice and a cake when he comes to visit in the same way that she did when she lived in her own home? How does this make Mrs Jones feel and has anyone ever asked?

Standards in this grouping are also about social activities and community participation. Care services in particular can become extremely insular and closed environments. This is the right breeding ground for abusive practice to become established. Again the care service should be about helping people to maintain lifestyles or one which is close to the old one. While it is helpful when care services have a hairdresser visiting or the weekly religious service, these only respond to the functional aspects of the activity, not the wider social role.

### GOOD PRACTICE POINT

Practitioners should ask questions: 'How does the care service respond to the cultural, recreational and occupational needs of the person using the service?' 'What is in place to help the person maintain their old lifestyle?' 'Are users seen as the person they once were rather than a condition to be looked after?'

## Complaints and protection

'Complaints and protection' standards essentially do what it says on the can! They remind the registered person of their duty to protect users and what they should do if abuse occurs. They set out some important principles about policies and make reference to other key agencies. What they fail to do is make the vital link with the overall way in which the service operates and for some providers they, too, will fail to make the link. However, the key risk area of managing money belonging to people who use the service is well covered and can be supplemented with the Commission's most recent publication, *In Safe Keeping: Supporting People Who use Regulated Care Services with their Finances* (CSCI 2007).

## GOOD PRACTICE POINT

Find out if the care service has a safeguarding policy. Question/ decide whether it is in line with the local authority procedures.

Much has been made over recent years that the regulator has been too concerned with the environment in which services operate – with an obsession on room sizes. There has been some shift on this with the introduction of the Commission but concerns with service and facilities in care services remain important and a key factor in minimising abuse. How can users be protected from harm and potential abuse if the right equipment is not in place? If Mr Cooper is assessed as needing a hoist to support him from his bed to a standing position, the absence of the equipment will expose him (and others) to harm. As the need is identified and the potential harm is known, the deliberate harm must amount to abuse. If Mrs Bradford uses a hearing aid and the provision of audio aids is not in place, we can describe this in a number of ways, but it is abusive and even more so if it leads to greater isolation for her or denies her access to her favourite television or radio programmes. Small rooms have probably not caused anyone too much harm in themselves, but the cumulative effect with other deficits in a service will result in a detriment to the person especially if a significant period of time is spent in the room.

## GOOD PRACTICE POINT

Check out with the provider or manager of the service if they have in place equipment and adaptations to meet the specific needs of the person whom you are supporting.

The final group to be considered in this section from this set of NMS covers staffing. After the people who use services, who are the income generators, staff are probably the greatest asset to a service but also the greatest liability in terms of potential for abuse. These standards do not only focus on numbers, but what is also important, on how staff are recruited, their qualifications, background and expertise, as well as how they are trained. There is a view that social care is easy and caring for people is even easier, requiring very little training – getting it right is very difficult and requires much more than instinct. The process of staff recruitment coupled with good induction is vital to ensure that staff quickly understand and grasp the culture and ethos of the home. The requirements of the other standards are designed to make sure people get a good service free from harm and abuse.

Staff training and ongoing professional development is essential and should start from the moment the new employee takes up the post. The Common Induction Standards designed by Skills for Care (Skills for Care 2005) provide an important framework which should be the start of a training and development plan for all workers. The induction standards deal with the practicalities of the care settings, such as safety in the work place, but also safeguarding and protection. The underlying principle of the Common Induction Standards makes it clear that the worker should meet the outcomes for each of the standards before they are deemed to be 'safe to leave' – this means that they understand their role and can be left unsupervised. Access to other training as part of the overall training and development programme is essential and this should include individuals working towards National Vocational Qualifications (NVQs). The Commission is explicit in its general guidance that staff training is vital if staff are to fully understand and deliver safe working practices.

A staff development programme ensuring the continuous professional development of all workers is required to make sure that standards are maintained over time. Good quality staff working to well thought-out policies and supervised by competent managers will not eliminate abuse. It will, however, minimise the likelihood, and in the event of occurrence it will be in spite of all endeavour and should be reported and dealt with in a timely manner.

## GOOD PRACTICE POINT

It is worth remembering that abuse can occur in any care service, and acceptance of this is no reflection on the service itself, but is a responsible and necessary approach to the care of vulnerable adults.

## INSPECTION

The inspection of care services is now based in part on risk-assessment following on from the work of the Commission in awarding quality ratings. All services are rated as 'poor', 'adequate', 'good' or 'excellent' and these will be represented as star ratings with the range being from zero to three stars. The inspection process is the way in which the Commission tests out whether or not providers are delivering good quality outcomes and safe environments. Although all services will be assessed each year it is possible for good and excellent services to have an annual service review which does not involve a visit to the care home or agency for up to three years. The way in which the Commission learns of suspected abuse or poor practice therefore relies less on the inspection process.

The frequency for inspection as set out in The Commission for Social Care Inspection (Fees and Frequency of Inspections) (Amendment) Regulations 2006 means that the Commission will focus its attention on those services which are rated as poor (zero stars) or adequate (one star). The frequency of inspection will mean that for the worst performing services inspection will take place at least twice in a 12-month period and once in the same period for adequate services. However, it is important to stress that the Commission will not allow services to languish at poor and adequate performance for long.

As part of the regulatory programme the Commission will require the provider to complete and submit an Annual Quality Assurance Assessment (AQAA). This is a self-assessment of what the service does well, what it could do and how good outcomes are secured for people who use the service. There is the concern that providers may be less than accurate in their assessment of the service and this is provided for within the regulations. The service-specific regulations have been amended to make it a legal requirement that the provider must submit an AQAA when requested to do so by the Commission. The AQAA must be supported by evidence and must be a reasonable assessment of the service by the provider. The AQAA together with other information about a service will determine the type, intensity and timing of regulatory activity. As part of this decision making process the inspector will make decisions about obtaining information from other sources – people who use the service, their carers, relatives and sponsors, care managers and general practitioners. This information will be used to determine the focus of the inspection. The majority of inspections are now unannounced and are designed to test not only what happens on the day but to assess the quality assurance processes to guarantee consistent compliance with legislation, guidance and good practice. In assessing services the Commission will use established benchmarking tools to check how each service scores against the expected standard. This document is known as the Key Lines of Regulatory Assessment (KLORA). A KLORA is available for each service type and sets out what the inspector is looking for in order to decide if they are giving poor, adequate, good or excellent outcomes for people who use the service. The KLORA is a public document and allows users, service providers, purchasers and commissioners to see how judgements are made and what can be done to improve the service.

## GOOD PRACTICE POINT

Visit the CSCI website and look at the KLORA – check that the provider is doing what is expected of them. Encourage users to use the KLORA so that they know what is expected and what they can expect from good and excellent services.

Services which are rated as poor or adequate will receive a Key Inspection at least once a year. A Key Inspection always includes a visit to the home or agency. This is an opportunity to explore first-hand what life is like for people who use the service. The inspector will be looking to see if policies and procedures which are designed to protect people are in place, understood and translated into practice. If there are concerns about the way the service operates or fails to deliver good outcomes then the Commission will make a judgement about the risk to determine the action it will take. The Commission recognises its broader role in safeguarding users but will expect other agencies to take the lead and to support this would make an alert to the local social services department. The Commission will also make a requirement in the inspection report giving timescales for compliance.

The Commission is now engaging people who use the service as part of the inspection process. These are known as Experts by Experience. These are people whose knowledge about social care services comes directly from using social care services. The Expert will be able to make an assessment about services from a user perspective and comment on the level to which services meet needs.

It is unlikely that inspectors or Experts by Experience will observe first-hand abuse but they will identify systems or ways of working which may lead to or have caused poor outcomes for users. The inspection regime provides opportunities to test out what systems are in place to protect users.

## CASE STUDY 6.1

Hollybank House is registered to provide a service for up to 30 older people. In line with national averages a number of the people are receiving prescribed medication. The manager has taken charge of all medication and passively discourages self-medication. As part of administering medication the manager removes medication from the original container and places it in individual pots to be dispensed by care workers after meals.

Is this abusive? The first response is usually 'No, it's only poor practice'. The practice runs the risk of people getting the wrong medication or the medication may deteriorate being left out in this way. The result of this is that the person for whom the medication was prescribed is at risk of not getting it or it being of poorer quality. This is known because the guidelines are explicit. It could be argued that the risk is due to ignorance – does this make it better? No.

This practice is abusive and has the potential to cause harm – whether this is due to ignorance or not is not the issue. In addition to denying users the chance to maintain previous lifestyles and manage their own medication, it is also an abuse of power.

The inspector, in observing the practice at the time of inspection, makes a requirement that medication must be administered in line with best practice.

## DEALING WITH POOR SERVICES

Services which are assessed as poor are required by law to submit an improvement plan to the Commission. These services are assessed as providing poor outcomes for the people using the service and, in line with the Commission's commitment to stamping out poor practice, they are on the radar. The improvement plans place the responsibility on the provider to improve the service and the Commission to monitor when this is being achieved. As stated previously, poor services will not be allowed to drift and if improvement is not secured enforcement action will be taken.

## INSPECTION REPORTS

Reports are published following the inspection and detail what is good about a service, what has improved and what, if any, action the provider has to take to

## GOOD PRACTICE POINT

Visit the CSCI website, download inspection reports and share them with people who use the service. Ask the provider what action has been taken in response to requirements and look for evidence that the action has made a difference.

make further improvement or respond to any shortfalls. They will indicate if users are at risk, why and what has to be done about it.

### THE ROLE OF THE CSCI IN RESPONSE TO SPECIFIC ALLEGATIONS OF ABUSE

The Commission has agreed a joint protocol with the Association of Directors of Adult Social Services (ADSS) and the Association of Chief Police Officers (ACPO) called *Safeguarding Adults Protocol and Guidance* (CSCI *et al.* 2007). This protocol sets out the respective roles of the key agencies and details what providers, social services, practitioners and others can expect from the Commission. This protocol has significantly changed how the Commission as a regulator responds to allegations of abuse. This change has been viewed by other agencies and practitioners as the Commission taking a 'back seat' or 'being difficult to engage'. The section in conjunction with the protocol should set out what can be reasonably expected. The Commission recognises three main levels at which it would become involved in response to an alert about alleged abuse:

- Serious risk to a person's life, health or wellbeing. These are the grounds that would result in the Commission considering urgent or immediate cancellation of regulation. The Commission would work with other agencies but would pursue action in line with its statutory responsibilities.

- Breach of regulation or standards identified through an investigation by other agencies or as part of the initial alert. If information suggests that the alleged abuse involves a registered person the Commission may undertake an inspection or other enquiries, the purpose being to identify what action the Commission should take in respect of enforcing compliance.

- Incidents where there is no suggestion of serious risk and the information from an investigation undertaken by other agencies or the registered person will determine what, if any, further action the Commission will take. (CSCI *et al.* 2007, p.5)

## ALERTS

The Commission receives from a number of sources concerns about practice within care facilities. In line with the protocol information will be considered by an inspector and decisions made as to whether the information indicates abuse and will refer the matter to social services as the lead agency. Systems are in place to ensure that this takes place on the day the information is known to the Commission. In passing on information decisions will be taken as to whether any regulatory action is required. Any additional action taken by the Commission will be made known to the lead officer in social services. Regardless of this an alert would still be made to social services as it is best placed to consider the needs of individual users while the Commission can consider the broader operation of the service. If an alert is about a regulated service and has not come via the Commission then the lead officer in social services will notify the local office.

It is for social services in line with its procedures to determine if the alert is accepted as a referral and if so this would lead to a strategy meeting. The Commission is clear about which strategy meetings it would attend and the criteria is set out in the protocol, but as minimum key information will be provided which will assist the meeting in making decisions. Strategy meetings are a key stage in the process as they are the forum in which action can be agreed and resources allocated.

## STRATEGY MEETING

It is recognised that the new protocol has not yet been fully implemented at a local level and work is ongoing within the Commission and within local social service authorities to make sure that this is addressed. If practitioners consider that the vision of the protocol is not being translated into practice then they should raise this with their own manager who in turn can raise it with key staff in the Commission. It is important that practitioners have an understanding of the protocol and how the Commission now expects its staff to be involved in safeguarding. The role of this Commission is different to predecessor bodies and therefore CSCI staff conduct must be measured against the existing protocol, not what the Commission or individuals used to do. The Commission should be notified of every strategy meeting to be convened in respect of a regulated service and would attend in person if the alleged incident included one or more of the registered persons, including the manager, or if there are already concerns about the service where enforcement action is being considered or has taken place. When the Commission does not attend the meeting, it will provide key information in advance and will receive the minutes of the meeting to inform any decision to take action itself.

## GOOD PRACTICE POINT

If practitioners are concerned that local CSCI staff are not working in line with the protocol they should raise their concerns with the local Regulation Manager.

### REGULATORY ACTIVITY BY THE COMMISSION

Where the allegation suggests that there are breaches of legislation and standards the Commission would undertake enquiries using its own methodologies. This is most likely to be an inspection of the service and would probably be unannounced. However, although an inspection may in itself deal with the immediate issue and collect information to provide evidence of the breach, the key outcome must be to stop the practice which is causing harm.

The indicators which would prompt the Commission to undertake an inspection would include:

- one or more registered persons being implicated
- current quality rating of the service and any identified risks
- enforcement action being considered or initiated
- whether urgent action would be required if the allegation proved to be founded
- indications to suggest that the poor practice is complex and/or is institutional or cultural abuse or neglectful practice.

The Commission would report its findings back to social services and would share information to be used solely as part of the broader safeguarding investigation.

### SCOPE OF ACTION AVAILABLE TO THE COMMISSION

Following an inspection or other enquiries by the Commission or an investigation by partner agencies the Commission will decide what action it will take. The following list shows the range of possible interventions together with the desired outcomes.

- *Statutory requirements*

  Specific requirements are set out together with timescales indicating what the registered person must do and why. The outcome would be that the provider would stop doing what was causing the harm or start taking action to eliminate the harm. Failure to comply could lead to a statutory notice being served.

- *Statutory notice*

    A notice is served under the specific regulations setting out the breach, what action the registered person must take and the timescale for compliance, a period not exceeding three months. Failure to comply could lead to the prosecution in a magistrate's court.

- *Imposing conditions*

    This can be achieved by agreement, or by imposition if the registered person does not agree. It permits the Commission to impose restrictions which can limit the way in which the service operates. Examples of this could include reduction in numbers to be accommodated or changes to the service user categories. This can be through application to a magistrate's court where action is needed urgently.

- *Cancelling registration*

    If the concerns indicate a serious risk to the life, health or wellbeing of people using the service the Commission may submit an application to a magistrate's court for an urgent closure to cancel the registration. If the magistrate is satisfied that if the order is not made the risk will continue then an order will be made and the service must cease to operate. If the risk is not immediate the Commission may make a proposal to cancel registration but this process takes more time. During the process the Commission would continue to monitor the service to ensure compliance with regulations and standards leading to good outcomes for users. During this period any new alerts would be referred to social services and if the situation deteriorated then emergency cancellation could be considered.

---

## CASE STUDY 6.2

Stanmore Court is a home registered to provide a service for up to 24 people with mental disorder and specifically provides care for those with dementia. The Commission has rated the service an overall quality rating of level 2 – providing adequate outcomes for people who use the service. The Commission has been concerned about the way in which the manager operates the service and in particular the reporting of adult safeguarding issues to external bodies including both the CSCI and the local authority.

A student nurse had a placement in the service and witnessed an incident which at the time she did not report outside the home because the manager advised her that it was 'one of those things that happened and it was best not to raise as it would cause embarrassment to the people involved'. The student nurse continued to be concerned about the incident and following a discussion with her practice supervisor she realised that the incident should be reported and contacted the local CSCI.

The reported incident which she witnessed was between two people who use the service when one forcibly masturbated the other. It was clear from the report that this was not something that the recipient wanted, welcomed or enjoyed and it would appear was distressed by the incident. It is without doubt that the incident was abuse – it was something against the person's express wish and a violation of their right. It is also likely to be a criminal act and the matter has been reported to the police.

**WHAT ARE THE ISSUES?**
Provider failing to report the incident – this perpetuates the notion that abuse can be dealt with in-house. Raises concerns about the thresholds the manager uses in reporting incidents. Raises the possibility that other incidents have occurred and have not been dealt with. Denies people using the service appropriate interventions to manage behaviours which may be outside their control. Gives the wrong message to staff by failing to model good practice in safeguarding the rights of people using services and protecting people from harm.

**WHAT ACTION IS REQUIRED?**

- The matter must be reported to the police – it is not for social care practitioners to decide whether or not a crime has been committed. Clearly social care staff must work with and support the police in deciding in the best interest of users.

- A strategy meeting is required and the CSCI must be involved. The judgement of the manager cannot be relied upon and therefore the safeguarding of people using the service is compromised.

- The local social services must assess whether or not the safety and wellbeing of the people using the service is being upheld and, if not, must put in place actions to protect – this could include moving people to alternative accommodation.

- The CSCI must determine what action it will take in response to the provider's failure to comply with his legal obligations.

**WHAT ACTION COULD BE TAKEN?**

- CSCI – statutory notice, impose conditions on certificate, cancellation of registration

- Local Authority – assess the situation to see what, if any, immediate action is required to safeguard the people living there, for example, put staff in the home, move users to alternative accommodation.

**CONCLUSION**

The Commission has both a proactive and reactive role in the safeguarding of adults using regulated services. The proactive role is broad and is concerned with ensuring that standards are in place which support the development of environments which minimise risk and protect people from harm.

In the event that the Commission is unable to secure compliance or in the event of abuse occurring there is a range of interventions which the Commission can take using its own statutory powers or in partnership with key agencies. Although the idea that the Commission takes a back seat or is difficult to engage is acknowledged, situations which give rise to this criticism are perhaps caused by individual responses to safeguarding issues and do not feature as part of the agreed protocol. What is clear is that the Commission has become explicit about its role and this is a shift from that adopted by its predecessors. The Commission, like all other regulatory bodies, should be adhering to the Better Regulation Principles, which include being proportionate, transparent, accountable, targeted and consistent. These principles, individually and collectively, should enable others to hold the Commission to account, ensuring that a consistent delivery of the protocol is delivered throughout England.

**NOTE**

1   The protocol can be found at the Commission website: www.csci.org.uk/ professional.

## REFERENCES

Challis, D., Hughes, J., Qiu Xie, C., Jacobs, S., Reilly, S. and Stewart, K. (2004) *Social Services before the Influence of Modernisation: Baseline Study (BS2)*. Manchester: PSSRU.

Commission for Social Care Inspection (CSCI) (2007) 'In safe keeping: supporting people who use regulated care services with their finances'. *In Focus: Quality Issues in Social Care. Social Care Policy and Practice* 6 (May), pp.1–32.

Commission for Social Care Inspection (CSCI), Association of Directors of Social Services (ADSS) and the Association of Chief Police Officers (ACPO) (2007) *Safeguarding Adults Protocol and Guidance*. London: CSCI.

Department of Health (DH) (2002) *Care Homes for Older People: National Minimum Standards*. London: DH.

Department of Health (DH)(2006) *Our Health, Our Care, Our Say: A New Direction for Community Services*, White Paper. London: DH.

Department of Health (DH) (2007) *Modernising Adult Social Care – What's Working*. London: DH.

Skills for Care (2005) *Common Induction Standards*. Leeds: Skills for Care.


## STATUTES

Care Homes Regulations 2001. London: The Stationery Office

Care Standards Act 2000. London: The Stationery Office

Health and Social Care (Community Health and Standards) Act 2003. London: The Stationery Office

Registered Homes Act 1984. London: HMSO

The Commission for Social Care Inspection (Fees and Frequency of Inspections) (Amendment) Regulations 2006. London: The Stationery Office


## WEBSITE

The Government's Principles of Good Regulation, Better Regulation Taskforce (1997) see website: www.berr.gov.uk/bre/index.html (accessed on 4 June 2008).

# CHAPTER 7

# THE ABUSE IN INSTITUTIONS AND THE RESULTING INQUIRIES

## DEBORAH KITSON

### INTRODUCTION

This chapter will look at recent inquiries investigating the abuse of vulnerable adults with a particular focus on specific ones that have had/should have had a significant impact on practice issues. It will explore what instigates an inquiry, the relevant legislation, the role and responsibility of the inquiry and its investigators, the recommendations that result, the responsibility of agencies to implement those recommendations and the impact of inquiries on policy decisions and future planning of services.

I will be looking at inquiries involving the most vulnerable people in our society. Why are older people, people with mental health needs and people with learning and/or physical disabilities so vulnerable? There are a number of common factors for these groups that help us to understand their increased vulnerability and reinforce the need for us to look closely at why poor practice and abuse occurs in institutions established to care and support them. This will enable us to learn and adjust services accordingly. These factors include:

- *Difficulty with clear verbal communication.* We rely heavily on verbal communication without enough consideration of alternative forms of communication.

- *Disempowerment.* People are so often excluded from being involved in choices and decisions that affect their lives and this further reinforces their feelings of worthlessness and vulnerability.

- *Dependence.* Many people in institutional care rely on others to provide their basic needs and to assist them on a day-to-day basis.

- *Not being listened to.* There are many examples of staff not allowing the people they are caring for the time to talk and be listened to, and further, of staff not believing them if they do raise concerns.

'Institutional abuse includes individual acts or omissions and managerial failings in which the regime of the institution itself may be abusive' (Evans and Garner 2001). The concerns raised that instigated the following inquiries relate closely to this definition.

The specific inquiries covered will include background information and why the inquiry was initiated along with its main findings and recommendations. Common themes that emerge from these inquiries and their recommendations will be explored together with their impact across services internally and nationally. The following inquiries will be looked at in some detail – they have been selected because they have all presented common themes which are discussed later and have introduced change as a result of lessons learned:

- Portsmouth Healthcare NHS Trust, 1998

- Longcare, 1998

- Rowan Ward, 2002

- Cornwall, 2006

- Sutton and Merton, 2007.

**WHAT IS AN INQUIRY?**

There are many ways that allegations of abuse are dealt with and some understandable confusion about the decision making process for how allegations or concerns within an organisation are investigated. These include:

- internal investigations

- serious case reviews

- inquiries.

The majority of incidents will be reported and acted upon with reference to the local policy and procedures. *No Secrets* (DH and Home Office 2000) offered guidance on developing multi-agency policies and procedures to protect vulnerable adults from abuse and many authorities now have adult protection (or safeguarding) units and adult protection committees (or safeguarding boards) which coordinate and monitor this activity in their area. Many of these units also now produce annual reports and statistical information about the investigations carried out including their outcomes and other details. These investigations are useful, particularly in the light of the creation of adult protection committees set up since the implementation of *No Secrets*. They both enable and encourage an organisation critically to review the effectiveness of their internal procedures and to implement relevant changes and introduce necessary safeguards.

Serious case reviews, as referred to in *Safeguarding Adults* (ADSS 2005), were introduced as a requirement under the Department of Health Guidance *Working Together to Safeguard Children* (DH *et al*. 1999). *No Secrets* did not offer specific guidance on such reviews in adult protection but the ADSS, under Standard 1 (ADSS 2005, p.10), included them in their guidance and referred to the need to have a 'safeguarding adults' serious case review protocol and an agreed multi-agency protocol for the commissioning and undertaking of such review. The purpose of the review is to learn from past experience, improve practice and enhance procedures in the light of lessons learned.

So when would adult abuse concerns warrant an inquiry rather than an internal investigation or a serious case review? And how does the process and its outcomes vary?

The following definitions are useful in understanding the meaning of an 'inquiry' and its aims and objectives:

- *Inquiry* is any proceeding or process that has the aim of augmenting knowledge, resolving doubt, or solving a problem. A theory of inquiry is an account of the various types of inquiry and a treatment of the ways that each type of inquiry achieves its aim. (Wikipedia)

- A systematic investigation of a matter of public interest; a search for knowledge; an instance of questioning. (Wordnet)

- *in·quir·y* also *en·quir·y*

  1    The act of inquiring

  2    A question; a query

  3    A close examination of a matter in a search for information
       or truth

  Synonyms: inquiry, inquest, inquisition, investigation, probe, research. These nouns denote a quest for knowledge, data, or truth. (The free dictionary)

So the focus of the inquiry is to gain insight and knowledge into why something has occurred, in this instance why abuse has occurred, its context and its repercussions, whereas an internal investigation will deal commonly with an allegation, the perpetrator and the victim and will result in risk assessments, disciplinary action, internal policy and strategic changes required to minimise the risk of further abuse.

There have been key pieces of legislation that have impacted on abuse and protection and that refer to the format and status of an inquiry.

## RELEVANT LEGISLATION

### Care Standards Act 2000

In April 2002 previous legislation regulating residential and nursing homes – the Registered Homes Act 1984 and attendant regulations – were repealed and replaced by the Care Standards Act (CSA) 2000.

The CSA is a far more broad-ranging piece of legislation than the 1984 Act. It applies to and regulates a wider range of services than previously, applies across all aspects of care and brings for the first time previously unregulated care services under the regulatory umbrella including domiciliary social care providers, independent fostering agencies and residential family centres.

Those services previously regulated, including residential care homes for adults and nursing homes, continue to be registered and inspected but the powers of registration and inspection were removed from local and health authorities and passed over to a new national public authority called the Commission for Social Care Inspection (CSCI).

The Act refers to the instigating of an inquiry:

> The Secretary of State may cause an inquiry to be held into any matter connected with the exercise by the Commission of its functions. (10,1)

> The appropriate Minister may cause an inquiry to be held into any matter connected with a service provided in or by an establishment or agency. (10,2)

The Act goes on to say that:

> The report of the person who held the inquiry shall, unless the Minister who caused the inquiry to be held considers that there are exceptional circumstances which make it inappropriate to publish it, be published in a manner which that Minister considers appropriate. (10,7)

### Health and Social Care (Community Health and Standards) Act 2003

This Act also refers to inquiries instigated by the Secretary of State by either the Commission for Healthcare Audit and Inspection (CHAI) or the Commission for Social Care Inspection (CSCI) and reiterates sections of the Care Standards Act with reference to privacy and publications.

### Inquiries Act 2005

This Act gives the power to establish an independent inquiry as follows:

> (1) A Minister may cause an inquiry to be held under this Act in relation to a case where it appears to him that–

> (a) particular events have caused, or are capable of causing, public concern, or

> (b) there is public concern that particular events may have occurred. (Inquiries Act 2005, 1.1)

## WHO IS RESPONSIBLE FOR INQUIRIES?

The Commission for Healthcare Audit and Inspection, commonly referred to as the Healthcare Commission, was created under the Health and Social Care (Community Health and Standards) Act 2003 and has responsibility for investigating allegations of serious failings in healthcare. It has discretion with regard to investigations but,

> generally, the Healthcare Commission will only commence an investigation where it possesses credible information that suggests that there may have been, or there may be, a serious failing in the provision of healthcare by or for an NHS body that has resulted, or is resulting, in an adverse impact on the safety of patients, clinical effectiveness, or responsiveness to patients. (Healthcare Commission 2008)

They were responsible for the most recent inquiry discussed below looking at the learning disability services in Sutton and Merton and had joint responsibility with the CSCI in the Cornwall inquiry six months previously.

The CSCI inspect and report on care services in England and aim to 'promote improvements in social care and stamp out bad practice' (CSCI 2008)

It is the single inspectorate for social care in England and is responsible for regulating and inspecting all social care providers in both the public and the independent sectors. It also assesses the performance of local councils in delivering their personal social services functions.

Independent inquiries, instigated with reference to the Inquiries Act 2005, are undertaken '(a) by a chairman alone, or (b) by a chairman with one or more other members', and with reference to the appointment of the inquiry panel 'Each member of an inquiry panel is to be appointed by the Minister by an instrument in writing' (Inquiries Act 2005).

## INQUIRIES: A BRIEF HISTORY

In 1967 the *News of the World* reported on the appalling conditions at Ely Hospital, Cardiff, and forwarded to the Minister of Health a statement by a man containing allegations of various forms of misconduct on the part of members of the staff at Ely Hospital which resulted in an inquiry by the Department of Health and Social Security (1969). Similar living conditions were reported by *The Guardian* at Harperbury Hospital (1968) and there followed a number of subsequent inquiries which led to public outcry and pressure on the government to respond with changes to services. A number of significant government initiatives followed which impacted significantly on future services for adults with learning disabilities and for other vulnerable adults including:

- *Better Services for the Mentally Handicapped* (DH 1971)

- Jay Report, 1979: advocated a faster pace of change and promoted the social model of disability
- Griffiths Report, 1984: highlighted the difference between 'rhetoric and reality' in the provision of community services and called for market-led reforms
- NHS and Community Care Act, 1990: community services to be *accessed* via systematic assessment of need, but can be *provided* by independent sector.

Since the implementation of the NHS and Community Care Act 1990 there has been significant progress towards the protection of vulnerable adults. 'It is in this field, of abuse prevention and vulnerable witness protection, that inquiries can be seen to have played a significant role in the development of new statutory frameworks and policy guidance' (Fyson, Kitson and Corbett 2004, p.223). These include:

- *Speaking up for Justice* (Home Office 1998)
- *No Secrets* (DH and Home Offfice 2000)
- *Valuing People* (DH 2001)
- *Achieving Best Evidence* (Home Office 2002)
- Sexual Offences Act 2003
- Safeguarding Vulnerable Groups Act 2006.

**MORE RECENT INQUIRIES**

There have been a number of inquiries in recent years concerning vulnerable adults. Concerns have been raised in various ways but all of the resulting inquiries have made recommendations requiring both local and national changes. But for 20 years inquiries have revealed the same issues and have subsequently recommended relevant changes in services – so what is the real impact of these inquiries and why does it not seem to have significantly reduced the risk of abuse to vulnerable adults living in institutions? A sample of inquiries are referred to here to give examples of the process of an inquiry and its recommendations. I will then draw on the common factors which will be discussed later in this chapter.

**Longcare**

Between 1983 and 1993, many adults with learning disabilities who lived at the Longcare residential homes, near Slough, were beaten, tormented, drugged, neglected, indecently assaulted and raped. The main perpetrator was the owner of Longcare, Gordon Rowe, but other members of staff, including his wife Angela, and managers of the service were also responsible for neglecting and ill-treating residents.

The Independent Longcare Inquiry's remit (Burgner *et al.* 1998) was restricted mainly to the role of Buckinghamshire County Council as an inspection and registration body. The investigation by Buckinghamshire's inspection unit that finally brought an end to Rowe's regime was sparked by complaints from members of staff, but it took nearly ten years for that to happen. So why didn't they speak up sooner?

Gordon Rowe used power and control not only over the people living in his care but also over his staff. 'Gordon had such power, and not just over the residents, over the whole staff. I think some of us were frightened we would never get another job in the caring profession' (anon. in Pring 2005). He created an environment where staff felt unable to raise concerns, convinced others that his practices were acceptable ways of working with people with learning disabilities and used threats and bribes to prevent disclosure. This inquiry raised significant issues about whistleblowing and the importance of creating systems whereby staff would feel able to raise concerns without fear of repercussions and reprisals.

As a result of this inquiry, Buckinghamshire County Council agreed to pay an estimated £1 million compensation to 54 former Longcare residents, because of its failure to prevent and halt the abuse. This civil case served to highlight the government's failure to address the flaws that existed in the criminal justice system. The trial clearly highlighted the inadequacies of the criminal justice system which failed to deal effectively with these crimes. In his summing up Judge John Baker said that the Mental Health Act 1983 had provided him with inadequate sentencing powers and he called for a parliamentary review. Indeed Gordon Rowe's wife had received only a 30-month sentence despite her involvement in the most serious abuses seen at Longcare.

This resulted in a further outcome of the Longcare inquiry – the following year, civil servant Tom Burgner, who led the independent inquiry, called for a new offence, of causing harm to or exploitation of a vulnerable adult, with a maximum penalty of ten years in prison, as with child neglect.

John Pring, news editor for the journal *disabilitynow* and author of *Silent Victims* (2004) which discusses the Longcare case in detail, supported this and launched the Justice for Survivors campaign calling for a new, arrestable offence of harming or exploiting a vulnerable adult, with a maximum penalty of ten years in prison. The Mental Health Act 2007 increases the maximum sentence for staff in care homes and hospitals who ill-treat or neglect residents and patients with learning difficulties or mental health problems from two years to five years, so there has been some progress made.

## Portsmouth Healthcare NHS Trust

The Commission for Health Improvement (CHI) (2002) undertook this investigation looking at the care and treatment of frail older people at Gosport War Memorial Hospital provided by Portsmouth Healthcare NHS Trust. Between 1998 and 2001 the police investigated an unlawful killing on the ward and five patient deaths and in 1998 had made a referral to the CHI for a formal investigation. Recommendations from the report included issues relating to the following.

---

### Recommendations

- Medication
- Daytime activities
- Staff training
- Risk and incident reports
- Whistleblowing
- Levels of support

---

There were also recommendations made to the Department of Health concerning clarity of the understanding of the terms relating to levels of care and the need to work more closely with the Association of Chief Police Officers (ACPO) to develop a protocol for sharing information.

## Rowan Ward

The Greater Manchester Strategic Health Authority contacted the CHI in October 2002. Following allegations of physical and emotional abuse of patients in Rowan Ward it was asking for an investigation into its older age services. Rowan Ward was an isolated facility for older people with mental health problems. In this inquiry the CHI looked at systems and processes as opposed to the allegations themselves which were already being dealt with by the police and by the internal investigation. They looked at the quality of care and levels of safety prior to and following the allegations (CHI 2003).

The following issues were identified as key contributory factors:

- geographical isolation
- low staffing levels
- lack of training

- lack of nursing leadership
- lack of clinical governance.

Recommendations from the CHI included the following:

---

## Recommendations

- Strengthen management capacity
- Accountability
- Implementation of clear policies
- Professional development
- Improved reporting systems
- Robust information systems
- Integration into services

---

In 2005 the Care Services Improvement Partnership published *Moving On: Key Learning from Rowan Ward*, endorsed by Stephen Ladyman, the then Parliamentary Under Secretary of State for Community, who said: 'we need to ensure that an older person with mental illness is treated in the same way as any other citizen and offered the best possible support and care. There must never be another Rowan Ward' (Foreword).

## Cornwall

The Healthcare Commission and the Commission for Social Care Inspection jointly investigated services for people with learning disabilities provided by Cornwall Partnership NHS Trust in May 2005. The concerns were raised by East Cornwall Mencap Society and resulted in a formal investigation, an internal disciplinary investigation and subsequent dismissal of five staff. The investigation found that poor and abusive practices had been evident for many years and had resulted in various actions that had clearly not been effective. The Trust had carried out several internal investigations dealing with individual allegations of abuse and there was clear evidence of physical, emotional and environmental abuse. Cornwall Partnership NHS Trust had investigated 57 members of staff in all involving 46 incidents prior to October 2005.

Immediate changes in the Trust's services for people with learning disabilities was considered necessary and were implemented immediately by an external team as it was agreed that there were significant failings that required action before the conclusion of the investigation. Institutional abuse was widespread with people with learning disabilities being denied their right to independence, choice and inclusion.

> Poor practice has become ingrained within management of learning disability services and the provision of care. (Healthcare Commission/CSCI 2006, p.5)

> A damning report has raised serious concerns about the treatment and care of people with learning disabilities. (BBC News 24, 5 July 2006)

The media picked up on this report and although public attention was short lived it did have an impact and Cornwall, coupled with just six months later the report from Sutton and Merton again detailing institutional abuse on a wide scale, resulted in a national review of learning disabilities services (see the section on Sutton and Merton following).

## Sutton and Merton

Following on only six months after the Cornwall inquiry, the Healthcare Commission made a decision in February 2006 to investigate services in Sutton and Merton Primary Care Trust provided for people with learning disabilities after being contacted by their Chief Executive. This followed a number of incidents and allegations including physical and sexual abuse. 'The aim of the investigation was to establish whether the ways of working at the PCT were adequate to ensure the safety of people using the service' (Healthcare Commission 2007, p.3). Because it was the second formal investigation carried out by the Healthcare Commission in six months its impact appears at this comparatively early stage to have been significant at creating service and strategic changes. For this reason I have offered information and detail of this more recent inquiry and its recommendations.

The findings of the investigation were published in its final report in February 2007 and included a catalogue of examples of poor care and institutional practices. Between 2002 and 2005, prior to the investigation, there had been 15 serious incidents, two of which had resulted in criminal proceedings. One care assistant was charged with the rape of a woman in his care and received a six-year sentence. A second man was charged with indecently assaulting a male in his care, but the case was discontinued. Apart from these incidents which formed a part of the investigation, there were also numerous examples of abuse that reflected a cultural acceptance of poor standards of care and included issues of:

- communication
- management
- morale

- training
- person centred planning
- risk management
- culture of acceptance
- resources.

## COMMUNICATION

Communication was limited between staff and service users, summed up by one comment from a manager who said: 'staff do not require communication training because the client does not speak' (Healthcare Commission 2007, p.5). Staff were not encouraged to explore alternative methods of communication or to use an advocate to assist in understanding the individual. This resulted in the service users' increased dependency and lack of participation in their own decision making and choices.

## PERSON CENTRED PLANNING

Without effective communication and with little understanding of the person's individual needs there was no commitment towards developing person centred planning. Institutional care and a 'one size fits all' approach was adopted throughout the service.

## TRAINING

A significant lack of training contributed to the institutional services that had developed and there was evidence that some staff had not attended even the mandatory training involving health and safety. Training on person centred planning and values, crucial if a service is to ensure that individuals are treated with respect and dignity, was not available. There were examples of institutional care that staff had considered to be acceptable practice in the absence of any professional support, guidance and training.

## MANAGEMENT

There had been seven Chief Executives in the last decade resulting in a lack of continuity. The Primary Care Trust (PCT) covered four organisations and three health authorities and there appeared to be a lack of commitment in the PCT towards learning disability services generally. Coupled with staff shortages and subsequent poor supervision and staff support the service was inevitably going to feel the effects of this structure. Inadequate recording and reporting were also inevitable shortcomings from a service that has little regard for either its staff development or the rights of its service users.

## RESOURCES

Many service users lived in environments that lacked individuality with poor furnishings, insufficient adaptations and inadequate access. One service user had been without the use of his electric wheelchair for a considerable time as nobody had considered sorting out its repair and many others did not have the appropriate aids and adaptations to meet their needs.

## INSTITUTIONAL PRACTICES AND ACCEPTANCE

Many of the practices reported were those seen so often in the last century – service users were reported to be 'fed' wrapped in paper, they participated in few activities, with some reportedly only spending three to four hours a week in the community; a culture of dependency was evident. Relatives and carers, though few had complained, were not referred to in decisions affecting their relatives and advocacy services were not referred to as they should have been.

## RISK ASSESSMENTS

The management of risk was found to be ineffective in part of the learning disability service despite systems in place. Numbers of incidents were not reported and so there was no appropriate response to safety that left people at continued risk.

The report acknowledges that much of the abuse was unintentional and that staff, through lack of training and management support, were unaware that their practice was abusive and degrading to service users. The effect on many of the staff in the PCT must have been devastating when the report was published and the repercussions began – media, further investigations, disciplinaries.

The Healthcare Commission concluded its report with a number of recommendations addressed to Sutton and Merton PCT.

---

### Recommendations

- Quality of care
- Staff development and training
- Empowering people who use services
- Governance and strategic arrangements
- Redesigning services

As well as local recommendations the Healthcare Commission included in their report significant national recommendations:

> In light of the learning from this and the Healthcare Commission's previous investigation into Cornwall Partnership NHS Trust, clarification from the Department of Health on what a modern learning disability service should look like would help PCTs to commission services for people with learning disabilities. (Healthcare Commission 2007, p.82)

It went on to carry out an audit of learning disability services across England in the NHS and the independent sector which should have a significant impact on the future management and structuring of these services. Following debate about the practicality of learning disability services being managed as they are currently across health, social services and the independent sector there are expectations that the service will, in future, be managed outside of health services. This also reflects the principle that many endorse that learning disability should be perceived in social rather than medical terms.

Interestingly, an inquiry led by Peggy Jay in 1975 was set up to look at just this issue in response to the then Labour health minister David Owen's idea to set up a 'mental handicap executive' to establish the service in local authority social services. By the time the report was published in 1979 the plans had been abandoned due to the impending general election. There is a certain irony that 30 years on this is being reconsidered in the light of further evidence of abuse and poor services.

## CURRENT INQUIRIES

There are also a number of current inquiries being undertaken that have been instigated by significant concerns in adult care. It is hoped that the following two inquiries will result in significant outcomes for vulnerable adults.

### Inquiry into the deaths of people with a learning disability in National Health Service (NHS) care

In May 2007 the Department of Health announced that an inquiry had been established into access to healthcare for people with a learning disability. This followed Mencap's *Death by Indifference* report published in March 2007 which featured the cases of six people who had died within NHS care. The inquiry will investigate why they died and whether their deaths could have been avoided. They include the following:

- Martin, aged 43, went without food for 26 days whilst he was in hospital following a stroke.

- Emma died of cancer on 25 July 2004. They decided not to treat her as they believed she would not cooperate with treatment.

- Tom's expressions of pain weren't listened to and he died on 25 May 2004. He had profound and multiple learning disabilities.

### The Joint Committee on Human Rights – Inquiries

Chaired by Andrew Dismore MP, the Joint Committee on Human Rights consists of 12 members appointed from both the House of Commons and the House of Lords. Two inquiries recently have been of particular interest with reference to protection of vulnerable adults:

- *The Human Rights of Older People in Healthcare* – looking at the victimisation or neglect of older people within the healthcare system, who may be particularly vulnerable to ill-treatment, raises important issues of substantive human rights law.

- *The Human Rights of Adults with Learning Disabilities* – the Committee intends to consider the practical application of human rights principles to people with learning disabilities.

## WHAT CAN BE LEARNED: AN EXAMINATION OF THE COMMON THEMES

There are a number of recurring themes that appear in recent inquiries clearly showing that these issues are not being addressed and lessons are not being learned despite the recommendations in the inquiry reports. These include the following:

### Whistleblowing

All the inquiries, and in particular the Longcare investigation, highlighted concerns that practices had not been reported and the culture of abuse was allowed to continue over significant periods of time. The Longcare Report highlighted a number of reasons for the reluctance of staff to raise concerns, and research by the Ann Craft Trust (ACT 2005) supported this – that whistleblowing on abuse is fraught with difficulties, but that it is essential in protecting vulnerable adults. In response to the Public Interest Disclosure Act 1998, most employers have developed whistleblowing policies to enable workers to raise concerns. However, little is known about how whistleblowing legislation interacts with adult protection procedures, nor whether it is succeeding in protecting staff and the people with learning disabilities with whom they work.

Blowing the whistle can help protect adults with learning disabilities from abuse but doing so can have a profound impact on the whistleblower and on wider relationships within a care setting. The way in which whistleblowing incidents are perceived and managed in the workplace makes a huge difference to the experience of care staff. Support, protection and feedback for the whistleblower are crucial. Almost all care providers now have whistleblowing policies to allow staff to raise concerns, but the implementation of these policies varies widely. ACT's research found that whistleblowing continues to be regarded negatively and people may be reluctant to self-identify as a whistleblower, so they may not access the protection and support offered by a whistleblowing policy. Changes in organisational culture are necessary so that workers can speak out without fear of reprisal and have the confidence that their concerns will be listened to.

## Person centred planning

All the inquiries referred to a lack of individual care and respect for the individual with a casual disregard of their right to be included in a decision making process that had an impact on decisions about their lives. Advocacy services were seldom accessed and relatives and carers were very often excluded from future planning. Without the implementation of person centred planning few care plans or records detailed specific needs. This resulted in inconsistencies in the care provided by staff, in specific medical and social needs not being met and in few structures being put in place to assess risk and review needs – all of which play a part in increasing a person's vulnerability.

## Management

There were issues in all the inquiries about management on a strategic level and on a day-to-day basis including lack of supervision and support for staff and poor recording and individual planning. It is no surprise that a PCT with seven Chief Executives in ten years should reveal a lack of strategic direction and a poor commitment to the quality of the service (Sutton and Merton). The current discussions about changes in the way that learning disability services are managed may have some benefits but there still needs to be consideration of these issues for older people and those with mental health needs.

## Training

A lack of commitment to training has been exposed in all the recent inquiries looking at the abuse of vulnerable adults in institutions, sometimes including even the mandatory training on health and safety and values. New, inexperienced staff, without training, will be dependent on other staff to show them models of practice. They will often, as in the case of the appalling poor practices at Sutton and Merton, be unaware that they are copying institutional practices that are both outdated and abusive. As a result they will not be competent to follow procedures, to record and report appropriately or to introduce person centred planning. In many situations new staff who recognise the poor practices look elsewhere for work and others imitate current practices and so the culture of abuse and poor practice becomes increasingly widespread and accepted.

## CONCLUSION

There are a number of significant government initiatives that have resulted from or been influenced by the outcome of inquiries (see above). Inquiries have also had an impact on existing legislation, for example *No Secrets* is likely now to be reviewed and reproduced in the light of the more recent inquiries where its implementation had failed to protect the people in the care of those services, and there is currently consultation about whether adult protection legislation should be introduced, modelled on child protection. These are positive outcomes from inquiries – they highlight deficiencies, generate debate and do create pressure for change.

Although not an inquiry that came out of institutional abuse and therefore not for discussion in detail in this chapter, the deaths of Holly Wells and Jessica Chapman in 2002 also had a significant impact on the safeguarding of vulnerable adults. Holly and Jessica, both aged 10, went missing in August 2002. Their bodies were found on 17 August 2002 and Ian Huntley, their school caretaker, was charged with their murders three days later. The Bichard Inquiry was an independent inquiry arising from the Soham murders and chaired by Sir Michael Bichard with the following terms of reference:

> Urgently to enquire into child protection procedures in Humberside Police and Cambridgeshire Constabulary in the light of the recent trial and conviction of Ian Huntley for the murder of Jessica Chapman and Holly Wells.

> In particular to assess the effectiveness of the relevant intelligence-based record keeping, the vetting practices in those forces since 1995 and information sharing with other agencies, and to report to the Home Secretary on matters of local and national relevance and make recommendations as appropriate. (House of Commons 2004, p.19)

The Safeguarding Vulnerable Groups Act 2006 which incorporated the findings of this inquiry established the Independent Safeguarding Authority (ISA) which replaced the Protection of Vulnerable Adults list established in July 2004. As from the autumn of 2008 the safeguarding of vulnerable adults and children is enhanced by the adoption of new working practices by the ISA by preventing those who are deemed unsuitable to work with children and vulnerable adults from gaining access to them through their work. This is done by providing employers with a more effective and streamlined vetting service for potential employees and by barring unsuitable individuals from working, or seeking to work, with children and vulnerable adults at the earliest opportunity.

The Healthcare Commission launched a national audit of learning disability services in response to the Cornwall Inquiry and there is likely to be a huge change in the delivery of learning disability services nationally.

Internal policies and procedures have been reviewed as well as the strengthening of structural processes that should minimise risks in the agencies that instigated the inquiries. These initiatives are to be cautiously celebrated.

But do they really impact on national debate and public attitudes, both of which are essential if we are really going to make a difference to the lives of the most vulnerable in our society? Inquiries looking at the abuse of vulnerable adults receive little public attention. Sutton and Merton and Cornwall, for example, shocked those of us working in this area, but media attention lasted 24 hours. Unless we can shift attitudes and ensure that vulnerable adults are treated with the dignity and respect that are their right, investigations and inquiries will only scratch the surface of the problem and produce little real change. It is time that we recognise that vulnerable adults have the right to be treated with respect and dignity and to be supported in services that minimise the risk of them being harmed. How many more inquiries will it take to get the basics right?

## REFERENCES

Ann Craft Trust (ACT) (2005) *Blowing the Whistle on the Abuse of Adults with Learning Disabilities.* Nottingham: ACT.

Association of Directors of Social Services (ADSS) (2005) *Safeguarding Adults.* London: ADSS.

BBC News 24 (5 July 2006) 'Patients "suffer extensive abuse"'.

Care Services Improvement Partnership (CSIP) (April 2005) *Moving On: Key Learning from Rowan Ward.* London: CSIP.

CSCI (2008) www.csci.org.uk/about_csci.aspx (accessed on 25 June 2008).

Department of Health (DH) (1971) *Better Services for the Mentally Handicapped.* London: HMSO.

Department of Health (DH) (2001) *Valuing People: A New Strategy for Learning Disability for the 21st Century.* London: DH.

Department of Health (DH) and Home Office (2000) *No Secrets: Guidance on Developing and Implementing Multi-Agency Policies and Procedures to Protect Vulnerable Adults from Abuse.* London: DH.

Department of Health, Home Office and Department for Education and Employment (1999) *Working Together to Safeguard Children.* London: Department of Health.

Evans, S. and Garner, J. (2001) 'Institutional abuse of older adults'. *Psychiatric Bulletin 25*, p.364.

Fyson, R., Kitson, D. and Corbett, A. (2004) 'Learning disability, abuse and inquiry'. In N. Stanley and J. Manthorpe (eds) *The Age of the Inquiry.* London: Routledge.

Healthcare Commission (2008) www.healthcarecommission.org.uk/serviceprovider information/investigationcriteria/afm (accessed on 25 June 2008).

Home Office (1998) *Speaking Up for Justice: Report of the Interdepartmental Working Group on the Treatment of Vulnerable or Intimidated Witnesses in the Criminal Justice System.* London: Home Office.

Home Office (2002) *Achieving Best Evidence in Criminal Proceedings: Guidance for Vulnerable or Intimidated Witnesses including Children.* London: Home Office Communication Directorate.

Mencap (2007) *Death by Indifference: Following the Treat Me Right Report*. London: Mencap.

Pring, J. (2004) *Silent Victims*. London: Gibson Square Books.

Pring, J. (2005) 'The long-term effects of the abusive regime at the Longcare homes'. *Journal of Adult Protection 7*, 2 (August), pp.37–43.


## INQUIRY REPORTS

Burgner, T., Russell, P., Whitehead, S. *et al.* (1998) *Independent Longcare Inquiry*. Aylesbury: Buckinghamshire County Council.

Commission for Health Improvement (2002) *Portsmouth Healthcare NHS Trust at Gosport War Memorial Hospital*. London: The Stationery Office.

Commission for Health Improvement (2003) *Investigation into Matters Arising from Care on Rowan Ward, Manchester Mental Health and Social Care Trust*. London: The Stationery Office.

Department of Health (1979) *Report of the Committee on Enquiry into Mental Handicap Nursing and Care*, Cmnd. 7468 (Jay Report). London: HMSO.

Department of Health and Social Security Committee of Inquiry (March 1969) *Report of the Committee of Inquiry into Allegations of Ill-Treatment of Patients and Other Irregularities at the Ely Hospital, Cardiff*, Cmnd. 3975. London: HMSO.

Healthcare Commission (2007) *Investigation into the Service for People with Learning Disabilities Provided by Sutton and Merton Primary Care Trust*. London: Commission for Healthcare Audit and Inspection.

Healthcare Commission/CSCI (2006) *Joint Investigation into the Provision of Services for People with Learning Disabilities at Cornwall Partnership NHS Trust*. London: Commission for Healthcare Audit and Inspection.

House of Commons (2004) *The Bichard Inquiry Report*. London: The Stationery Office.

House of Commons Social Services Committee (1984) *Griffiths NHS Management Inquiry Report*. London: HMSO.

House of Lords/House of Commons, The Joint Committee on Human Rights (March 2007) *The Human Rights of Adults with Learning Disabilities*. London: The Stationery Office.

House of Lords/House of Commons, The Joint Committee on Human Rights (July 2007) *The Human Rights of Older People in Healthcare*. London: The Stationery Office.


## STATUTES

Care Standards Act 2000. London: The Stationery Office

Health and Social Care (Community Health and Standards) Act 2003. London: The Stationery Office

Inquiries Act 2005. London: The Stationery Office

Mental Health Act 1983. London: HMSO

Mental Health Act 2007. London: The Stationery Office

National Health Service and Community Care Act 1990. London: HMSO

Registered Homes Act 1984. London: HMSO

Safeguarding Vulnerable Groups Act 2006. London: The Stationery Office

Sexual Offences Act 2003. London: The Stationery Office

# CHAPTER 8

# OLDER ADULTS IN PRISON
## VULNERABILITY, ABUSE AND NEGLECT

## ADRIAN J. HAYES AND SEENA FAZEL

### INTRODUCTION

Older prisoners are a doubly hidden population. Whilst it is reported that older people in the community have felt ignored and overlooked (e.g. Help the Aged 2002), the issue has, at least, been highlighted in the media. Media access to prisons, on the other hand, is very limited, so the general public do not have a clear idea of what goes on in such institutions, or who is contained there. Many people are surprised that there are older people in prison, or presume that they are people who began life sentences many years ago. In fact the fastest-growing group of prisoners today is those aged 60 and over (Home Office 2005). Despite this, older prisoners do not represent a large proportion of the prison population as a whole (at around 2% of all prisoners), and their different health and social needs can remain undetected and unaddressed.

In this chapter, we hope to set out the context of the older population in English and Welsh prisons, to discuss issues relating to their health and social need, and explore ways in which they could be met. An important aspect of unmet need amongst this group is how far this could be said to fall under definitions of 'abuse' and 'neglect'. This chapter also aims to set out current definitions of abuse and neglect as they apply to older adults and evaluate their relevance to prisoners.

### THE OLDER PRISON POPULATION
#### The policy

At present, there is no national strategy for the care and management of older people in prison. However, the recent publication of several policy documents does have implications for their treatment. *National Service Frameworks*, published by the Department of Health to improve standards of care in priority areas, are applicable to prisoners and one of these has focused on the care of older adults (DH 2001). The document stated:

> The NHS and Prison Service are working in partnership to ensure that prisoners have access to the same range and level of health services as the general public... It is important that there is good liaison between prison healthcare staff and their colleagues in health and social care organisations in the community to ensure that prisoners who are being released are assessed for and receive services which meet their continuing health and social care needs. (DH 2001, p.4)

In the wake of this, Her Majesty's Inspectorate of Prisons (HMIP) published *No Problems – Old and Quiet* – a thematic review of the care of older prisoners in 2004 (HMIP 2004). This report included several recommendations as to how older prisoners should be treated, and some key areas (described below) where their different needs demanded alternative or additional services. Finally, building on these documents, the Department of Health produced a 'toolkit' for working with older offenders (DH 2007). The guidance provided very practical recommendations for assessment and care planning as well as preparation for integration of services in the community on release and it is hoped this will form the basis for development in individual prisons in this area.

However, whilst drawing attention to the issue of older prisoners, establishments are not required to implement any of these recommendations, and it will take the publication of a national strategy to ensure their needs are properly addressed.

*No Secrets* (DH and Home Office 2000) was a document published by the Department of Health which offers guidance on using policies and procedures to protect vulnerable adults from abuse. This is of specific relevance to prisoners, as the guidance states:

> Abuse can take place in any context. It may occur when a vulnerable adult lives alone or with a relative; it may also occur within nursing, residential or day care settings, in hospitals, custodial situations, support services into people's own homes, and other places previously assumed safe, or in public places. (DH and Home Office 2000, p.11)

Six categories of abuse are described in the document, which are usefully outlined as:

- *physical abuse*, including hitting, slapping, pushing, kicking, misuse of medication, restraint, or inappropriate sanctions

- *sexual abuse*, including rape and sexual assault or sexual acts to which the vulnerable adult has not consented, or could not consent or was pressured into consenting

- *psychological abuse*, including emotional abuse, threats of harm or abandonment, deprivation of contact, humiliation, blaming, controlling, intimidation, coercion, harassment, verbal abuse, isolation or withdrawal from services or supportive networks

- *financial or material abuse*, including theft, fraud, exploitation, pressure in connection with wills, property or inheritance or financial transactions, or the misuse or misappropriation of property, possessions or benefits

- *neglect and acts of omission*, including ignoring medical or physical care needs, failure to provide access to appropriate health, social care or educational services, the withholding of the necessities of life, such as medication, adequate nutrition and heating

- *discriminatory abuse*, including racist, sexist, that based on a person's disability, and other forms of harassment, slurs or similar treatment. (DH and Home Office 2000, p.9)

Vulnerable adults are defined in the document as those using or in need of community care, and this is relevant to prisoners who are detained in institutions where they have little control. It is relatively straightforward to see how definitions of the more direct forms of abuse (e.g. physical, psychological, sexual) may be of relevance to prisoners as perpetrators or victims. Older prisoners may be seen as more vulnerable from such abuse as being less physically and/or mentally able in some cases. However, prisoners can also experience indirect abuse, for example where services are withheld or not available, and this chapter will focus on such neglect, arguing that by ignoring the health and social needs of older prisoners (which are clearly elevated), they could be said to suffer neglect under the above definitions.

### Facts and figures

In 1989 there were 345 prisoners aged 60 or over in England and Wales (Katz 2001). By 2004, the number had risen to just under 1700 (HMIP 2004; more recent figures are unfortunately only available for sentenced prisoners); a rise of nearly 500 per cent over 15 years. The population as a whole is ageing, and sentencing practice has been getting tougher; Campbell and Allison (2006) report that prisoners serve 50 per cent more time than ten years ago, with life and indeterminate sentences particularly rising. With longer sentences, there are more people growing old in prison. Among prisoners aged 60 and over, around half are convicted of sexual offences, a much higher proportion than that of the overall prison population (where it is 19%). Victims may come forward later in life for incidents that happened when they were children or younger adults, so that offenders are older by the time they are convicted of these offences.

There are a small number of units or wings in prison service establishments dedicated for the use of older prisoners (e.g. HMP Frankland, HMP Wymott and HMP Kingston). These have been on the basis of local need or expertise rather than as direct initiatives by HM Prison Service. As well as being sparsely situated around the country, these units are also small, so the majority of older prisoners will be located with their younger counterparts in the general prison population. Prisoners are often located with reference to the length of their sentence or the availability of specific rehabilitation programmes. This means there are some prisons with fairly large older populations, for example in prisons with a large 'Vulnerable Prisoner Unit' (such as HMP Wymott) or lifer units (e.g. HMP Kingston). On the other hand, there are many more prisons that house just a few older prisoners.

## Defining the older prisoner

So far we have discussed the group of prisoners who are aged 60 and over. But why is this thought of as a useful age cut-off for defining older prisoners? One reason may be the availability of information. The Ministry of Justice (and previously the Home Office) produces quarterly statistics on the prison population, including the number of prisoners aged 60 and over. In the community, of course, health services for older adults are for those aged 65 and over. Various international studies have used a definition of older prisoners of aged 65, 60, 55, 50, 45 and even 40. There is no clear consensus, though Fazel and Jacoby (2002) found that 60 years was probably the age used most commonly in the forensic psychiatry literature. Amongst older female prisoners, 50 is more frequent (e.g. Wahidin 2004), but this could be due to the small numbers of women over 60 in prison (less than 20 in England and Wales according to the latest statistics from the Ministry of Justice).

However, there is a need to look beyond age boundaries towards definitions of need. The important cut-off is where prisoners' health and social need is different to that of younger prisoners. Aday (1999) and Wahidin (2004) have both suggested that people aged 50 in prison are similar in terms of their health to people aged 60 in the community. For those who have served a long time in prison, this may be due to institutionalisation. Furthermore, those who come into prison are more likely to be from a lower socio-economic group, to have misused illicit substances and to have had itinerant lifestyles, thus contributing to ageing. There is no clear research evidence from the UK comparing the health of different age groups, but emerging findings from some ongoing research suggests that prisoners aged 50 to 59 may not be dissimilar in physical health to prisoners aged 60 and over (Hayes et al. 2006). If we take 50 and over as a cut-off age for older prisoners, then the group is much larger at 8 per cent of the entire prison population.

To summarise, we know that there is a group of older people in prison which is growing in numbers faster than any other in the prison population. Currently there is no national strategy for the care of older prisoners, nor is there agreement on what age cut-off should be used. They may be found in large groups in some prisons or specialised wings, but more commonly are scattered throughout the general prison population where their needs may not be recognised. But what are their needs, and how are they different to those of younger prisoners?

## THE NEEDS OF OLDER ADULTS IN PRISON

The Inspectorate thematic review into the care of older prisoners was entitled *No Problems – Old and Quiet* (HMIP 2004), after a comment in one prisoner's case files, noted in the course of the study. The Inspectorate highlighted that this was a common representation of older prisoners amongst prison staff. However, it is one that holds a dangerous assumption; that being quiet indicates a lack of problems. The reality can often be very different.

---

### CASE STUDY 8.1

Mr M is 62 and nine months into a two-year sentence. He was shocked by the length of his sentence and says his mind was a mess as he was brought to prison and received into custody. The induction was a blur and he cannot remember a lot of what he was told. He was so upset that he was seen as a suicide risk on reception and for the first few days. He has requested no contact with his family since he came to prison and does not mix with the other inmates. He was prescribed antidepressants by the prison doctor when he was thought to be at risk of suicide, but these did not seem to make a difference to his mood so he stopped taking them after a couple of weeks. He has not had any contact with the health care department since he was first prescribed the tablets. Although he feels he is not at risk of self-injury, he still feels very down and cannot see this improving. He has periods when he becomes very upset and cannot stop crying, particularly in the evening and night-time. Staff describe him as 'quiet and sensible' and do not see him as a management problem, so have little contact with him.

---

## The health of older prisoners

In 2001, Fazel and colleagues from the University of Oxford interviewed sentenced prisoners in establishments holding at least ten prisoners aged 60 or over, within 100 miles of Oxford; the most comprehensive study of older prisoners' health in the UK (Fazel *et al.* 2001a, b). A total of 203 prisoners were interviewed at 15 establishments, representing about a fifth of the English and Welsh population of sentenced prisoners in this age group. Most (74%) of the group had served under four years with 16 per cent having served over ten years, and common convictions were for sexual offences (50%), violent offences (25%) or drug offences (14%). The group was predominantly spread between 'training prisons' (52%), which concentrate on rehabilitation, and 'local prisons' (37%), where those on short sentences or in the early stages of long sentences are housed.

The interviews showed a significant physical health need, with the majority reporting a chronic illness or disability. The most common areas to be affected by chronic illness were the musculoskeletal system, the cardiovascular system and the respiratory system. The most common diagnosed conditions were ischaemic heart disease or angina, osteoarthritis, diabetes, chronic obstructive pulmonary disease and asthma. In comparison with previous research into the health of the prisoners, older prisoners were shown to have more illnesses than the general prison population. Furthermore, in comparison with the health of older people in the community, they had more illnesses in seven of the nine body systems under study, and this comparison was with people aged 65 and over.

The research also uncovered serious mental health problems. Psychiatric disorder was diagnosed in over half of the older prisoners, with depression being the most common illness at a prevalence of 30 per cent. Again, this was higher than comparative rates of psychiatric disorder and depression in younger prisoners and older adults in the general population, and the rate of depression was found to be around five times higher for older prisoners than the age-matched general population. Adults with mental ill-health are deemed 'vulnerable' according to Department of Health policy (Lord Chancellor's Department 1999), therefore prisoners of any age with mental health problems are a particularly vulnerable group.

Two prisoners had symptoms indicating dementia, which appeared to have emerged during imprisonment. As Fazel, McMillan and O'Donnell (2002) argue in a more detailed discussion of these cases, there are ethical questions over the feasibility of rehabilitation for these prisoners and their capacity for future reoffending. Dementia would also render these prisoners more vulnerable to abuse by other inmates, as well as neglect if their psychiatric and associated social needs are not recognised or met.

Despite the complex and significant health needs of older prisoners, there is an indication that their needs are not being met. In Fazel *et al.*'s sample (2004) of those where depression was indicated, only 18 per cent had been prescribed antidepressant medication. This indicates an unrecognised and undertreated mental health need; HMIP (2004) suggested that prison mental health services are geared towards younger people. With regard to physical health, HMIP also found variable provision for the management of chronic conditions and a need for improved medication management services.

### Social needs and neglect

To date there has been no systematic study of the social needs of older prisoners, or physical/emotional neglect amongst this population. However, some exploratory work has been carried out by Frazer (2003) who interviewed staff and policy makers, and also the Inspectorate review (HMIP 2004). A key aspect from Frazer's interviews was the issue of prisoners who needed assistance with getting around the prison, and caring for themselves. Although most older prisoners are functionally independent, those with problems in this area caused difficulties for prisons. Helping prisoners to dress or wash themselves, or to move around the establishment are aspects of care that fall between the job descriptions of nurses and prison officers. Local social services very rarely work within prisons, though they may assess prisoners in preparation for release, and this seems to be a key omission in the care of older prisoners. Other prisoners will often help those who are less able, for example by bringing food to them or helping them keep their cell clean, but this should be factored into official health and social services within prison.

The physical environment can also be difficult for older people to negotiate. The Inspectorate (HMIP 2004) noted that prisons are designed with young men in mind, often with many stairs and long distances between buildings. This is potentially a form of discriminatory abuse (as it adversely affects those with physical disability), under definitions in *No Secrets* (DH and Home Office 2000). There is an emphasis in the prison regime on strict timekeeping, and prisoner movements (for example from wings to places of work or education) need to be completed in very short times. Older prisoners receive no additional consideration and must keep up with the younger prisoners. If they are unable to climb stairs, their range of work and even education options may be severely affected. Converted cells for those with disabilities are rare, and gates are often too narrow for wheelchairs; again, both issues of discrimination on the grounds of physical disability.

Although prisoners have the option of retiring at age 60, prisons tend to encourage them to remain in work or education. In fact, many older prisoners want to work to keep active and supplement the small pension provided by the prison. However, many of the available options for work in prisons are unsuitable for this group due to the need for either strength or agility, for example in industrial workshops or the laundry. The Inspectorate found that older prisoners did not always use exercise facilities, often because there was nowhere to sit down, their perception that they may not be allowed back before the period was finished, and a concern over suffering physical or emotional bullying. Being engaged in purposeful activity can be a protective factor for depression, and regular physical activity can maintain physical health and dexterity.

Loss of contact with family and friends is also associated with depression. Because prisoners are located on the basis of their sentence and rehabilitation, there is no guarantee they will be close to their home area. Older prisoners' partners and family are more likely to be older themselves and have physical problems, thus less able to visit their relatives and partners in custody. Isolation within the prison is also common, resulting in possible psychological abuse (DH and Home Office 2000). Prison wings are noisy places, particularly at night when younger prisoners play loud music and shout between cells. Older prisoners can feel they have nothing in common with younger inmates so may keep out of their way. At worst, bullying may take place where older prisoners are exploited for cigarettes or other possessions (meeting *No Secrets'* definition of financial/material abuse). On the other hand, younger prisoners may look up to their older counterparts, and it is common for the more educated to help others with filling in forms and education work.

Finally, the resettlement of older prisoners on release has been criticised and the Inspectorate (HMIP 2004) suggested that many are rehoused inappropriately. Resettlement of older people convicted of sexual offences is particularly difficult, as they may not be allowed to return to their home area where they have social support, and release plans may require them to remain in a hostel for a period. Another group where this was perceived as difficult was for those who had served very long sentences, and those with health difficulties (Frazer 2004).

## Institutional abuse

This section has considered ways in which the health and, particularly, social needs of older prisoners are elevated, and how they can remain unmet. As mentioned previously, such a failure of services falls under the Department of Health category of 'neglect or acts of omission' (DH and Home Office 2000) and can be conceptualised as abuse. This is different, but no less harmful, than the other direct forms of abuse discussed in that document. Indeed, it is feasible to see such neglect as 'institutional' or 'systemic' abuse (as used in Australia and North America), where people suffer abuse due to the systems themselves rather than any individual. A good example for this argument is the current position that social services departments should assess but not address the functional needs of people in prison. A concerted effort should be made to ensure that older prisoners are not neglected or abused in this way. The introduction of a national strategy would be a first, major step towards protecting this group, but in the meantime, there is much that prison, health and social care agencies can do to assist with meeting the needs of older people in custody.

Older prisoners have higher rates of physical and mental health problems compared to both younger prisoners and older people in the community. They also have social needs specific to their age group. These health and social needs can often go undetected in prison, resulting in possible neglect.

## MEETING THE NEEDS OF OLDER PRISONERS

In the absence of a national strategy for the care and management of older prisoners, we would make the following recommendations for prison staff working with this group. Several prisons have developed services and approaches for their older populations.

### Assessment

In order to meet the needs of older prisoners, these needs must first be identified. This is particularly important for prisons with small numbers of older people as, without a visible, recognisable population, they may not come to the attention of prison or health staff. Older prisoners may not themselves make the first move to complain of their problems, especially depression. Therefore, a comprehensive, standardised assessment is needed which takes into account issues specific to older people. Social and health needs should be quantified, as well as prisoners' risk to and from others and to themselves through self-harm and self-neglect.

The *National Service Framework for Older People* (DH 2001) brought in the idea of a 'Single Assessment Process'. This was designed to ensure that, on contact with health or social care staff, older people received standardised assessments of their needs on which care programmes could be built. There was a big push for the Single Assessment Process to be used in the community from the publication of the Framework, but not within prisons. There is, however, a pilot project in HMP Wakefield where the Single Assessment Process is being used. We hope this pilot will be successful, and will demonstrate how an appropriate early assessment can inform older prisoners' care throughout custody.

### Management

The next stage, once needs have been identified, is to design care pathways outlining what happens to those with specific needs. These may be existing health services; for example, if a prisoner is found to have diabetes, prisons will have specified actions such as regular reviews, chiropody and optician appointments and an adapted diet. Chronic disease management, criticised in the Inspectorate review, needs to be a priority to ensure prisoners' health does not unnecessarily deteriorate. Of course, this is true for all inmates, not only older prisoners, but the effect of not managing these illnesses will be more detrimental to the continued health of older people. Mental health services, too, need to be carefully aligned to assessment so that an appropriate level of care can be provided. As well as screening for depression, psychosis and other common mental health problems in prison, older prisoners at high risk could be monitored for cognitive impairment, and specialist assessment provided for those with symptoms of dementia.

Prisoners with health problems are likely to need continued care throughout their sentence or when on remand, so care plans and regular review are necessary to note any change in circumstances. Prisons need to link to existing geriatric health services available to the local Primary Care Trust so that specialist opinion can be sought. Training of health staff in emergency procedures (such as use of a defibrillator) may limit the frequency with which older prisoners must be transported to hospital by ambulance. So-called 'blue lights' followed by inpatient stays with officers on bedwatch are very unsettling for the ill prisoner, as well as those in neighbouring cells, not to mention the cost implications for the Prison Service.

**Social care**

The current gap in roles relating to social needs should be examined as a matter of priority. At present, services available for prisoners with mobility or self-care needs are insufficient or provided on an unofficial basis by staff or prisoners who should not be doing so. Local social services departments should engage fully not only in assessment of prisoners' needs in preparation for release, but in the provision of assistance during the prison sentence. As it has been widely accepted that health services for prisoners should be of equivalent quality and scope to those provided in the community (Joint Prison Service and NHS Executive Working Group 1999), the same should be true for social services. Until this occurs, prisoners with difficulties in these areas will continue to be neglected.

---

## CASE STUDY 8.2

HMP Wymott has devoted an entire wing to what is known as the 'Elderly and Disabled Community'. Prisoners aged 60 or over, and those with physical disabilities, can apply to be housed in the

Community. Staffing levels are slightly lower than in the rest of the prison, and there is space for 64 prisoners. The creation of the wing aimed to create a supportive atmosphere and to encourage self-help and responsibility, and the wing is certainly much calmer than other areas of the prison. The prison made considerable effort to find contracts with external companies for light work that could be done on the wing by prisoners who wished to remain active. In the early stages, this included packing combs and tea bags, and, later, drawing string through plastic bags. Gym and yoga classes suitable for older people were also convened and regularly attended by prisoners on the wing. The Elderly and Disabled Community appears to be a success, with a waiting list of prisoners wanting to be relocated there, and praised by internal inspections. However, there are older prisoners elsewhere in the prison who would not want to be moved to the Community, and enjoy mixing with younger prisoners, whom they describe as keeping them young. The element of choice concerning where prisoners are located is important in their quality of life.

---

## Additional considerations

Activity is a very important aspect for older prisoners to keep themselves physically and mentally healthy. Prisons should assess activities as to their suitability for people with chronic health conditions or mobility issues. If there is an insufficient range of suitable activities, they should make a concerted effort to introduce alternatives. The benefits in terms of continued health costs and access to health services should be enough to encourage prisons to do this. The prison environment must also be examined as to its suitability for older or less able prisoners. Cells and washing facilities may need to be adapted, and care should be taken to ascertain whether there are areas that are inaccessible to these prisoners, and the likely effect of this.

Contact with friends and family should be encouraged, and facilitated where possible. Staff should be aware of the additional problems faced by older people wanting to visit prisons, and not allow prisoners to become isolated simply because their community links are not easily accessed. Staff should also be aware and monitor for the possibility of bullying and exploitation by younger prisoners, particularly over medication. Currently, prisoners should have 'personal officers': named prison officers with whom they have monthly meetings to discuss their welfare. Prisons should ensure that these take place for older prisoners and that officers build up a rapport so that prisoners feel safe about disclosing any concerns.

**Prisons**

HMP Wymott is a training prison and, as such, prisoners can be expected to stay at that establishment for some time. Local prisons have a much faster turnover, with prisoners often being transferred or discharged at almost no notice. Many prisoners in such prisons are detoxifying from drugs and alcohol, and suicide is a particular risk. Therefore, it is difficult for local prisons to deliver medium- or long-term treatments, or to address many of the problems associated with coming into custody. It would not be possible for local prisons to have dedicated wings for older prisoners due to this turnover and the relatively small numbers of older prisoners received. However, local prisons are an ideal place for assessment at the beginning of custody.

Most other establishments have small populations of older prisoners, where it does not appear feasible to introduce dedicated accommodation or alternative work placements. However, the Disability Discrimination Act (introduced in 1995, but applicable to prisons in 2004) enshrines the approach that all services should be accessible by every prisoner. Thus it does not appear to be possible to have centres for older prisoners, perhaps on a regional basis, as prisoners may not now be relocated because an establishment cannot accommodate them. This means older prisoners will continue to be scattered throughout the prison estate. Every prison should have a named 'older prisoners lead', in the same way as they should by now have a disability liaison officer. Where the disability liaison officer has audited the prison environment for accessibility, the older prisoners lead should examine the facilities for older prisoners, including work options, family contact and access to health and social care services. Prisons would also be advised to place older prisoners together to reduce isolation and create an area where the noise from younger prisoners is limited. Wings are usually separated into smaller areas (e.g. spurs or landings), and older prisoners can be located together without the need for entire dedicated wings.

**CONCLUSION**

Research has demonstrated the different and elevated health and social needs of older prisoners. This chapter has argued that where these are not addressed, older prisoners are in danger of 'institutional abuse', including individual abuse as well as abuse by the system itself. All prison staff need to be made aware of the challenges faced by this group, and the harm that can be done by ignoring their issues. This can be achieved by comprehensive assessment early in custody followed by individualised care plans and reviews. Every prison should consider the suitability of their environment and services for older prisoners, and have a named person responsible for doing so. Older prisoners should be given the option of being located together, whether on a dedicated unit for older inmates, or as part of an existing wing.

## REFERENCES

Aday, R. H. (1999) *Responding to the Greying of the American Prisons: A 10 Year Follow Up.* Unpublished report. Murfreesboro, TN: Middle Tennessee State University.

Campbell, D. and Allison, E. (2006) 'Number of prisoners given life doubles in ten years'. *The Guardian*, 17 June, and at www.guardian.co.uk/guardianpolitics/story/0,,1799831,00.html. (accessed on 10 March 2008)

Department of Health (DH) (2001) *National Service Framework for Older People.* London: The Stationery Office.

Department of Health (DH) (2007) *A Pathway to Care for Older Offenders: A Toolkit for Good Practice.* London: DH.

Department of Health (DH) and Home Office (2000) *No Secrets: Guidance on Developing and Implementing Multi-Agency Policies and Procedures to Protect Vulnerable Adults from Abuse.* London: DH.

Fazel, S. and Jacoby, R. (2002) 'Psychiatric aspects of crime and the elderly'. In R. Jacoby and C. Oppenheimer (eds) *Psychiatry in the Elderly.* Oxford: Oxford University Press.

Fazel, S., Hope, T., O'Donnell, I. and Jacoby, R. (2004) 'Unmet treatment needs of older prisoners: a primary care survey'. *Age and Aging 33*, pp.396–8.

Fazel, S., Hope, T., O'Donnell, I. and Jacoby, R. (2001a) 'Hidden psychiatric morbidity in elderly prisoners'. *British Journal of Psychiatry 179*, pp.535–9.

Fazel, S., Hope, T., O'Donnell, I., Piper, M. and Jacoby, R. (2001b) 'Health of elderly male prisoners: worse than the general population, worse than younger prisoners'. *Age and Ageing 30*, pp.403–7.

Fazel, S., McMillan, J. and O'Donnell, I. (2002) 'Dementia in prison: ethical and legal implications'. *Journal of Medical Ethics 28*, pp.156–9.

Frazer, L. (2003) *Ageing Inside: School for Policy Studies Working Paper Series, Paper Number 1.* Bristol: School for Policy Studies.

Hayes, A.J., Shaw, J., Burns, A., Byrne, J. *et al.* (2006) *The Needs of Older Adults at HMP Wymott.* Manchester: University of Manchester.

Help the Aged (2002) *Age Discrimination in Public Policy: A Review of Evidence.* London: Help the Aged.

H M Inspectorate of Prisons (HMIP) (2004) *'No Problems – Old and Quiet': Older Prisoners in England and Wales.* London: HMIP.

Home Office (2005) 'Offender management caseload statistics 2004'. *Home Office Statistical Bulletin 17/05.* London: Home Office.

Joint Prison Service and NHS Executive Working Group (1999) *The Future Organisation of Prison Health Care.* London: Department of Health.

Katz, I. (2001) 'Grey area'. *The Guardian*, 30 January and at www.guardian.co.uk/prisons/story/0,,467180,00.html (accessed on 10 March 2008).

Lord Chancellor's Department (1999) *Making Decisions: The Government's Proposals for Making Decisions on Behalf of Mentally Incapacitated Adults.* London: The Stationery Office.

Wahidin, A. (2004) *Older Women in the Criminal Justice System: Running Out of Time.* London: Jessica Kingsley Publishers.

## ACKNOWLEDGEMENTS

The authors would like to thank Professor Jenny Shaw for helpful comments on a draft of this chapter.

# CHAPTER 9

# BRAIN INJURY, CASE MANAGEMENT AND FINANCIAL ABUSE
## A COMPLEX AFFAIR

## LUCY NAVEN AND JACKIE PARKER

### INTRODUCTION

Much of the literature around financial abuse focuses on older people, the largest population at risk of this type of abuse. However, those people who have sustained brain injuries are also at significant risk of exploitation and this is rarely documented. Acquired (traumatic) brain injury is most commonly caused by road traffic accidents, assaults, falls or medical negligence and can happen to anyone at any time. While some may sustain severe physical disabilities as a result, most are likely to sustain less obvious disabilities. These 'walking wounded' may have no apparent physical disability but present with complex impairments in cognition, emotions and behaviour. Difficulties in areas such as memory, judgement, decision making, planning, organising, insight and awareness into their own difficulties can all result in high levels of vulnerability. This chapter will make reference to real case examples to illustrate the ways in which individuals with brain injury are being financially abused and some of the ways this has been dealt with. It will demonstrate the difficulties in not only detecting such abuse but also in providing a safe enough environment so that the abuse does not happen in the first place. And finally it will explore good practice points to assist practitioners working in this field.

Brain injury does not always fall neatly into the three main social care categories of mental health, learning difficulties and physical disabilities and as a result the needs of these vulnerable adults can sometimes be missed or may be not met by statutory services. Guidance for the provision of services is available, for example, in the *National Service Framework for Long Term Conditions* (Department of Health 2005) which provides guidelines on good practice for working with individuals and what services should be available for people with brain injury.

People with a brain injury can find themselves financially vulnerable in all aspects of their day-to-day lives, from remembering how much was in their wallet, to being able to problem solve why they appear to be running out of money so frequently. They may blame themselves or the effect of their brain injury rather than consider that others may be taking advantage.

---

### CASE EXAMPLE

Fred was constantly complaining of having no money, but when questioned about what he was spending his money on he was never able to remember. His partner would claim that he was spending money on food shopping and cigarettes, but the carer reported that there was frequently no food in the house. Fred's family felt strongly that his partner was abusing him financially. Fred didn't know whom to believe.

---

## THE ROLE OF THE BRAIN INJURY CASE MANAGER

Some people who have sustained a traumatic brain injury may pursue personal injury compensation claims (for further discussion see Whiteley and Wright 2006). Some will have catastrophic injury and require assistance to manage their everyday lives. This assistance can be provided privately by brain injury case managers who will work closely with the person, those close to them and professionals, such as therapists and Court of Protection and litigation lawyers, to support the person to reach their greatest potential.

Case management is 'a process devoted to the coordination, rehabilitation, care and support of people with complex, clinical needs. It aims to facilitate clients' independence and improve their quality of life, while acknowledging safety issues' (Clark-Wilson 2006, p.15). In working toward this aim, brain injury case managers will assess need and implement recommendations. This could include the employment of brain injury support workers who will work with the client in their home and community with the aim of supporting the client[1] to achieve their goals.

The British Association of Brain Injury Case Managers (BABICM) hold to a number of principles. On the issue of protection, the principle reads: 'Clients, especially children or vulnerable adults, shall be safeguarded in accordance with recognised written policies from physical, financial, material, psychological or sexual abuse, neglect, discriminatory abuse or self-harm, inhuman or degrading treatment, whether through deliberate intent, negligence or ignorance'(BABICM 2005, p.4).

It is likely that many clients within this vulnerable group will have financial awards as a result of their compensation claims, be it through interim payments or final settlement. Access to such funds, often large amounts of between £250,000 and £6 million, can create a perception of wealth that could be exploited, in some cases relatively easily.

Brain injury case managers will work closely with professional receivers within the Court of Protection (an office of the Supreme Court) in assisting clients who are deemed incapable of managing their own financial affairs under the Mental Health Act 1983, to access their money safely. Suto, Clare and Holland (2002) estimated that 12 per cent of 'patients' within the Court of Protection have an acquired brain injury that impacts significantly on their day-to-day lives, leaving them vulnerable to financial abuse.

## CASE EXAMPLES

- Diane's parents had lived in her home for a number of years and refused to contribute to household bills or maintenance claiming that they were providing free care for their daughter. When Diane employed a 24-hour care package, her parents continued to refuse to pay, claiming that their daughter did not want them to. Diane reported that her dad had told her that he would move out and never see her again should she agree that they pay their own way.

- Sam's support worker was struggling with maintaining professional boundaries and found himself 'pulled in by the client' who saw him more as a friend than a support worker. A culture of borrowing and lending money with each other developed.

- Steve's claim was settled and due to his impulsivity he found himself telling anyone who would listen about his new multi-millionaire status. He suddenly went from a young man with few friends to having a wide circle of friends who were more than willing to help him out in his new home. All of his new 'friends' required paying for any help they provided and, when Steve forgot to pay them, he was threatened with violence.

**DEFINITION OF FINANCIAL ABUSE**

While it is recognised that financial abuse does not necessarily occur in isolation, this chapter focuses solely, as far as is possible, on this area of abuse. The Department of Health guidance *No Secrets* defines financial abuse as follows:

---

### Definition of financial abuse

Financial or material abuse, including theft, fraud, exploitation, pressure in connection with wills, property or inheritance or financial transactions, or the misuse or misappropriation of property, possessions or benefits. (DH and Home Office 2000, p.9)

---

In considering this definition, is this support worker abusing her client?

### CASE EXAMPLE

Sue would take her client shopping every week to the supermarket. Her client would have cash to pay for her groceries and each week Sue would hand over her own rewards point card and get the points associated with the sale. Sue was then able to use the points towards her own shopping, reducing her own bill each week. The client did not have the cognition to understand the purpose of the rewards point card, nor that it may benefit her support worker financially.

This is, sadly, an all too frequent example of financial abuse where the support worker may not be aware of how serious their actions are. It is important, therefore, that organisations have clear policies and guidelines regarding the management of client finances, along with codes of practice about what workers can and cannot do.

**IDENTIFICATION OF FINANCIAL ABUSE**

Financial abuse can be very difficult to identify despite it probably being the most common form of abuse of vulnerable adults (Pritchard 2007). At its extremes it can take the form of overt abuse and involve large amounts of an individual's assets, or it can involve very small amounts that could easily go unnoticed. There are a number of possible variables when considering how financial abuse might present itself. It could occur anywhere and be carried out by anyone. One victim could respond to the abuse entirely differently from another. It is perhaps, therefore, one of the most difficult types of abuse actually to uncover.

The Department of Health guidance *No Secrets* contains clear examples of what to look for and how to respond to abuse of vulnerable adults. It is important that all practitioners who may come into contact with vulnerable adults make themselves familiar with this document.

---

### Signs of financial abuse

- Unexplained loss of money or inability to pay bills
- Sudden withdrawal of money
- Sudden disappearance of favourite or valuable possessions
- Loss of financial documents such as pension books, building society books, etc.
- Benefits cashed and money not given out
- Someone is supposed to buy food, pay bills, etc. but does not
- Shopping award points are allocated to a card other than that belonging to the vulnerable person
- The vulnerable person is persuaded to transfer savings/property/financial affairs over to another person

---

## MAKING A DIFFERENCE

There are a number of points that organisations and practitioners should consider when working with vulnerable adults, be they people with brain injury or others.

### Policy and procedure

All organisations involved with vulnerable adults should set a strategy for protecting a potentially vulnerable client from abuse. Organisational policies and procedures on safeguarding adults are bound to cover all aspects of abuse and therefore will not be specific to financial abuse per se. However, principles that should be within good policies and procedures dealing with financial abuse specifically include the following:

- Vulnerable adults should be able to make informed choices, in accordance with the Mental Capacity Act 2005. At the very core of this Act is the requirement of social care practitioners to support and encourage clients to manage their own financial affairs wherever they have the capacity to do so.

- All support and guidance with regard to assisting someone with their financial affairs should be open and transparent.

- The client's need for assistance in managing financial affairs should be identified during the assessment process. This should include assessment of their ability, risk and undue influence. Any support or assistance required should be clearly recorded in the client's care/support plan.

- It would be good practice to encourage those vulnerable adults with capacity to think ahead with regard to financial matters and consider legal advice with regard to Lasting Power of Attorney in order to protect them financially.

### Translating policy into practice

Thompson (2000) outlines the complexities of the translation of social and organisational policy into practice. He notes the necessity and indeed importance of professional judgement when attempting to relate an organisational policy and/or procedure to a specific situation and this is particularly pertinent to financial abuse.

It must be acknowledged that perhaps the reason that financial abuse is possibly the most common form of abuse is that it is often hard to identify and the evidence can be hidden. High levels of professional judgement are required to ensure that risk is minimised as far as possible. The clarity of whether or not financial abuse is present is perhaps blurred further by one of the 2005 Mental Capacity Act's main principles that 'A person is not to be treated as unable to make a decision merely because he makes an unwise decision' (Mental Capacity Act 2005, Part 1, 1.4). Clearly the definition of 'unwise' is open to interpretation. Therefore, if a client chooses, for instance, to allow his daughter free access to his bank account, despite recognition that she has abused this access in the past, is it still abuse if she takes more money than agreed?

### Staff induction and training

All practitioners should be introduced at induction to the local area's inter-agency policy and procedures on adult protection work as well as their employer's guidance. Should action be required, the local inter-agency policy would take precedence. These documents should be supported by training during at least the first six months of employment (Department of Health 2003). The aim of such training should be to raise awareness about issues related to adult protection, including what constitutes abuse, how to recognise possible abuse and what the practitioner's role should be when abuse is suspected/identified. This initial training should be followed by updated/refresher training every two years (Department of Health 2003). The requirement of specific induction and ongoing training stems from the Care Standards Act 2000 which established provision to regulate and inspect care services throughout England and Wales.

### Assessment and investigation

It is essential at any point of assessment that information is taken from both the person with the brain injury and those close to them. Without this additional supporting information, it is highly possible that the assessment will be flawed. Many people with brain injury have little insight and awareness into the ways in which their brain injury affects them in day-to-day life. They may speak expertly about what they can and cannot do, but this can often not translate into the actualities of daily life. It is often only when speaking to those close to the person that the discrepancy between what they say and what they do becomes clear. While this has been considered good practice in the brain injury field for many years, the Mental Capacity Act 2005 now requires practitioners, when determining what is in the client's best interests, to consult the views of others. Assessors, however, should also be mindful of the possibility that family and/or friends may have their own agendas in the information they might provide.

Clearly this approach to assessment would need to take account of the importance of client confidentiality and respect should be given to clients' wishes, while being mindful of occasions when it may become necessary to override a client's self-determination (such as if a crime has been committed or other people may be at risk of harm in the future). In such situations, *No Secrets* states that the practitioner should inform the relevant agency which will, in most cases, be the local social services department who should manage any investigation. In brief, the process of any investigation should be to establish the facts of the incident, ensure the safety and protection of the vulnerable adult and determine a way forward.

### Recording

As the need to provide evidence of suspicions and observations is so important, good record keeping is essential. All practitioners should make

## GOOD PRACTICE POINTS

### RECORD KEEPING

- Keep your contemporaneous notes, even if you write up more fully at a later time – they are crucial in evidencing.

- Make sure the reasons for decisions/actions are documented.

- Record facts which are relevant.

- Record opinions on matters qualified to do so.

- Record all incidents of vulnerability and/or decision making clearly in order that patterns of behaviour can be easily developed.

- Record discussions with managers – including if you do not agree with the action the manager has recommended, and why you disagree.

- Record as much detail as possible.

- Remind yourself regularly of the purpose of record-keeping and how/why your notes may be required in the future.

sure that they are familiar with the recording guidelines of their employing agency. Basic requirements that should be included in all guidance include: making sure notes are legible, written in black ink, jargon-free, signed and dated and with a note of the time; the client's name must be clearly noted on every page.

Good practice would also instil that written details of all allegations and incidents of abuse and action taken should be recorded in the personal file of the client held by the practitioner, and that these be duplicated in a specific file held centrally by the organisation.

One other aspect of record keeping falls in line with the Mental Capacity Act 2005 and the importance attached to the need for practitioners to record clearly any incidents of their own decision making about empowerment and/or capacity. The *Mental Capacity Act 2005 Code of Practice* (Department of Constitutional Affairs 2007) states that good practice for professionals involved in assessing a person's capacity to make certain decisions includes recording findings in the relevant professional records. There is little further guidance at this stage and the authors anticipate that this will develop with case law.

## Supervision

Perhaps because of the difficulty of determining the existence of financial abuse, all practitioners should have the opportunity to benefit from both regular, formal supervision and the more instantaneous support and supervision that would be required when issues require discussion immediately.

Practitioners should have planned clinical supervision sessions at predetermined regular intervals. An open door policy is also important (if possible) to ensure that practitioners have access to their supervisors/managers at times when either they need to think something through in a safe environment or when they simply need a decision, and the reasons behind that decision, to be agreed by management, in line with any agency policy or procedure guidelines.

Supervision should not only be based around decision making and action planning but also the more human side of this work: how it feels. This might include discussions around what to do when a practitioner suspects financial abuse but cannot find the evidence; what happens when they get the evidence and what that might mean to the client (separation from family for instance); how to deal with how long the process may take and what this means not only to the client but also to the practitioner; how to deal with a potentially difficult and possibly irreconcilable relationship with the client, their family and/or friends; and how to cope if the outcome is not what the practitioner had hoped for.

## MANAGEMENT OF FINANCIAL ABUSE

There are many ways in which a brain injury practitioner can work with a vulnerable client to reduce the risk of financial abuse.

## GOOD PRACTICE POINTS

- Treat all personal financial information with respect and confidentiality.

- Follow the financial procedures outlined in the care/support plan.

- Keep accurate written records of accounts as requested regarding any relevant expenditure.

- Raise any concerns regarding malpractice or any suspected irregularities.

- Highlight any concerns regarding procedures or managing of the client's finances with the manager in supervision or, if necessary, immediately.

### Procedural guides for field workers

Any worker assisting a client in the community may have access to client finances. They should be made aware that their duty and responsibility to the client includes certain good practice points (see Good Practice Points box). A procedural guide should list all the financial responsibilities and procedures that the worker uses to assist the client with their finances. All recording procedures should be listed.

If workers have access to or can claim expenses during the shift, a procedure for expenses should also be provided (see box below).

---

### CASE EXAMPLE

Extract from the financial section of a support plan

- There is a weekly allowance of £10, kept in the locked cash box in the bottom drawer in the day room.
- Save all the receipts.
- Return all change to the cash box.
- Complete the expenses balance sheet.
- Number all the receipts as listed on the balance sheet.
- File the numbered receipts with the balance sheet.
- All balance sheets and receipts to be given to the case manager each month for checking and filing.

---

### Forms

Forms can be used for monitoring purposes as well as to support a client to feel empowered about how their money is being used. Clients and carers can use these forms, which can be designed to meet a specific purpose. They should be kept as basic as possible in order to promote use.

### Receipt collection

It should be standard practice for all carers/support workers to collect and submit receipts for all expenditure be it the client's or their own money (where the latter is to be refunded through wages). However, it can also be empowering for clients to do the same and families may also agree to keep records in this way.

## Staggered access to funds

For those clients in the Court of Protection, a common system used to support clients to have more control over their own funds can be to stagger their access to funds. For instance, if a client has, say, £150 per week spending money, it might be that funds are deposited into their bank account throughout the week on three different days. This enables them to ensure that their money lasts throughout the week and protects them by ensuring that others cannot access the larger sum at any one time.

## TAKING ACTION

Brain injury case managers, much like many other practitioners in the health and social care field, have a responsibility to act on any occurrence or suspicion of financial abuse toward their clients. It is sometimes the case that clients with private practice brain injury case managers have an array of professionals involved who specialise in brain injury provision where a clear multi-disciplinary approach to risk management is taken. It is often these professionals, such as professional receivers, who would be a first port of call in instances of suspected financial abuse.

### CASE EXAMPLES

People who may become involved in an investigation

- Court of Protection/Receiver
- Litigating Lawyer
- Police
- Commission for Social Care Inspection (CSCI)
- Local Social Services Department
- Protection of Vulnerable Adults panel (POVA List)
- Independent Mental Capacity Advocate (IMCA)
- Family

A few of these are considered below.

## Role of the receiver

In the field of brain injury case management, it is often the professional receiver (usually a lawyer) to whom the suspicions are referred in the first instance and it can be that it is the receiver, who has an overriding duty to the

Court to ensure that their clients are financially protected, who will lead any action to reduce or remove the risk.

## CASE STUDY 9.1

Mary, very physically and cognitively impaired, is in her forties and lived in her own home with support after a brain injury sustained some eight years previously. She has no verbal communication. She expresses her emotions and frustrations by hitting out and by loud grunting and shouting.

Mary needed 24-hour care to meet her physical, social and emotional needs. This was provided during the day by paid care staff funded via a limited personal injury settlement and in the evenings and overnight by her two adult sons and a nephew (the 'boys') also living in her home.

The case manager spent a lot of time dealing with difficulties that arose between the family members and the care team. The care team reported that the 'boys' could not be relied upon to arrive in time to take over the evening care. The 'boys' were eating all the food in the house leaving nothing for Mary and they were verbally abusive and disrespectful to Mary and to the care team.

Mary's finances were managed by a receiver who had agreed with the 'boys' that they would contribute a very small amount of money each week to the household budget. They rarely made the payments. The care team then became aware that the 'boys' were taking money directly from Mary's purse to buy her cigarettes and sweets but then would consume them themselves, leaving Mary without. Neighbours began to complain about loud drunken behaviour at night and household furniture was damaged by the 'boys' when drunk.

Mary told the case manager that she wanted the 'boys' to live with her, that she was happy for them to eat her food and smoke her cigarettes. She did not want to challenge the 'boys' as they were her only family.

The case manager was concerned that Mary was not only being financially but also emotionally abused and suffering from neglect once the paid carers went off duty. The case manager called a strategy meeting attended by Mary, the 'boys', the receiver and the social worker. It was agreed that the 'boys' would pay the agreed weekly rent to the receiver. Social services confirmed that they would take no action.

The two sons paid but the nephew did not. Eventually the receiver gave the nephew notice to leave the house, which he did, and things improved for Mary. Once the nephew had gone, Mary's own sons' behaviour did not give as much cause for concern, although the case manager continued to deal with concerns that Mary was being physically and emotionally neglected.

---

### Role of social services

When referring to social services it is important to have as much information as possible in order to demonstrate the possibility of the suspected abuse and the threat this may have to the client. *No Secrets* is clear that social service departments should manage adult abuse investigations. Strategy meetings should be called where a clear plan is determined with regard to a way forward. In the current climate of limited resources, where the threat to the client may perhaps not be considered substantial, and where private services and/or a professional receiver are involved, it is often the professional receiver that the social services department will encourage to lead any action agreed and brain injury case managers will work closely with them to ensure that the situation is rectified in the best possible way for the client.

### Role of the police

The *Mental Capacity Act 2005 Code of Practice* (Department of Constitutional Affairs 2007) notes that many forms of financial abuse will constitute a criminal offence and therefore it becomes a police matter. The criminal investigation then takes priority over all other forms of investigation, while working alongside the social services department, which would manage issues of health and social care. Therefore, an ongoing criminal investigation does not preclude the need for strategy meetings, case conferences and the development of a protection plan for which the social services department has the ultimate responsibility.

### Role of family and those close to the client

The Mental Capacity Act 2005 promotes family and friends as an integral part of considering a vulnerable adult's best interests, be that for financial matters or matters of welfare. It is clear that in most circumstances, those closest to the client will have valuable knowledge about both the client's aspirations and the values held within the family and/or community. Therefore it could be that whilst the vulnerable adult may be unable to have insight into potential abuse, those closest to the client may be able to shed some light on a situation whilst maintaining the client as central to any discussions.

However, it can also be the case that it is those closest to the client who are the perpetrators of financial abuse. It could also be that the client is either unaware or unwilling to take any potential accusation further. In these circumstances it is crucial that the vulnerable adult is protected whilst taking into account their own wishes. Issues need to be dealt with sensitively and a case manager or perhaps receiver will spend time reiterating procedures to family members in an attempt to manage the situation.

## CASE STUDY 9.2

Steven is a 21-year-old man who sustained a traumatic brain injury in a road traffic accident at the age of four. There had been much history of antisocial behaviour prior to the case manager becoming involved and it was clear that he had been regularly abusive to his mum. She reported that he had taken money from her purse regularly and had sold her belongings, including the TV and washing machine, to make money to buy drugs. When the case manager became involved, Steven agreed to attend a residential rehabilitation unit. Steven engaged well initially but gradually began to disengage and his behavioural difficulties increased significantly. Both the case manager and the rehabilitation team worked closely with Steven to determine the reason for the gradual decline and he eventually disclosed that his mum had been pressurising him to give her money, now that he had some funds from an interim payment. He reported that she was emotionally blackmailing him, reminding him of what monies he stole from her in the past and frequently telling him how she was struggling financially.

With support, Steven was able to decide that he did not want to give his mum any money and wanted the requests to stop; however, he did not want her confronted, as this would break their relationship. Steven was therefore supported to monitor his phone calls with his mum, only taking them when he felt strong and had a worker nearby.

As there was no actual evidence other than Steven's reports, the case manager, in liaison with the receiver, decided not to involve social services. Instead the receiver spent time discussing with Steven's mum why the Court of Protection was in place and the procedures that Steven needed to go through to access his funds.

## POTENTIAL OUTCOME

Taking a person centred approach to practice with this vulnerable client group where clients are enabled to make choices and are encouraged to make decisions is not without its risks. Practitioners will be aware that this approach will mean that some clients will make choices and decisions that could be considered unwise and unsafe. Actively encouraging empowerment for our clients is paramount to the spirit of the Mental Capacity Act 2005. However, the balance between self-determination, empowerment, risk taking and risk management is not always easy to achieve: 'A key difficulty remains the need not to lose sight of acceptable or more positive risks, and how these might be enhanced, not just how the risk of "significant harm" can be reduced' (Titterton 2005, p.54).

Brain injury practitioners need to be alert to the possibility of their client being financially abused. Reference to the Good Practice Points summary box may assist.

## SUMMARY OF GOOD PRACTICE POINTS

- Have an understanding of the Department of Health's guidance *No Secrets* (DH and Home Office 2000).

- Have a clear understanding of the organisation's policy and procedure regarding financial abuse.

- Become familiar with the relevant laws associated with financial abuse.

- Use professional judgement in translating policy into practice.

- Induction and initial training on safeguarding vulnerable adults should take place within the first six months of employment and be updated every two years.

- Where appropriate, supporting evidence from those close to a vulnerable adult should be sought while being mindful of confidentiality, client wishes and hidden agendas.

- Maintain a good standard of record keeping.

- Records of allegations and incidents of abuse should be duplicated and stored centrally.

- Utilise both formal and informal supervision to consider both decision making/action planning and how it feels.

- Introduce a procedural guide for all field workers with regard to all financial matters relating to the client.

- Put in place risk management strategies such as forms, receipt collection and staggered access to funds.

- Refer allegations, incidents and suspicions to the relevant agencies as outlined in the organisation's policy and procedure.

- Be confident that all that can be done has been done to minimise risk of significant harm for the client.

## NOTE

1   The medico-legal context in which most brain injury case managers work has provided a language that can differ from the prevailing language of statutory services. One such difference is that, currently, individuals receiving brain injury case management services are neither referred to as 'patients' nor 'service users' but by the legally coined term 'clients'.

## REFERENCES

British Association of Brain Injury Case Managers (BABICM) (2005) *Principles and Guidelines for Case Management Best Practice*. Cranbrook: BABICM.

Clark-Wilson, J. (2006) 'What is brain injury case management?' In J. Parker (ed.) *Good Practice in Brain Injury Case Management*. London: Jessica Kingsley Publishers.

Department of Constitutional Affairs (2007) *Mental Capacity Act (2005) Code of Practice*. London: The Stationery Office.

Department of Health (DH) (2003) *Domiciliary Care: National Minimum Standards. Care Standards Act 2000*. London: DH.

Department of Health (DH) (2005) *National Service Framework for Long Term Conditions*. London: DH.

Department of Health (DH) and Home Office (2000) *No Secrets: Guidance on Developing and Implementing Multi-Agency Policies and Procedures to Protect Vulnerable Adults from Abuse*. London: DH.

Pritchard, J. (2007) *Working with Adult Abuse: A Training Manual for People Working with Vulnerable Adults*. London: Jessica Kingsley Publishers.

Suto, W. M. I., Clare, I. C. H. and Holland, A. J. (2002) 'Substitute decision-making in England and Wales: a study of the Court of Protection'. *Journal of Social Welfare and Family Law 24*, pp.37–54.

Thompson, N. (2000) *Understanding Social Work: Preparing for Practice*. Hampshire: Palgrave.

Titterton, M. (2005) *Risk and Risk Taking in Health and Social Welfare*. London: Jessica Kingsley Publishers.

Whiteley, N. and Wright, J. (2006) 'The role of the case manager in personal litigation'. In J. Parker (ed.) *Good Practice in Brain Injury Case Management*. London: Jessica Kingsley Publishers.

Act 2000. London: The Stationery Office

Act 2005. London: The Stationery Office

1983. London: HMSO

# CHAPTER 10

# USING THE MENTAL CAPACITY ACT TO PROTECT VULNERABLE ADULTS

## SIMON LESLIE

Mental capacity is a fundamental, preliminary issue in work to safeguard vulnerable adults. We need to know if someone has the capacity to make a particular decision. We need to be clear about a person's capacity to consent to being interviewed or medically examined. We may need to know if they have the capacity to apply for an injunction or ask the police to investigate suspected abuse. Neglecting someone who lacks mental capacity can be a criminal offence, as can sexual activity with someone whose impaired capacity means they are unable to give a valid consent. Mental capacity should always be addressed when thinking about protecting people or supporting them to protect themselves.

This chapter summarises the Mental Capacity Act 2005 as it affects work to protect vulnerable adults. It focuses particularly on:

- what we mean by capacity or incapacity to make a decision
- why capacity matters in adult protection work
- how we work out what is in the best interests of someone who is incapacitated and at risk
- how far the Mental Capacity Act can be used to protect adults from risk.

What do we mean by capacity? Capacity is the ability to make an informed decision about a particular decision at a particular time. '[T]he test of capacity is the ability...to understand the nature and quality of the relevant transaction.'[1] Capacity is specific to the individual and the issue that has to be decided.[2]

## THE ORIGINS OF THE MODERN LAW OF CAPACITY

The Mental Capacity Act 2005 started as a legislative proposal from the Law Commission as long ago as 1995.[3] However, the principles in the Act and the test of capacity derive from case law developed over the past century and more.

Two modern cases illustrate the approach the courts have taken to capacity.

---

### The elements of (in-)capacity: Ms MB*

*Facts of the case*: Ms MB was 40 weeks pregnant when it was discovered that the baby was in the breech position. She was told that a vaginal delivery would pose serious risks to the child (assessed at 50%) and that a Caesarean section would substantially improve the child's chances of survival. She had consented to the Caesarean, but later withdrew her consent due to her irrational fear of needles required for the anaesthetic.

Ms MB was in labour and was not responding to those caring for her. The hospital asked the Court to make declarations that a) her phobia incapacitated her from making a decision about being anaesthetised and b) the anaesthetic would be in her best interests.

*The Court's decision*: The High Court made the declarations as asked. Subsequently the Court of Appeal endorsed this and gave the following general guidance:

1.  Incapacity involves being *unable to comprehend and retain the information which is material to the decision*, especially as to the likely consequences of deciding either way.

2.  Being *unable to use the information* in arriving at a decision would also amount to incapacity.

A compulsive disorder might stifle belief in the information presented, as might a phobia such as Ms MB's fear of needles. Ms MB (and the unborn child's father) wanted the child to be born alive and she would be likely to suffer significant long-term damage if the anaesthetic and section were not carried out. (The Court considered the child's best interests, but rejected this as a contributory basis for the decision, since foetuses only acquire the protection of the law when born.)

* *Re MB (Medical Treatment)* [1997] 2 FLR 426.

---

The MB case sets out the test not only for capacity to consent to medical treatment, but also capacity to decide where to live and with whom to have contact with.[4]

---

### A person's condition does not determine their capacity: Mr C

Mr C* was in prison for an offence of violence when he was diagnosed with chronic paranoid schizophrenia and transferred to Broadmoor. While there, he developed severe gangrene and was advised to have his leg amputated below the knee or face a high likelihood of death. Mr C sued the hospital when they refused to undertake not to amputate without his written consent.

The High Court decided that Mr C's capacity was reduced by his chronic mental illness. However, he still understood the nature, purpose and effects of the proposed amputation and hence he had capacity validly to refuse consent.

In the event Mr C accepted treatment with antibiotics and less invasive surgery, and the risk of death had receded by the date of the hearing.

* *Re C* [1994] 1 All ER 819, Thorpe J.

---

Three important points can be drawn from Mr C's case:

1. Whether someone has capacity has to be judged in the context of the particular decision at the time it arises. A person's condition (schizophrenia, dementia, learning disability, etc.) does not of itself tell us whether they are able or unable to take the decision in question.

2. The fact that someone proposes to do something against advice does not of itself mean they lack capacity. The issue is whether they have capacity, not how they use that capacity. The question of a person's 'best interests' only arises once incapacity is established. No-one can impose a decision on a person with capacity just because they think it is in their best interests.

3. If his case arose now, Mr C would be considered a vulnerable adult as defined in the Department of Health guidance *No Secrets*,[5] whether in prison, secure hospital or any other setting.

## WHAT IS INCAPACITY TO MAKE A DECISION?

The Mental Capacity Act gives a broad, essentially functional definition of incapacity. Someone lacks capacity to make a particular decision if 'at the material time, [s]he is unable to make a decision for [her- or] himself in relation to the matter because of an impairment of, or a disturbance in the functioning of, the mind or brain'.[6]

This definition includes people incapacitated by mental illness, learning disability and (among others) brain injury acquired in adulthood.[7]

---

### Elements of incapacity

What does 'unable to make a decision for oneself' mean? There are four elements.* These are being unable:

1.  to *understand* the information relevant to the decision [this includes the reasonably foreseeable consequences of deciding one way or another, and of failing to make a decision]

2.  to *retain* that information [for as long as required to make a decision]

3.  to *use or weigh* that information in making the decision

4.  to *communicate* one's decision (whether by talking, sign language or any other means).

* Section 3(1) Mental Capacity Act 2005.

---

Someone must be able to do all four of these things to be considered as having the capacity to make a decision. The four elements are closely modelled on the test of capacity developed in case law, including the cases of *MB* and *C* discussed above.[8] The most important elements are often likely to be a) understanding the information needed and b) being able to use or weigh it in coming to a decision.

## MENTAL CAPACITY ACT CODE OF PRACTICE

The *Mental Capacity Act 2005 Code of Practice* (DCA 2007) is available online.[9] It provides both practical advice and a number of case examples to illustrate how the principles of the Act can be applied in work with vulnerable adults. Professional staff must 'have regard to' what the Code of Practice says before doing anything to, or on behalf of, someone who lacks capacity.[10]

## CAPACITY: APPLYING THE CORRECT TEST TO EACH DECISION

Generally speaking, the more complex an issue, the more information one needs to assimilate and process in coming to a decision. Hence there are vulnerable people who are able to decide relatively straightforward things, but who cannot make more complex decisions. It is important to be clear where each individual's threshold of 'manageable complexity' lies. Whether someone has capacity to make a particular decision is a legal test, depending on input from a range of people, from family members as well as professionals.

The courts have repeatedly stressed that incapacity to decide one issue does not mean the person lacks capacity to decide about something else.[11] The tests are different.

### Capacity to litigate

In many cases it is important to be clear whether a vulnerable adult has the capacity to make an application to court themselves. If they lack this capacity, they will need a 'litigation friend' to represent their best interests. How does one decide if someone has this 'capacity to litigate'? The answer is that one needs to be able, with appropriate advice, to understand 'the issues on which [her/] his consent or decision is likely to be necessary in the course of those proceedings'.[12] For example, if someone is being harassed by a gang of youths, the court could make a restraining order under the Protection from Harassment Act.[13] If capacitated to litigate, the victim can apply; otherwise a litigation friend will be needed.

### Capacity to marry

This will be particularly important in cases of suspected forced marriage. The test of capacity to marry is whether the person understands the 'duties and responsibilities' of marriage. It is not enough to understand the words of the ceremony, although the marriage 'contract' is essentially simple and 'can readily be understood by anyone of normal intelligence'.[14]

In assessing capacity to marry in general, the court is not examining the wisdom or otherwise of the person's particular choice of partner.[15] Also, since marriage depends on consent, the court cannot give a best interests approval to marriage for someone who lacks capacity to give consent.[16]

Capacity to marry is particularly important to consider in cases where financial abuse is suspected as a motive, for example a younger person marrying someone with dementia for money.

### Capacity to consent to sexual relations

The test of capacity to agree to sexual relations is whether or not one understands the nature, character and implications of intercourse.[17] The 2007 case of *MM* makes clear that someone may have capacity to consent to intercourse, but lack capacity to decide the more complex question of whether to pursue a long-term relationship.[18] For example, if someone with a severe learning disability lacks the capacity to consent to sexual contact, the risk of exploitation should be borne in mind in devising and implementing plans to protect them.

### Capacity to create an Enduring Power of Attorney

A person does not need to be able to manage their own property and affairs at the time they give someone else an Enduring Power of Attorney (EPA). The questions are whether the person (the donor) understood a) that they were giving the attorney authority over their affairs and b) that the power would be irrevocable if the donor became incapacitated.[19]

The same is likely to apply to Lasting Powers of Attorney (LPAs) under the Mental Capacity Act. Unlike EPAs, LPAs can be expressed to give authority (once the donor has become incapacitated in this respect) to make decisions about healthcare and personal welfare matters.[20]

### MENTAL CAPACITY ACT PRINCIPLES

In deciding whether someone has capacity to make a particular decision – and what to do on their behalf if they lack that capacity – it is important to bear in mind the following principles which appear in section 1 of the Mental Capacity Act.

*The presumption of capacity.* 'A person must be assumed to have capacity unless it is established that he lacks capacity.'[21] However, where capacity to make key decisions appears borderline it should be assessed, particularly if there is concern that the person may be at risk of abuse.

*The right to be supported in making decisions.* 'A person is not to be treated as unable to make a decision unless all practicable steps to help [her or] him to do so have been taken without success.'[22] This principle imposes a duty on professionals and family to do all they can to help the person make an informed decision before concluding they lack the capacity to do so. In some cases, providing this support will call for a substantial range and depth of expertise.

*The right to reject advice and make 'unwise' decisions.* 'A person is not to be treated as unable to make a decision merely because he makes an unwise decision.'[23] Making a decision that professionals and one's family may disagree with is not of itself evidence of incapacity.[24] However, capacity

## GOOD PRACTICE POINTS

Ways to help people make decisions for themselves – points to consider:

- What information the person needs in order to make the decision

- How this information can be presented – and by whom – so the person can best absorb and retain it

- Whether visual or other aids may help communication or memory

- How the person can be supported to use and weigh the information

- Whether the person would be more at ease in one setting than another

- Whether there are people who can support the person by being present, and/or people (such as possible abusers) who should be excluded.

For further detail, see Chapter 3 of the *Mental Capacity Act Code of Practice*.

should be investigated if there is a pattern of repeatedly making unwise decisions that exposes one to significant risk, or if the person makes an unwise decision that is clearly irrational or out of character.[25]

This principle may pose dilemmas in cases of adults at risk. For example a person may choose, despite advice, to expose themselves to physical or financial abuse. This does not necessarily mean they lack capacity to make an informed choice about whether – or how – to protect themselves. However, decisions which place the person at serious risk should prompt enquiries about possible incapacity, whether cognitive or situational.

*Least restrictive intervention.* 'Before the act is done, or the decision is made, regard must be had to whether the purpose for which it is needed can be as effectively achieved in a way that is less restrictive of the person's rights and freedom of action.'[26] For example, if an incapacitated person at risk could possibly be safeguarded by receiving support (or additional support) at home, this should be carefully considered before the more restrictive step of removal to another setting is contemplated.

*Best interests.* 'An act done, or decision made, under this Act for or on be-half of a person who lacks capacity must be done, or made, in his best inter-ests.'[27] Note that 'best interests' does not arise, still less justify action, unless it is clear the person is incapacitated to make the decision them-selves.

## HOW DO WE DECIDE WHAT IS IN THE 'BEST INTERESTS' OF SOMEONE WITHOUT CAPACITY TO DECIDE FOR THEMSELVES?

The Mental Capacity Act gives guidance on some of the aspects of deciding what is in the best interests of someone who lacks capacity to make the decision themselves.[28] For example, regarding *equal consideration and non-dis-crimination*. Best interests must not be decided 'merely on the basis of' someone's 'age, appearance or…behaviour which might lead others to make unjustified assumptions about what might be in [her/] his best interests'. For example, protection plans for incapacitated adults at risk must be firmly based on a detailed knowledge of their circumstances rather than on generalisation.

Decisions about someone's best interests 'must take account of all the relevant circumstances and, in particular, take the following steps':

- *Regaining capacity?* The decision-maker must consider 'whether (and when) it is likely the person will in the future have capacity to make the decision'.[29] If the person may regain capacity in a few hours or days, a decision should not be rushed if it will wait. Any urgently needed action should not pre-empt any longer-term decision the person may be able to make later.

- *Permitting and encouraging participation.* The decision-maker 'must, so far as reasonably practicable, encourage the person to participate as fully as possible in any act done for them and any decision affecting them'.[30] Even though the person cannot themselves make a valid decision, they can and should be encouraged to participate.

- *The person's wishes and feelings, beliefs and values.* The decision-maker 'must consider, so far as reasonably ascertainable, the person's past and present wishes and feelings, the beliefs and values likely to have influenced them if they had capacity and any other factors they would consider if they could'.[31] Where the person's values or past wishes are known, these should influence what is now decided on their behalf – what would the person have done if they still had capacity? Thus, if someone wants to make a payment to an individual or organisation they supported when they had capacity, this could be consistent with their best interests now. If on the other hand they propose making a payment they would not have made before, greater caution would be needed before meeting the person's expressed wish.

- *Withholding treatment.* The decision-maker 'must not be motivated by a desire to bring about the person's death'.[32] The best interests approach cannot be used to support euthanasia, voluntary or otherwise.

This list of factors is not comprehensive in deciding what is in the best interests of someone without capacity.[33] 'Best interests' is not a single, objective standard, rather 'its value is in requiring decision-makers to think carefully before acting' and 'it demands that a decision be given a context that is informed by factors that are important'.[34]

However, the Code of Practice emphasises[35] that best interests does not mean the decision-maker asking themselves what they themselves would have done, or what they personally consider to be best for the incapacitated person. This is important for practitioners to bear in mind when dealing with carers and others who may have strong but possibly misguided views about the best interests of the person for whom they care.

### INDEPENDENT MENTAL CAPACITY ADVOCATE SERVICE

With some decisions, an Independent Mental Capacity Advocate (IMCA) should be involved. The IMCA's role is to represent and support the incapacitated person and examine the proposed decision critically to ensure that it is the least restrictive and that it will serve the person's best interests.[36]

An IMCA is required where there is no relative or other person close to the incapacitated person, and the decision involves:

- proposed serious medical treatment
- a proposed stay in hospital of more than 28 days
- a proposed move to a care home (or to a different care home) for more than eight weeks.

Local authorities are responsible for operating the IMCA service. They can also provide an IMCA when someone lacking capacity:

- is undergoing a care review or
- is subject of adult protection procedures.

### INCAPACITATED PEOPLE AND THEIR CARERS

A large number of 'substituted' decisions are made every day by carers – paid and unpaid – on behalf of people with impaired capacity. Section 5 of the

Mental Capacity Act lays down rules for such substituted decision-making. The decision-maker must:

1.  take reasonable steps to establish whether the person has capacity to make the decision themselves:

2.  reasonably believe that the person lacks capacity to decide, and that the proposed step is in their best interests.

If the decision-maker follows these rules under Section 5, they will not be criticised (and cannot be sued), unless they act negligently.[37]

Section 5 provides protection for people who provide personal care, or help with mobility. The Act also authorises carers to buy necessary items with the person's money and to pledge their credit.[38] Carers' powers also extend to restraint, provided this is used proportionately and to protect the incapacitated person from harm.[39]

Section 5 may well provide reassurance to carers. It may not have much direct impact on the majority of vulnerable adults who may be at risk. However, there will be a small number of such people whose carers claim to be acting in their best interests under the Mental Capacity Act, but who may in fact be misguided, neglectful or abusive. Practitioners will need to engage such carers in dialogue, and if necessary challenge their views about capacity, or best interests.

Particularly in matters of personal care, section 5 does not give anyone exclusive or overriding authority to act.[40] If at all possible, family members and professionals need to cooperate in exercising their shared responsibility.

The authority under section 5 does not cover proposed care decisions which are disputed or finely balanced – see below.

## PROTECTING INCAPACITATED PEOPLE THROUGH THE COURTS: THE NEW COURT OF PROTECTION

If a contentious decision has to be made on behalf of an incapacitated person, the High Court can be asked to make declarations:

1.  that the person lacks capacity to make the decision themselves

2.  that the proposed step is in their best interests.

Such declarations might be about healthcare, or about where the person is to live or with whom they are to have contact.

Where there is no consensus about a step proposed for an incapacitated adult, the court can make declarations to resolve the dispute. Similarly, if the step is unusual or the risks and benefits finely balanced, the court may be asked to decide, even where family and professionals agree about what should be done.

Best interests declarations have been developed by the High Court in the exercise of its 'inherent jurisdiction' rather than under any statute. Such declarations can now be made under the Mental Capacity Act, and are an important means to safeguard vulnerable incapacitated adults who cannot be protected in other ways.

The leading case on best interests declarations about the care and welfare of adults is *Re F.*[41]

---

## High Court declarations to protect vulnerable incapacitated adults

*Case background*: T was an 18-year-old woman with a severe learning disability. She and her younger siblings had experienced prolonged neglect and poor parenting. A consultant paediatrician found that T had been sexually abused.

T's siblings were made subject of care orders, but this was not possible in T's case as she was over age 16. She and her parents wanted her to return home. Guardianship under the Mental Health Act was rejected by the court* because, as a person with a learning disability, T's wish to return home was not 'seriously irresponsible'.

The local authority asked the High Court to make declarations:

a)   that T lacked capacity to decide

b)   that she should not return home

c)   that her contact with her family should be restricted.

*The Court's decision*: The Court of Appeal held that since there was no other legal means to protect T as a very vulnerable young woman, the 'doctrine of necessity' applied and the Court could make declarations to avert the risk.

* On application to 'displace' the parents as Nearest Relative under the Mental Health Act.

---

Best interests declarations about health or personal care can now be applied for under sections 15 to 17 of the Mental Capacity Act, although the High Court's inherent jurisdiction will remain important, particularly for people who are incapacitated by their situation.

## CAPACITY AND THE CRIMINAL LAW

The criminal law offers some protection from abuse and neglect to people with impaired capacity.

Under section 30 of the Sexual Offences Act 2003 it is an offence to engage in sexual activity with someone who is 'unable to refuse because of or for a reason related to a mental disorder'. This covers any intentional sexual touching and, in the case of intercourse, carries a maximum penalty of life imprisonment. 'Mental disorder' means the same as in the Mental Health Act and includes mental illness and learning disability. The mental disorder can make someone 'unable to refuse' if they either lack the capacity to choose whether to agree to the touching, or are unable to communicate their refusal. This offence only applies if the victim has a mental disorder.

Under section 44 of the Mental Capacity Act it is an offence to ill-treat or neglect someone one is looking after who 'lacks capacity'. It is not clear whether this applies to victims with impaired capacity or only those who lack any capacity at all.[42] The maximum sentence is five years' imprisonment.[43]

## SITUATIONAL INCAPACITY

What if a vulnerable adult needs protection because they are incapacitated by their situation rather than cognitively? Although the Mental Capacity Act probably does not cover such people,[44] the High Court has made clear that it will use its inherent jurisdiction to protect them.

The leading case is *Re SA*.[45]

---

High Court declarations in cases of situational incapacity

*Case background*: SA was a young woman who required protection from an unsuitable arranged marriage. SA was deaf and had no speech or oral communication. She functioned at the intellectual level of a 13- or 14-year-old. She could communicate in British Sign Language but not in Punjabi, the main language within the family.

SA wished to marry a Muslim man of her parents' choosing, but someone who spoke English and was prepared to live in the UK. She was able to give an informed consent to marry, but only if provided with a full understanding of what was proposed.

The Local Authority applied to court because of concern that SA was about to be taken to Pakistan to be married against her wishes. The concern was that she would not be able to communicate with people around her, and would feel isolated. This would affect her wellbeing and mental health, and make her possibly unable to recognise risk to herself.

> *The Court's decision*: The High Court held that it had power to make declarations to protect SA, even though her incapacity arose from her situation rather than her cognition:
>
> > The inherent jurisdiction can be exercised in relation to a vulnerable adult who, even if not incapacitated by mental disorder or mental illness, is, or is reasonably believed to be, either
> >
> > (i)   under constraint or
> >
> > (ii)  subject to coercion or undue influence or
> >
> > (iii) for some other reason deprived of the capacity to make the relevant decision, or disabled from making a free choice, or incapacitated or disabled from giving or expressing a real and genuine consent.

The *SA* case raises three categories of situational incapacity.

'Constraint' – which can be less than incarceration, and applies whenever there is 'some significant curtailment of the freedom to do those things which in this country free men and women are entitled to do'.[46]

'Coercion or undue influence' will apply where

> a vulnerable adult's capacity or will to decide has been sapped or overborne by the improper influence of another…[particularly] where the influence is that of a parent or other close and dominating relative, and where the arguments and persuasion are based upon personal affection or duty, religious beliefs, powerful social or cultural conventions, or asserted social, familial or domestic obligations, the influence may…be subtle, insidious, pervasive and powerful. In such cases, moreover, very little pressure may suffice to bring about the desired result.[47]

'Other disabling circumstances' – where

> circumstances…may so reduce a vulnerable adult's understanding and reasoning powers as to prevent him forming or expressing a real and genuine consent, for example, the effects of deception, misinformation, physical disability, illness, weakness (physical, mental or moral), tiredness, shock, fatigue, depression, pain or drugs. No doubt there are others.[48]

The *SA* case establishes an important – and possibly very wide – precedent for protecting people who may be incapacitated from making decisions to protect themselves not by cognitive deficit but by the constraints or undue pressure of their situation.[49]

## CASE SNAPSHOTS: HOW DO WE APPLY THE INCAPACITY RULES IN SAFEGUARDING ADULT CASES?

### CASE STUDY 10.1: MRS A – POSSIBLE PHYSICAL ABUSE

*Case snapshot*: Mrs A has Alzheimer's disease. She lives with her husband, who is finding her needs and behaviour increasingly difficult to manage. Mrs A attends a day centre, where staff have on a number of occasions seen her with bruises to her face and arms. Mrs A has reportedly spoken of her husband having caused the injuries, but no detail is available.

*Discussion*: The first question is whether Mrs A has capacity to give a reliable account of the way she has been treated. If she does, and if her account suggests abuse, professionals will need to be clear whether she has capacity to decide what to do to protect herself. This could include formally asking the police to investigate and possibly taking legal advice.

   If Mrs A has capacity in these respects, it will be for her to decide what action (if any) to take to protect herself. If she lacks capacity, it will be for professionals, in consultation with any other family members, to decide what protective measures are in Mrs A's best interests.

### CASE STUDY 10.2: MS B – POSSIBLE SEXUAL ABUSE

*Case snapshot*: Ms B has a history of mental health problems going back to childhood and repeated sexual abuse by her father. She appears to be of at least average intelligence, and has fairly consistently said she does not want to see her father. Twice in the past, such contact has led to serious self-harm and other setbacks to Ms B's mental health. However, when approached by her father Ms B often finds she is unable to refuse to see him. This is partly because of sympathy for him (which professionals consider misplaced) and partly because of the hold he appears to have over Ms B.

*Discussion*: It appears Ms B may be cognitively capacitated, but that the dynamic of her relationship with her father may undermine her ability to make informed decisions about the risks of seeing him. In other words, she may be situationally incapacitated by 'circumstances [which] so reduce a vulnerable adult's understanding and reasoning powers as to prevent [her] forming or expressing a real and genuine consent' (see note 45).

If this vulnerability cannot be addressed in other ways, an application will need to be made to the High Court, under its inherent jurisdiction, rather than under the Mental Capacity Act, because the incapacity is essentially situational rather than cognitive.

---

## GOOD PRACTICE POINT

Mental capacity – a key question in every adult protection case:

*Is this person able to decide this issue at this time?*

If YES, the decision is theirs to make. The role of others is confined to supporting and advising.

If NO, the decision needs to be made for them on a best interests basis by carers, clinicians and other professionals involved.

## ADULT PROTECTION LAW: SAFETY NET OR STRING OF GAPS?

The remainder of this chapter explores the question of whether current law and policy go as far as they can in promoting the protection of adults at risk.

The Mental Capacity Act and the programme of implementing it have helped bring to the forefront of many people's minds the crucial issue of the ability of vulnerable people to make informed decisions about how they live their lives and what protection – if any – they need from abuse.

However, for adults at risk and practitioners working with them, the Act is disappointing in at least three respects:

- *Little new substance.* The Act is more accessible than case law, but it adds few substantive measures. It is essentially a codification of the case law about incapacity as at around 2000–1 and now lags behind the High Court's inherent jurisdiction,[50] particularly in failing to address situational incapacity.

- *Little to protect adults.* The Law Commission's 1995 report on 'Mental Incapacity' recommended clarifying decision-making on behalf of incapacitated people. That has been achieved through the Mental Capacity Act. However, the Law Commission also recommended – as an integral part of their proposed package of reforms[51] – improving 'the protection of vulnerable adults by imposing on local authorities a duty to investigate suspected abuse or neglect of an incapacitated adult, and powers to remove under court order in an emergency'.

This reform was put to one side in 1999, without explanation.[52] When what became the Mental Capacity Act was being debated in Parliament, the Government rejected the recommendation of the Joint Parliamentary Committee that 'the statutory authorities should be given additional powers of investigation and intervention in cases of alleged physical, sexual or financial abuse of people lacking the capacity to protect themselves from the risk of abuse'.[53]

The Government said in response to this recommendation that there were already sufficient safeguards in the form of the Department of Health guidance *No Secrets*[54] and the role of the Public Guardian.[55]

- *Little role for the State?* Unlike other legislation aimed at protecting vulnerable groups, the Mental Capacity Act focuses more on private relationships (principally between incapacitated people and their carers) than on the role of the State in affording protection.

By contrast, the Mental Health Act (MHA) confers a range of powers and duties on central and local government to assess and care for those who are mentally disordered and are either at risk themselves or pose a risk to others. The MHA confers some powers on individuals, principally the statutory Nearest Relative. However, the thrust of the MHA is that identifying and addressing risks to – and posed by – people with a mental disorder is a task for the State.

Or take the Children Act 1989; some of its measures belong in the domain of private law, for example governing residence of and contact with children when their parents and others cannot agree. But the Act is also the principal vehicle for protecting children through the courts from abuse and neglect. It confers a wide range of responsibilities on central and local authorities. These include duties to investigate suspected risk, to provide services to avert risk and to apply to court for orders to protect children who cannot be protected in other ways.

The Mental Capacity Act takes a different approach. In its 69 sections and seven schedules the Act confers only one responsibility on local authorities – to operate the Independent Mental Capacity Advocate service. There is no duty to investigate, and no statutory duty on agencies to cooperate to promote safeguarding.

Perhaps most surprising is the class of people who may apply to the Court of Protection as of right. This is limited to individuals – the person themselves, anyone with an LPA, a court-appointed deputy, anyone named in a court order about the person and, if the person is under 18, anyone with parental responsibility. All other people, including local authorities, will need the court's permission even to bring an application.[56] Anyone seeking the court's permission (including local authorities) will need to show their reasons for applying, the benefit to the person of the order being sought and whether this can be achieved in any other way.[57]

The Mental Capacity Act appears to be principally intended to regulate private relationships. The question is whether this takes adequate account of the protection needs of the small but most vulnerable minority of incapacitated people who are at risk.

## IMPLEMENTING THE LAWS WE ALREADY HAVE

There are examples, beyond the Mental Capacity Act, of legislation passed by Parliament to protect vulnerable adults, but not brought into force by UK Government departments.

### Applying on behalf of someone else

As indicated above, if someone lacks 'capacity to litigate', a litigation friend can act in their place to bring an application to court. But what if the victim is capacitated but fearful of the consequences of making an application themselves, particularly for an injunction? There is a measure already on the statute book (in section 60 of the Family Law Act 1996) to enable rules to be made so that applications could in specified circumstances be brought by one person on behalf of another. Clearly, section 60 could be used to help vulnerable victims of abuse. Unfortunately, it has not been implemented.

### Pre-recorded cross-examination at criminal trials

As long ago as 1989, the Pigot Report recommended that, in relation to child witnesses, both their answers to the prosecution (evidence-in-chief) and cross-examination or questions from the defence should be pre-recorded as early as possible, removing the need for the child to wait months or longer to give 'live' evidence at the trial itself.[58]

In 1998, a Home Office inter-departmental working group report *Speaking Up for Justice* made the same recommendations for vulnerable and intimidated adult witnesses. The working group recognised the logistical difficulties of arranging early recorded cross-examination, as well as the risk of pressure to cross-examine at trial a vulnerable witness who had already been cross-examined on video. The working group therefore recommended that there should be no further cross-examination in such cases unless new evidence came to light which could not reasonably have been identified earlier.[59]

The Youth Justice and Criminal Evidence Act 1999 enacted this recommendation among a number of 'special measures' aimed at improving the quality of the evidence given at criminal trials by both child and vulnerable adult witnesses.[60] Other special measures include giving evidence by 'live link' from another room or building, and (where a witness gives evidence in the courtroom) the use of screens to shield them from seeing and being seen by the defendant. But of these measures, it is only pre-recorded cross-examination which would:

- enable *all* the vulnerable person's evidence to be captured promptly (and hence more reliably)[61]

- enable them promptly to receive therapy without fear it will 'taint' their evidence, or that the therapist's records may have to be disclosed to the defence[62]

- avoid the stress and apprehension of the months of waiting for the trial itself.[63]

Video interviews with child witnesses are frequently used in place of examination-in-chief, though this is less commonly done with vulnerable adult witnesses.[64]

On the other hand video-recorded cross-examination, although enacted by Parliament in section 28 of the Youth Justice and Criminal Evidence Act, has never been implemented. In July 2004 the UK Government, having received a briefing paper on the difficulties of implementing video-recorded cross-examination,[65] decided 'not to implement section 28 as it stands'. A Review of Child Evidence was set up, which did not consider vulnerable adult witnesses. The Review identified 'considerable practical problems organising cross-examination before the trial proper. These concerned the availability of the relevant judges and advocates, who would need to be available for the pre-trial hearing as well as the trial. This could impede timeliness.'[66] It was not clear how far the Review had weighed these practical difficulties against the benefits for vulnerable witnesses.

In June 2007 the UK Government consulted on a proposal to retain and implement pre-recorded cross-examination for a much reduced group of child witnesses:

- very young children

- witnesses with a terminal/serious degenerative illness

- those with a mental incapacity but who are still capable of giving good evidence.

It did not appear that any adult witnesses would be included in this reduced scheme. It was estimated that there would only be 250 or so such witnesses each year[67] which (on the UK Government's own figures) is less than 1 per cent of the number of vulnerable and intimidated witnesses asked to attend court each year.[68]

Introducing video-recording of cross-examination will require major cultural and organisational changes, particularly for lawyers and the courts. This is likely to remain a major issue for those working with vulnerable victims and witnesses.

## A COMMITMENT BY GOVERNMENT

In 2006 the UK Government agreed to 'consider the benefits of introducing legislation to place adult protection work on a statutory footing'.[69] In June 2007 the Department of Health announced a review of *No Secrets*, published in 2000 and still the only UK Government guidance on adult protection.[70] In November 2007 the Department of Health indicated that this work had not yet started and 'the review will take between 12 and 18 months to complete. The review will also consider the case for legislation to protect vulnerable adults.'[71]

In the absence of both legislation and central government guidance it has been left to other local and national agencies to set the standards for protecting vulnerable adults. Particularly important is the Association of Directors of Social Services' National Framework of Standards *Safeguarding Adults* (2005) which, while not universally accepted, offers a comprehensive programme of strategic action to enhance the profile of adult protection work and the skills brought to bear on it.

In their own words, 'The Government is determined that vulnerable adults should be afforded the greatest protection possible from harm.'[72] Reference is then made to the establishment of National Service Frameworks, national minimum standards for regulated care services, and the schemes to bar from working with vulnerable people those who have placed such people at risk of harm.

These are important, but relatively modest, advances towards achieving the goal the UK Government have set themselves. Radical legislative and policy reforms are urgently needed if we are to make a meaningful difference to the lives of adults at risk.

## CONCLUSION

Capacity to make decisions should be a crucial issue in our minds throughout the process of investigating and responding to suspected abuse of adults. It is important to be familiar with the Mental Capacity Act and Code of Practice in judging whether someone who may be at risk has capacity to decide what to do; and in taking steps which meet the best interests of people who cannot decide for themselves.

## NOTES

1 *Local Authority X v MM and KM* [2007] EWHC 2003 (Fam) (Munby J) at para. 67.

2 'the test has to be applied in relation to the particular transaction (its nature and complexity) in respect of which the question whether a party has capacity falls to be decided': Chadwick LJ in *Masterman-Lister v Brutton and Co (No. 1)* [2002] EWCA Civ 1889 at para. 62.

3 'Mental Incapacity', report no. 231, Law Commission, 28 February 1995.

4 *Local Authority X v MM and KM* (see note 1 above) at paras. 77, 78.

5 Department of Health and Home Office (2000), para. 2.3.

6 Section 2 (1) Mental Capacity Act.

7 *Mental Capacity Act 2005 Code of Practice*, para. 4.12.

8 In the case of *Local Authority X v MM and KM* (see note 1 above), Mr Justice Munby held that there is 'no relevant distinction' between the tests of incapacity set out respectively in *Re MB* and in section 3 (1) of the 2005 Act (judgment paras. 73, 74 and 92).

9 www.justice.gov.uk/docs/mca-cp.pdf (accessed on 4 June 2008)

10 Section 42 (4) MCA.

11 See also MCA Code of Practice, para. 4.32.

12 *Masterman-Lister v Brutton and Co and Jewell* [2002] EWCA Civ 1889, Chadwick LJ at para. 75.

13 Protection from Harassment Act 1997, sections 3 (1) to (3).

14 *Sheffield City Council v E and S* [2004] EWHC 2808 (Fam) at para. 68.

15 *Sheffield City Council v E and S* at para. 102, citing Karminski J in *In the Estate of Park deceased, Park v Park* [1954], p 89 at p 107. See also the Forced Marriage (Civil Protection) Act 2007.

16 *Sheffield City Council v E and S* at para. 92.

17 *X City Council v MB, NB and MAB* [2006] EWHC 168 (Fam), [2006] 2 FLR 968, at para. 84.

18 *Local Authority X v MM and KM* (see note 1 above), judgement at para. 95.

19 *Re K (Enduring Powers of Attorney)* [1988] 1 All ER 358, Hoffman J.

20  Sections 9–11 MCA and Code of Practice, chapter 7.

21  Section 1 (2) MCA.

22  Section 1 (3) MCA.

23  Section 1 (4) MCA.

24  As the Court of Appeal said in the case of a severely physically disabled woman who did not wish artificial respiration, 'The doctors must not allow their emotional reaction to or strong disagreement with the decision of the patient to cloud their judgement in answering the primary question whether the patient has the mental capacity to make the decision.' *B v An NHS Hospital Trust* [2002] EWHC 429 (Fam) at para. 100.

25  MCA Code of Practice, para. 2.11.

26  Section 1 (6) MCA.

27  Section 1 (5) MCA.

28  Section 4 MCA.

29  Section 4 (3) MCA.

30  Section 4 (4) MCA.

31  Section 4 (6) MCA.

32  Section 4 (5) and (10) MCA.

33  'No statutory guidance could offer an exhaustive account of what is in a person's best interests, the intention being that the individual person and his or her individual circumstances should always determine the result.' Law Commission report no. 231, 'Mental Incapacity', para. 3.26.

34  John Coggon, Workshop on Best Interests, Cardiff Law School, 12 April 2007.

35  MCA Code of Practice, para. 5.61.

36  Sections 35–41 MCA.

37  Section 5 MCA.

38  Sections 7 and 8 MCA.

39  Section 6 MCA.

40  Code of Practice, para. 6.21; Law Commission report no. 231, para. 4.1. Note that the position is different with decisions about healthcare for incapacitated people, which fall to be made by the responsible clinician.

41  *Re F (adult patient)* [2000] 2 FLR 512, Court of Appeal.

42  Section 44 MCA. The bare phrase 'lacks capacity' seems at variance with the Principles in section 1 of the MCA and the Code of Practice, which treat capacity as graduated rather than bipolar. The section also does not say what it is that the alleged victim has to lack of capacity to decide.

43  The Crown Prosecution Service indicates that across England and Wales, in the first seven months after it was implemented, three charges were brought to court under section 44.

44  Section 2 (1) MCA (discussed above) defines incapacity as the inability to make a decision 'because of an impairment of, or a disturbance in, the functioning of the mind or brain'.

45  *Re SA, A Local Authority v MA, NA and SA* [2005] EWHC 2942 (Fam), Munby J.

46  This apparently includes the potential situational incapacitation of being denied contact with close relatives: *Re SA*, judgement para. 78, citing the case of *Re C (Mental Patient: Contact)* [1993] 1 FLR 940.

47  *Re SA*, judgement para. 78.

48  *Re SA*, judgement para. 78.

49  See also *Re G (an adult) (mental capacity: court's jurisdiction)* [2004] EWHC 2222 (Fam), Bennett J, which concerned a woman incapacitated when her father was allowed to pressurise her but who recovered capacity when his influence was removed.

50  Paper delivered by Mr Justice Munby to Community Care Law Reports seminar, 14 November 2007.

51  Law Commission report no. 231, 'Mental Incapacity', para. 1.9.

52  'Making Decisions', Lord Chancellor's Department 1999, para. 12.

53  Joint Committee on the Draft Mental Incapacity Bill – First Report, 17 November 2003, para. 2.66.

54  See note 5 above.

55  The Government Response to the Scrutiny Committee's Report on the draft Mental Incapacity Bill, February 2004, response to recommendation 79.

56  Section 50 (1) MCA.

57  Section 50 (3) MCA.

58  Report of the *Advisory Group on Video Evidence*, Home Office 1989.

59  *Speaking Up for Justice*, Report of the Interdepartmental Working Group on the treatment of Vulnerable or Intimidated Witnesses in the Criminal Justice System, Home Office, June 1998, paras. 8.55–8.61.

60  Adult witnesses are entitled to 'special measures' under the YJCEA if the quality of their evidence is likely to be reduced by intimidation, mental disorder, physical disability or disorder or a significant impairment of intelligence and social functioning (sections 16 and 17 YJCEA).

61  *Speaking Up for Justice* (see note 59), para. 8.38, citing A. Sanders, J. Creaton, S. Bird and L. Webster (1996) 'Witnesses with Learning Disabilities – A Report to the Home Office' Unpublished.

62  'Provision of Therapy for Vulnerable or Intimidated Adult Witnesses Prior to a Criminal Trial – Practice Guidance', Home Office 2001, paras. 3.6–3.15, 6.2. See also the case of *R (TB) v Stafford Combined Court and others* [2006] EWHC 1645 (Admin), where a 14-year-old victim, unrepresented and unsupported at court, was faced by the judge with a choice between delaying the impending trial and agreeing disclosure of all her therapeutic records.

63  *Speaking Up for Justice*, para. 8.57, citing Sanders *et al.* (see note 61).

64  Hamlyn, B., Phelps, A. and Sattar, G., 'Key findings from the Surveys of Vulnerable and Intimidated Witnesses 2000/01 and 2003', Home Office 2004, p.2.

65  Birch, D. and Powell, R. 'Meeting the Challenges of Pigot: Pre-trial Cross-examination under s.28 of the Youth Justice and Criminal Evidence Act 1999' (unpublished), cited in *Improving the Criminal Trial Process for Young Witnesses: A Consultation Paper*, Office for Criminal Justice Reform, June 2007, para. 3.3.

66  Summarised in *Improving the Criminal Trial Process for Young Witnesses: A Consultation Paper*, Office for Criminal Justice Reform, June 2007, para. 3.4.

67  *Improving the Criminal Trial Process for Young Witnesses: A Consultation Paper*, (see note 65) p.58.

68  Survey data and CPS statistics provided to the interdepartmental working group in 1998 put the number of prosecution witnesses asked to attend court each year at 100,000 in Crown Court and 60,000 in Magistrates' Courts (and defence witnesses at 25,000 for each tier): *Speaking Up for Justice*, para. 13.3. Home Office research in 2006 found that some 24 per cent of prosecution witnesses were likely to be vulnerable or intimidated (although only 9% or scarcely one in three of them was likely to be identified as such by the agencies working with them): Burton, M., Evans, R. and Sanders, A., 'Are special measures for vulnerable and intimidated witnesses working? Evidence from the criminal justice agencies', Home Office Online Report 01/06, pp.17, 22 (www.homeoffice.gov.uk/rds/pdfs06/rdsolr0106.pdf accessed on 19 June 2008). This suggests there are at least 35,000 vulnerable and intimidated witnesses required to attend court annually.

69  Letter from Gary Fitzgerald, Chief Executive, Action on Elder Abuse, 4 September 2007.

70  The announcement of a review of *No Secrets* coincided with the publication of research showing that 2.6 per cent of those over age 66 across the UK, or some 277,000 people, are likely to have been mistreated within the past year by a family member, close friend or care worker – 'UK Study of Abuse and Neglect and Abuse of Older People – Prevalence Survey Report', June 2007, p.3.

71  Email from Department of Health to the author, 23 November 2007.

72  Department of Heath website: www.dh.gov.uk (accessed on 4 June 2008).

## REFERENCES

Association of Directors of Social Services (ADSS) (2005) *Safeguarding Adults: A National Framework of Standards for Good Practice and Outcomes in Adult Protection Work*. London: ADSS.

Department for Constitutional Affairs (DCA) (2007) *Mental Capacity Act 2005 Code of Practice*. London: The Stationery Office.

Department of Health (DH) and Home Office (2000) *No Secrets: Guidance on Developing and Implementing Multi-Agency Policies and Procedures to Protect Vulnerable Adults from Abuse*. London: DH and the Home Office.

Home Office (1989) *Report of the Advisory Group on Video Evidence (the Pigot Report)*. London: Home Office.

Home Office (1998) *Speaking Up for Justice: Report of the Interdepartmental Working Group on the Treatment of Vulnerable or Intimidated Witnesses in the Criminal Justice System*. London: Home Office.

Law Commission (1995) *Mental Incapacity*. Report no. 231. London: HMSO.

Office for Criminal Justice Reform (2007) *Improving the Criminal Trial Process for Young Witnesses: A Consultation Paper*. London: Office for Criminal Justice Reform.


## STATUTES

Children Act 1989. London: HMSO

Family Law Act 1996. London: HMSO

Mental Capacity Act 2005. London: The Stationery Office

Mental Health Act 1983. London: HMSO

Protection from Harassment Act 1997. London: HMSO

Sexual Offences Act 2003. London: The Stationery Office

Youth Justice and Criminal Evidence Act 1999. London: HMSO


## ACKNOWLEDGEMENTS

I am grateful to a large number of people for their insights into and discussion around the issue of capacity, and particularly to Luke Clements and Penny Letts.

# CHAPTER 11

# DOING RISK ASSESSMENT PROPERLY IN ADULT PROTECTION WORK

## JACKI PRITCHARD

It has concerned me for a long time that many workers[1] are not regularly using formal risk tools in adult protection work. This is probably due to the fact that historically few policies and procedures concerned with vulnerable adults and adult protection work have included such tools. It is also worrying that few of the said workers have ever undergone formal training on risk assessment and risk management. Assessing risk of harm is an absolutely crucial part of all the work which is undertaken with victims and perpetrators of abuse. The objective in writing this chapter is to explain how the theory of risk can be applied to adult protection work.[2] This will be achieved by discussing in detail when and how risk assessment should be undertaken in the different stages of working with any adult abuse situation.

### WHAT IS RISK ASSESSMENT?

Very simply risk assessment is about assessing whether people and property are going to be harmed in some way. It has to be remembered that harm can be physical or emotional. In adult protection work it is necessary to focus on the following definition of significant harm: 'not only ill treatment (including sexual abuse and forms of ill treatment which are not physical), but also the impairment of, or an avoidable deterioration in, physical or mental health; and the impairment of physical, intellectual, emotional, social or behavioural development' (Lord Chancellor's Department 1997, p.68).

This is a difficult definition to adopt when working with vulnerable adults who have severe communication problems; in those cases the reality is that it is often impossible to measure the changes in functioning as required by the definition and to conclude how 'significant' the harm has been. Therefore, although the definition of significant harm must be acknowledged and utilised, practitioners need to focus on identifying specific physical and emotional harms.

## GOOD PRACTICE POINTS

- Practitioners must become familiar with and understand the definition of 'significant harm'.

- It is necessary to identify both physical and emotional harms which have resulted from abuse being inflicted on the victim and/or others.

### WHERE RISK ASSESSMENT FITS INTO ADULT PROTECTION WORK

Risk assessment is an ongoing task when working with adult abuse cases; it is not a one-off event. From the moment any worker suspects or witnesses that abuse is occurring, s/he is assessing the risk of harm. The worker should immediately make an alert to their own line manager, who in turn should immediately be thinking about the alleged victim's safety. So straight away the risk assessment has begun.

Safeguarding/adult protection policies and procedures require that if there is an allegation that a vulnerable adult is being abused information will be gathered and a strategy meeting will take place (either by telephone or in a formal sit-down meeting). Risk assessment should be on the agenda of any such meeting and it is possible to use a risk tool even at this early stage of the process. If an abuse investigation is to take place, then the investigating officers will be expected to be assessing risk as they proceed with the investigation.

## GOOD PRACTICE POINTS

The purpose of any abuse investigation is to:

- find out whether abuse has occurred and is likely to occur in the future

- ensure the safety of the victim

- gather evidence to prove abuse has happened

- assess the harm which has already occurred to the victim, others and property

- predict the risk of harm for the future.

The investigating officers will then bring their findings to a case conference by which time they should have started to complete the risk tool, which will be discussed and finalised during the course of the conference. If a person is likely to be abused in the future then a safeguarding/protection plan should be developed. All this will be discussed in detail below.

## GOOD PRACTICE POINTS

- Risk assessment is an ongoing process at all stages of adult protection work.

- A risk tool can be used at a strategy meeting.

- A partially completed risk tool should be presented to a case conference by the investigating officers.

- The risk assessment and risk tool are formally completed during a case conference.

- A safeguarding/protection plan should be developed if someone is likely to be abused in the future.

### TERMINOLOGY

Before introducing an example of a risk tool which can be used in adult protection work, there needs to be some discussion about the correct use of terminology. Both *No Secrets* (DH and Home Office 2000) and *Safeguarding Adults* (ADSS 2005) stress the importance of inter-agency working and working in partnership. Therefore, when risk assessment is being undertaken in relation to adult abuse cases it is vital that everyone involved is using the same terminology. I am only too aware from my own practice that even within single agencies or organisations different risk forms can exist. This is why there needs to be a good risk tool and related guidance within any adult protection policy, so that workers are clear about what they should be assessing.

Workers frequently say that someone is 'at risk' but fail to say at risk of what exactly. It is vital that the actual 'harm' is made explicit. A common occurrence is that workers often use the word 'risk' when in fact they should be using the term 'danger' (based on Brearley's theory of risk: Brearley 1982a, b). Workers need to be clear about the meaning of the following key terms in risk assessment:

- risk-taking action
- benefit

- hazard
- danger.

In addition they need to be clear about their tasks in the assessment and management of risk:

- prediction of positive and negative outcomes
- assessment of the likelihood of the harm(s) occurring
- grading the risk of harm.

Before considering the processes involved in risk assessment and adult protection, it is necessary to define the key terms.

### Risk-taking action

A useful question for a worker to ponder on is: 'What does the victim want to do?' If one thinks about the risk-taking action rather than just focusing on the word 'risk', it helps to avoid interchanging the words 'risk' and 'danger'. It is important to remember that some victims of abuse will be engaging in risk-taking actions and have no choice in the matter; that is, they are being controlled or forced to do something by their abuser. Some typical examples of risk-taking actions might be:

- to remain living with the abuser
- to hand money/assets over to a relative
- to allow strangers into the house.

### Benefit

A common failing is that workers never spend enough time thinking about the positive outcomes of a situation. It is only natural that a worker wants to protect an adult who is being abused. In an era when everyone is very conscious of working in a blame-culture and litigation is increasing there can be a tendency for a worker to be over-protective because of fearing the negative outcomes. Good practice says that a worker should acknowledge the fact that every human being has the right to take risks if they wish to do so and independence, choice and self-determination should be promoted (DH 2005, 2007). A very common scenario in adult abuse cases is that the victim chooses to remain in the abusive situation because the benefit is that s/he maintains the relationship with the abuser, who may be a loved one. Another example is that an adult who has no family or friends may be very isolated and may welcome strangers into the house for company (i.e. the benefit).

The benefits section of any risk tool should not be kept to a minimum. In many abuse cases the root cause of the abuse stems back to something which happened in the past. If social history is relevant to the current situation it is important to include this. The case study of Ena will illustrate this point.

---

### CASE STUDY 11.1: ENA[3] (PART 1)

Ena, aged 75 years, had regular admissions to hospital because she was regularly physically abused by her 21-year-old grandson, Craig, when he demanded money from her. Craig was a drug user who also was selling drugs from the house.

**RISK-TAKING ACTIONS**
Every time Ena was admitted to hospital:

- she refused to make a statement to the police
- she said she wanted to return home to live with Craig.

**BENEFITS**

- By returning home Ena maintained her relationship with Craig which was very important to her.

On the real risk assessment tool, there is a full social history in the benefits section which explains why Ena is so devoted to Craig. It explains in detail how Ena's daughter gave birth to Craig and on the same day left him; no-one knew who was Craig's father. Conse-quently, Ena had brought up Craig since the day he was born and felt a great sense of duty to him; she often talked about the guilt she felt for her own daughter's actions.

---

### Hazard

Workers can get confused between a hazard and a danger; I believe this is because some things could be a hazard *or* a danger depending on the situation. It is necessary to look at each individual case. What some workers fail to grasp is the concept that a hazard can be absolutely anything: a person, object, illness, situation, environment. It is important to remember the good practice point noted below.

---

### GOOD PRACTICE POINT

A hazard can stop a victim getting a benefit and/or it can directly cause a danger.

Some typical hazards in adult abuse cases are (and this list is not exhaustive):

- the behaviour/actions of the abuser (it is important when writing a risk assessment that the worker is explicit about the actions; that is what evidence has been gathered about: for example shouting, swearing, making threats, kicking, slapping, punching, stealing, showing pornographic material, etc.)

- fear of the abuser

- feelings of worthlessness

- low self-esteem

- lack of insight

- lack of confidence

- lack of capacity[4] in regard to [money, sexual relationships, etc.]

- disability/physical or mental illness (again this would have to be explained in detail *why* a condition was a hazard in the circumstances appertaining to abuse)

- being housebound

- physical dependency

- confusion

- inability to call for help

- loneliness

- no visitors/friends/family

- having wealth, assets

- abuser's history of violence, repeated offending, etc.

- abuser's particular problems, e.g. gambling, drug or alcohol misuse

- abuser's need for money

- abuser's knowledge of pin number

- abuser refuses access to services.

At this point it is useful to introduce the concept of *dangerousness*. The actions, behaviours or the problems being experienced by the perpetrator of abuse may be hazards, but a worker assessing the risk of harm must consider the dangerousness of that abuser. Simply dangerousness is about the potential to harm others. If an abuser is known to the prison or probation services it is imperative that they are contacted for information regarding past risk assessments in relation to re-offending behaviour (Kemshall 1997, 1998).

## Danger

A danger is a feared negative outcome. A worker has to predict what could happen in the future. Because we are focusing on adult abuse cases we have to relate this back to the definition of *significant harm*. It is important to remember the good practice point below.

---

### GOOD PRACTICE POINT

A danger can be a feared outcome which causes physical or emotional harm for the victim.

---

Workers usually find it easier to list physical harms rather than emotional ones. Investigating officers must try to gather evidence regarding how the abuse has affected a victim. It is important to talk to the victim about this; allowing enough time to build trust so that the victim can talk openly about their feelings – at the time of the abuse but also at the present time. Many victims will struggle with this and may not trust the people who are carrying out the investigation. It is also important to remember that victims are often threatened by their abuser and told not to tell anybody about what has been happening.

When writing in the dangers section of the risk tool for adult abuse cases, workers should first be thinking in terms of the categories of abuse; that is:

- physical
- sexual
- psychological
- financial/material
- neglect/acts of omission
- discriminatory
- institutional. (DH and Home Office 2000, pp.9–10).

Again it is important to emphasise that a worker should then expand on what forms of abuse occur in each individual category.

Some other dangers which are common in abuse cases are (again the list is not exhaustive):

- depression
- self-harm

- attempts at suicide
- lack of trust
- forming inappropriate relationships
- losses, e.g. contact with other people, money, self-worth
- debts
- disconnection of utilities, e.g. gas, electric
- permanent injuries.

Whilst looking at some of the dangers above, it is important to go back to the point made earlier that some things can be a hazard *or* a danger. It is very important to look at the individual case. Something like depression or forming inappropriate relationships can be the end result (i.e. long-term effect of abuse) in a particular case, but in another case they might be a hazard.

When considering dangers it is also vital that a worker is thinking about *public protection issues*. Risk assessment involves assessing harm to:

- the victim
- the general public (this would include service users, workers, visitors to a communal setting, people on the street)
- property.

Let us return to the case of Ena to consider just some of the hazards and dangers which were relevant in her case (see Case Study 11.1: Ena (Part 2)).

---

## CASE STUDY 11.1: ENA (PART 2)

### HAZARDS

- The violent behaviour of Craig. He had had a history of difficult behaviour in childhood and progressive violent behaviour as an adolescent. This was described in full in the risk tool with sources cited (professionals previously involved with him, e.g. psychiatrist, probation officer)
- Craig's own use of drugs, which often made him more violent
- Craig's dealing of drugs in the house
- Strangers coming to the house
- Syringes and other debris on the lounge floor

- Ena's poor mobility which made it impossible for her to remove herself quickly from any potentially dangerous situation
- Ena's love for Craig
- Ena's sense of duty and loyalty
- Ena's guilt about her daughter abandoning Craig at birth
- Craig's access to his grandmother's bank account
- Craig knowing Ena's pin numbers

**DANGERS**

- Physical abuse (by Craig; he always followed the same pattern of violence which was described in detail in this section)
- Emotional abuse (threats by Craig, verbal abuse, ridicule from strangers visiting the house to purchase drugs)
- Financial abuse (money taken from Ena's various bank and post office savings accounts)
- Infectious diseases (based on the possibility that Ena could fall onto a syringe lying on the floor)

At this point in the chapter it might be helpful for the reader to turn to Appendix 11.1 to look at an example of a risk tool. This was the tool I developed for the *North Wales Policy and Procedure for the Protection of Vulnerable Adults* (North Wales Vulnerable Adults Forum 2005) and has since been adopted by some other areas for their adult protection policies and procedures.

**HOW TO USE THE RISK TOOL**

As has already been said the risk tool can be used at the alert stage and within a strategy meeting. Information can be limited at these stages but the tool will help workers to focus on the issues surrounding safety and harm. The chairperson can lead people through the tool during a strategy meeting in a similar way as to how this should be undertaken during a case conference, which will be discussed below.

## Gathering information

During the course of an abuse investigation the investigating officers will be interviewing the victim and liaising with other people in order to gather evidence. At the same time they will be assessing risk, looking particularly at the hazards and possible dangers in the situation. The word 'evidence' needs to be used in two different senses during an investigation:

1.  The investigating officers will need to be gathering evidence to prove that abuse has occurred.

2.  Evidence will be needed to predict whether the dangers are likely to happen in the future.

In day-to-day risk assessment it is imperative that the service user is involved in the process; this is just the same in adult protection work – the victim should be made aware of the reasons why risk assessment is important and what will happen to the information obtained, i.e. with whom it will be shared. Good practice requires that the issues of confidentiality and information sharing are raised at the beginning of any interview. The victim must be made aware of the limits of confidentiality.

---

### GOOD PRACTICE POINTS

Investigating officers need to explain:

-   why information is being gathered

-   the limits of confidentiality, i.e it may have to be broken if someone is at risk of harm

-   that the principles of self-determination and choice may have to be over-ridden when public protection becomes an issue

-   what notes and records are kept and where they are located; who has access to these records

-   when and how information may be shared, e.g. telling the police when a crime has been committed; between participants attending a case conference.

---

### Completing and using the risk tool

Having interviewed the victim and liaised with other people the investigating officers should then complete Sections 1 to 4 on the risk tool. The tool should then be photocopied so that every participant can be given a copy during the case conference. Risk assessment should be an agenda item; it will usually be undertaken after everyone has presented their reports. The risk assessment process is where participants should have a full discussion about whether the victim may be harmed in the future.

The dangers are numbered on the risk tool so that the chairperson can guide the participants to consider each danger in turn. The chairperson should formally ask the key question: how likely is it the danger will occur?

---

### Key Question

'How likely is it the danger will occur?

---

Four gradings are listed on the tool:

- very likely
- quite likely
- not very likely
- not at all likely.

The chairperson has the difficult job of trying to get participants to reach a consensus of opinion for each danger. Grading can be very subjective and people should not just go with their 'gut-feeling'. The prediction of likelihood has to be based on evidence, which in turn will be based on facts from the past and the current situation. Everyone attending the case conference should have prepared their own reports with a view to contributing to the risk assessment. In order to predict the likelihood of a danger occurring a worker must think about:

- current circumstances
- environment
- past behaviours/incidents
- frequency
- duration
- vulnerability of the victim
- dangerousness of the abuser.

Where a participant refuses to go with the consensus of opinion, their reasons for not agreeing must be written in the conflict box (Section 6). During the course of any investigation there may be all sorts of conflict between different individuals – professionals and workers can argue between themselves, the victim may disagree with a worker. All this must be recorded in detail. The conflict box can also be used when a participant does not agree with the final decisions and recommendations; again reasons for refusal must be stated.

Let's return to the case of Ena and see how professionals predicted the likelihood of the dangers occurring (see Case Study 11.1: Ena (Part 3)).

---

### CASE STUDY 11.1: ENA (PART 3)

**KEY CONSIDERATIONS/INFORMATION NEEDED IN ORDER TO PREDICT THE LIKELIHOOD OF HARM OCCURRING IN THE FUTURE**

- Ena's current mobility
- Ena's current health problems
- Number of visits to accident and emergency
- Number of admissions to hospital
- Types of injuries sustained; whether non-accidental
- Calls to the police from neighbours (dates/times)
- Police visits to house (dates/times)
- Financial situation (accounts and card details)
- Amounts of money withdrawn from accounts by Craig (dates/times)
- Craig's use of Ena's cards (dates/times/amounts)
- Craig's use of drugs
- Visitors to the house (numbers/frequency)

**DANGERS**

- Physical abuse: *very likely*

  *Evidence*: Ena disclosed herself that Craig hit her at least three times a week. She had been to accident and emergency six times in a year; had had three hospital admissions in an 18-month period, although one was related to genuine health problems rather than non-accidental injury due to physical violence.

- Emotional abuse: *very likely*

  *Evidence*: Ena said Craig shouted and swore at her ~
  day. Neighbours had also witnessed Craig threatening Ena
  in the front garden and in the street. The manager of the
  post office recalled three occasions when Craig was
  verbally abusive to Ena when withdrawing money from
  her post office savings account.

- Financial abuse: *very likely*

  *Evidence*: Ena showed the investigating officers her bank
  statements and post office savings books. In the past
  year a total of £5000 had been withdrawn. On average
  withdrawals were made three times a month.

- Infectious diseases: *not very likely*

  *Evidence*: Although Ena's physical health is not good and
  her mobility is poor she has not fallen over in the past six
  months. She is very astute and knows the dangers of
  having syringes on the floor. She sits in a corner and
  accesses the hallway via the kitchen rather than walking
  across the lounge.

---

Good practice indicates that whenever possible a victim should attend a case
conference in order to participate in the discussion and engage in the risk
assessment. Obviously in some cases this is not possible (e.g. where a younger
person has a profound learning disability; an older person is in the advanced
stages of Alzheimer's disease; a person with a mental health problem is ill). In
these circumstances an advocate should attend.

### Developing a protection/safeguarding plan

Having predicted whether the victim is likely to be harmed in the future, participants at a case conference have to make decisions and recommendations
which will be developed into a protection (or safeguarding) plan. The main
aim of such a plan is to demonstrate how the risk of harm can be minimised.
This should be achieved by providing appropriate resources; sometimes this
will be resources for both the victim and/or the abuser. It has been said previously that a protection plan should be something which is developed *with* the
victim not something that is imposed on them. This is one of the main reasons
why a victim should be present at a case conference when possible and the protection plan should be written in conjunction with that person.

The decisions and recommendations made during the case conference should form the structure of a detailed protection plan. In reality many protection plans are written within the case conference minutes and lack the detail which is required. A good protection plan should be detailed enough to give insight into exactly how the victim is being protected without other information having to be made available. Because detail is needed it is good practice to nominate a key worker and a core group of people who will be involved in the plan. The main role of the key worker is to ensure that the core group of people carry out the tasks and responsibilities which have been agreed in the protection plan. The core group together with the victim should then meet to write the plan in detail; then it will be distributed with the minutes of the case conference. A pro forma for a protection plan which I developed some time ago is given in Appendix 11.3 and serves as an example of good practice.

It is important to say at this point that some alleged abusers will be vulnerable adults themselves. In such cases a separate case conference may be convened on the abuser and subsequently a protection plan may also be developed for that person.

### Grading the case overall

As well as predicting the likelihood of each danger occurring it is necessary to consider the seriousness of the case overall and give a general grading about whether the person is likely to be abused (i.e. experience physical or emotional harm) in the future. The overall gradings in the risk tool are:

- low
- moderate
- high.

### Signatures

The final task is for everyone who has contributed to and participated in the risk assessment to sign the last page of the tool. This page should be circulated around the case conference table in order to obtain original signatures. When the risk tool is typed up and circulated, the back page should be photocopied; the original signatures page should be kept on the victim's file.

### Typing up and distributing the risk tool

Ideally both the chairperson and the minute-taker should be recording on the risk tool as the case conference progresses. After the case conference has concluded the risk tool will be formally typed up based on the notes taken by the chairperson and minute-taker. The tool will then be copied and circulated with the minutes of the case conference together with the protection plan, which will be discussed below.

## THE NEED FOR A RISK TOOL SPECIFICALLY DESIGNED FOR USE IN COMMUNAL SETTINGS

A common occurrence in adult protection work is for people to have concerns about practices or situations which are occurring on a regular basis in communal settings. Abuse often remains hidden because people refer to actions as 'just a bit of bad practice'. There is often an unwillingness or reluctance to implement the abuse procedures.

Another common situation is where an alert is made regarding one particular service user and when the investigation starts other problems are highlighted. Investigations can become muddled at this point. Good practice would be for the original investigation to continue but for a separate strategy meeting to take place to assess the other concerns which have been brought forward. This is what happened in the following case.

---

### CASE STUDY 11.2: ROTTON PARK CARE HOME (PART 1)

Rotton Park is a care home for younger adults with learning disabilities. The local social services were contacted by the police after they had received a phone call from a woman who said she had been 'touched up on the street' by one of the residents whilst she had been out doing her shopping. The resident, Desmond, had been with a care worker at the time and she apologised for his behaviour. The woman rang the police to say she did not want to take any action herself but she felt that someone should 'do something about the young man'. The police did not go out to the care home but made an alert to social services, who convened a strategy meeting and decided to implement the protection of vulnerable adults policy. A social worker and a nurse from the learning disabilities team went out to see Desmond. Whilst at the home, they became very concerned about the conditions within the home, the appearance of many of the residents and the attitude of staff towards them. Another strategy meeting was convened in regard to the home and the Commission for Social Care Inspection were invited to attend.

---

As a result of the current research project I am undertaking[5] and from my own practice it seems that alerts regarding abuse or poor practices are increasing. I am not saying that abuse is increasing but thankfully more people are now alerting and whistle-blowing; a situation long overdue as highlighted by Deborah Kitson in Chapter 7. I am aware that the original risk tool has been used to consider risks in communal settings, but I felt another tool needed to be developed which was specifically designed to look not only at bad practices of staff but also in situations where a service user is abusing another service user (or where more than two service users are involved, e.g. in cases of bullying or discriminatory abuse). Case Studies 11.3 and 11.4 highlight such situations.

---

### CASE STUDY 11.3: MAGGIE AND LORNA (NOW AGED 101) (PART 1)

Maggie and Lorna were both 99 years old when concerns were raised about their violence towards each other. They live in a care home in a small village. Neither of them has ever been out of the village. The two women openly say they 'hate each other'. Staff at first were amused at their banter but gradually became aware that the women were very violent towards each other. They both had walking sticks which they used to hit each other. There was evidence that the violence was often pre-meditated. On one occasion Lorna travelled up in the lift and heard Maggie mumbling to herself as she was walking along the corridor. Lorna waited in the lift and then stuck out her walking stick so Maggie tripped over. The staff did nothing about this incident or others. Risk assessments had not been undertaken and the women's individual care plans did not address the issue of violence or highlight the fact that incidents were taking place on a regular basis. Everyone knew that the women hated each other because they had fought over a man 80 years ago (who is now dead); neither of them married him and they continue to fight over the matter, blaming each other for the fact that he left them and the village.

---

### CASE STUDY 11.4: DEVENDRA (AGED 24) (PART 1)

Devendra is an Asian man, who came to live in this country when he was 18 years of age. He struggles with the English language and prefers to speak Punjabi whenever possible. He went into hospital on a voluntary basis; he had been diagnosed as having schizophrenia four years ago. He was admitted onto a ward where there were only White British people. Three of the other patients started harassing Devendra. They made racist comments to him, ridiculed him when he went to say prayers and made various threats to harm him. The nursing staff were aware of what was going on; even when they heard what was being said to Devendra they did nothing at all. One evening when night staff came on duty, one of the nurses found Devendra huddled in the corner of a toilet cubicle. He had been badly beaten. He would not say who had done this to him.

## WHEN TO USE THE RISK TOOL FOR COMMUNAL SETTINGS

A major concern I have is that in many areas in the UK I am seeing a large number of inappropriate referrals for an adult abuse investigation. I say 'inappropriate' because it seems in many cases there *is* the potential for harm, but preventative work could and should have been carried out at an earlier time. There has often been a failure to assess the risk and develop a robust care plan. The typical scenarios I am alluding to are in care homes where older adults with dementia have some challenging behaviour and are violent towards other residents. Often an alert is made when staff are finding it difficult to cope or they have just attended a basic awareness course on adult abuse and they over-react. If an adult (young or old) does have problematic behaviour the workers should have assessed the risk immediately, and not waited until a crisis occurs. Hence, this was another reason I wanted to develop a tool which could be used not only in abuse investigation but also for preventative work.

The risk tool I have designed is in Appendix 11.2. It is still based on the terms which should be used in any risk assessment and were discussed previously: risk-taking action, benefit, hazard and danger – but it puts more questions to a worker who might be undertaking the risk assessment. I had in mind that some care workers might act as alerters and this might be a helpful tool for them to complete before making the alert. In other situations, this tool may be useful at a strategy meeting stage. Again a chairperson would lead participants through the form.

## USING THE RISK TOOL IN CASE STUDIES 11.2, 11.3 AND 11.4

It is not possible to present all the information which was gleaned by using the risk tool in Case Studies 11.2, 11.3 and 11.4, because of confidentiality issues and maintaining the anonymity of the people concerned. What follows are summaries of key information which was obtained by utilising the risk tool.

## CASE STUDY 11.2: ROTTON PARK CARE HOME
## (PART 2)

### MAJOR CONCERNS

- Needs of service users not being met
- Inappropriate, discriminatory comments by staff to residents
- Health and safety issues in the home
- All the staff employed in the home are related in some way to the owners – family, friends
- Lack of regular supervision
- Poor recording systems

### CURRENT PRACTICES/BEHAVIOURS/ACTIONS

- Residents are only bathed once a week
- Some residents wear old, torn clothes
- Clothing is generally dirty
- Three residents in particular constantly smell of urine and faeces
- Staff often ignore residents when they ask for help
- Two members of staff regularly swear at residents and make derogatory remarks about being learning disabled
- Desmond, a resident who regularly masturbates in public, is told to go to 'the garage' to do this. There is a disused garage at the end of the driveway to the home
- When it is considered that a resident has behaved badly they have to spend long periods of time in 'Desmond's garage'
- The deputy manager has tried to take action regarding concerns about loose handrails, ill-fitting carpets, exposed wiring; the manager said these repairs are not a priority

### FEARED NEGATIVE OUTCOMES

- Ongoing abuse: physical neglect; emotional neglect; discrimination
- Punishment/imprisonment

- Injuries as a result of falls
- Low self-esteem
- Depression
- Isolation
- Collusion between staff

## EVIDENCE

- All the above had been witnessed by a new deputy manager who has been brought in to cover long-term sickness. He said these behaviours happen on a daily basis
- Other professionals visiting the home have frequently witnessed derogatory comments by staff to residents (but not taken any action)
- One nurse said she knew three residents had been locked in the garage on one occasion
- Care workers in the home are reluctant to talk to the investigating officers
- Records are poor

## PEOPLE INVOLVED IN THE RISK ASSESSMENT

The risk assessment was carried out by two investigating officers who undertook an abuse investigation into the home (not the same two who had been appointed investigating officers for the original alert and investigation regarding Desmond). They eventually interviewed residents who could communicate in some way; manager; deputy manager; staff; administrator; professionals who regularly visited the home, e.g. community nurses, GP.

## PROTECTION PLAN

At the time of writing two residents have been moved to other care homes and three members of staff have been suspended (including the manager). The investigation is ongoing.

## CASE 11.3: MAGGIE AND LORNA (NOW AGED 101) (PART 2)

### MAJOR CONCERNS

- Both women wish to remain in the home as they have never left the village; therefore this could be an ongoing case of mutual abuse
- Physical abuse of both women
- Emotional abuse – long-term effect on other residents

### CURRENT PRACTICES/BEHAVIOURS/ACTIONS

- Both women are physically violent – they hit out with walking sticks; they also throw objects at each other
- They bully each other – physically and emotionally
- Verbal abuse – the women shout and swear at each other which has a detrimental effect on other residents who are frightened of the women, but some residents are also offended by the language they use

### FEARED NEGATIVE OUTCOMES

- Serious injury – to themselves; other residents; staff; visitors to the home
- Death due to the level of violence which is being perpetrated
- Emotional harm to other residents
- Physical damage to property

### EVIDENCE

The written records in the home were of a high standard and all the incidents (which happened on a daily basis) had been logged but no action taken. The problem was that staff did not raise concerns until a member of staff had attended a two-day training course on adult abuse. Records used to collate evidence for the risk were:

- service user files
- incident reports
- body maps
- communications book.

## ACTION

A strategy meeting was convened by the manager of the home; the local adult protection coordinator attended and chaired the meeting. It was decided not to implement the abuse procedures at that time but to first bring in an independent social worker in order to undertake in-depth risk assessments on both women. Interim protection plans were developed for both women.

## PEOPLE INVOLVED IN THE RISK ASSESSMENT

Manager of home; the two key workers in the care home who supported Maggie and Lorna; GP; independent social worker.

## PROTECTION PLANS

The plans were very detailed but the main subject areas covered were:

- The reasons *why* it was decided both women should remain in the care home.

- The work which would be done with each woman regarding their past and present situations – this included:

  - dealing with loss; giving the opportunity to talk about the man who left them

  - how to deal with anger/anger management

  - appropriate behaviour

  - how staff would supervise the women

  - location of the women's bedrooms

  - the women's use of lounges/dining areas.

---

## CASE STUDY 11.4: DEVENDRA (AGED 24) (PART 2)

## MAJOR CONCERNS

- That physical abuse, emotional abuse, discriminatory abuse by patients may have been ongoing for some time.

- Nursing staff had not taken any action when they witnessed incidents

- Nursing staff had failed to report and record the incidents they had witnessed

- All the nursing staff are White British; nothing has been done to facilitate Devendra with speaking in Punjabi

## CURRENT PRACTICES/BEHAVIOURS/ACTIONS
From other patients:

- racist comments

- physical attacks

- burning back with cigarettes

- putting head down toilet and flushing

- urinating on Devendra whilst being kicked on the floor.

From staff:

- some nurses stood and watched when the three patients made racist comments to Devendra; then laughed at the comments

- some nurses deliberately walked away when Devendra was being physically attacked; they did nothing to intervene

- when Devendra did not understand what was being said to him, no time or effort was put in to try to help him understand.

## ACTION

- Police were contacted after Devendra had been badly beaten in the toilet. A criminal investigation was carried out

- Vulnerable adults procedures were implemented

- Some nurses were suspended and disciplinary procedures followed

## EVIDENCE

- None of these incidents had been recorded by staff on the ward

- Other patients disclosed what they had witnessed

- One incident was witnessed by another patient's sister

- Racist comments were daily
- Violent incidents occurred two or three times a week

## PEOPLE INVOLVED IN THE RISK ASSESSMENT

An abuse investigation took place; the investigation officers were the police and an Asian social worker who was based in a community mental health team (i.e. not connected to the hospital). Statements were taken from Devendra, nursing staff, other staff on the ward (e.g. cleaners), patients on the ward and one patient's sister.

## IMMEDIATE PROTECTION PLAN

- On the day of the attack Devendra was moved to another hospital in the same city so his extensive injuries could be attended to

## CONCLUSION

The last case cited demonstrates how serious and life-threatening situations can become if workers fail to act. Devendra did survive physically but his mental health problems were exacerbated by the experience. Maggie and Lorna continue to be feisty women, but happily their violence towards each other has been reduced. The investigation into Rotton Park Care Home continues.

I hope this chapter has illustrated how vital it is to undertake robust risk assessments in every case. I am acutely aware that we are working in a time when workers across the sectors feel overworked and that there is just not enough time to get things done. However, everyone has to take responsibility for their own practice and we all have a moral responsibility to protect vulnerable human beings. Managers also have a responsibility to ensure that all their workers are trained properly to understand the theory of risk, the correct terminology to be used and how to use risk tools effectively. It is pointless producing all the paperwork – policies, procedures, monitoring tools – if workers are not trained how to use them properly. This chapter could be the start of such training.

## GOOD PRACTICE POINTS

- The primary focus of risk assessment should always be the service user.

- All vulnerable adults have rights and should be treated equally, i.e. they have the right to live their lives as they wish to do.

- Workers must consider whether the risk-taking action is currently or could become a public protection issue.

- Risk assessment is always undertaken *with* the service user; it is not something which is imposed on him/her.

- The issue of mental capacity will always be central to any risk assessment. It should be remembered that an individual may have the capacity to make decisions about certain aspects of their life, but may lack the capacity to make decisions about other aspects.

- It is important to involve other people in the risk assessment, but there must be clear protocols regarding obtaining permission from the service user and the sharing of information.

- Detailed recording is of paramount importance in order to ensure that it is clearly understood *why* decisions have been made and *how* risk of harm is to be minimised.

- Risk assessments should be written in a clear way, i.e. using plain language which everyone can understand.

## APPENDIX 11.1: RISK ASSESSMENT TOOL

| Name of service user | | | ID Code | |
|---|---|---|---|---|

Alleged/suspected/proven categories of abuse:

Name of worker(s) and job title completing the risk tool:

| **1** **RISK-TAKING ACTION (S)** | ① *What does the service user want to do?* |
|---|---|
| | |

| **2** **BENEFITS** | ① *Why does the service user want to take the risk? What will s/he get out of it?* |
|---|---|
| | |

| **3** **HAZARDS** | ① *Can be anything, e.g. person, behaviour, situation which stops the benefit or causes the danger.* |
|---|---|
| | |

| 4 | **DANGERS** | ⓘ | The worst feared outcomes/harms. Relate to definition of significant harm. |

| 1 |
| 2 |
| 3 |
| 4 |
| 5 |
| 6 |
| 7 |
| 8 |
| 9 |
| 10 |
| 11 |
| 12 |

**5** PREDICTION/LIKELIHOOD

ⓘ Key question: How likely is it the danger will occur?

Prediction Scale

| VERY LIKELY | QUITE LIKELY | NOT VERY LIKELY | NOT AT ALL LIKELY |
|---|---|---|---|

| | DANGER | EVIDENCE | PRESENTED BY | PREDICTION |
|---|---|---|---|---|
| 1 | | | | |
| 2 | | | | |
| 3 | | | | |
| 4 | | | | |
| 5 | | | | |
| 6 | | | | |

**5** PREDICTION/LIKELIHOOD ... cont'd

ⓘ Key question: How likely is it the danger will occur?

Prediction Scale

VERY LIKELY | QUITE LIKELY | NOT VERY LIKELY | NOT AT ALL LIKELY

| DANGER | EVIDENCE | PRESENTED BY | PREDICTION |
|--------|----------|--------------|------------|
| 7 | | | |
| 8 | | | |
| 9 | | | |
| 10 | | | |
| 11 | | | |
| 12 | | | |

**6** <u>CONFLICT BOX</u>

<u>NAME OF PERSON</u>

<u>EXPLAIN WHAT S/HE DISAGREES WITH</u>

**7** <u>DEVELOPMENT OF PROTECTION PLAN</u>

ⓘ *Detail needed about objectives, agencies, personnel, roles, responsibilities, tasks, contact, method of working, monitoring tools, written records.*

| 8 | GRADING OF CASE |
|---|---|

LOW ☐　　　MODERATE ☐　　　HIGH ☐

| 9 | DATE FOR REVIEW |
|---|---|

Date ☐　　　　　　　　　Time ☐

| 10 | SIGNATURES |
|---|---|

| NAME | JOB TITLE/RELATIONSHIP | SIGNATURE | DATE |
|------|------------------------|-----------|------|
|      | Service User           |           |      |
|      | Worker                 |           |      |
|      | Manager                |           |      |

## APPENDIX 11.2: RISK ASSESSMENT TOOL FOR COMMUNAL SETTINGS

Name of setting                                    Address

| **Type of setting** | For example: care home; day centre; hospital ward; day hospital; supported accommodation; education establishment; prison |
| --- | --- |

| **Alleged/suspected/proven categories of abuse:** | ☐Physical<br>☐Sexual<br>☐Psychological<br>☐Financial/material<br>☐Neglect/acts of omission<br>☐Discriminatory<br>☐Institutional |
| --- | --- |

**Alleged/suspected/proven bad practices**

| **How many residents/service users might be at risk of harm?  [  ]**<br><br>a._____<br>b._____<br>c._____<br>d._____<br>e._____<br>f._____<br>g._____ | List individuals if appropriate |
| --- | --- |

**Who are the alleged perpetrators?**

a._____

b._____

c._____

d._____

e._____

f._____

g._____

Name individuals and their status where possible.

---

## 1   <u>MAJOR CONCERNS</u>

What is giving cause for concern regarding the establishment/staff/service users?

---

## 2   <u>CURRENT SITUATION AND WISHES</u>

Do the service users wish to remain living in or attending the establishment?

Please state if the service users are detained, e.g. under the Mental Health Act; serving a prison sentence.

## 3   CURRENT PRACTICES, BEHAVIOURS AND ACTIONS

What is actually being done (by service users or staff)?

What is not being done?

Are there any practices or regimes which hinder the promotion of the basic principles of care, i.e. choice, independence, self determination, individuality, etc.?

a.

b.

c.

d.

e.

f.

g.

h.

i.

j.

k.

l.

m.

n.

o.

p.

q.

r.

## 4   <u>**FEARED NEGATIVE**</u><br><u>**OUTCOMES FOR THE FUTURE**</u>

What are people worried about?

What do they think will happen?

a. _____

b. _____

c. _____

d. _____

e. _____

f. _____

g. _____

h. _____

i. _____

j. _____

k. _____

l. _____

m. _____

n. _____

o. _____

p. _____

q. _____

r. _____

## 5 EVIDENCE

| a. | What evidence is available to support the belief that these actions/incidents have taken place? | What factual information is available?<br>Have there been verbal reports?<br>Are written records available? |
|---|---|---|

| b. | When did they happen? | State date, times, patterns of frequency and duration if possible. |
|---|---|---|

| c. | Has someone disclosed/talked about these incidents? | Who? (state name, position, e.g. service user, staff, relative, visitor)<br>When? (record dates and times) |
|---|---|---|

| d. | Has anyone witnessed these incidents? | Who? (state name, position, e.g. service user, staff, relative, visitor)<br>When? (record dates and times) |
|---|---|---|

e.  Have any records been kept?

State type of record
(service user file,
communications
book, incident report,
bodymap, complaint
letter/form)

Where are these
records located?

f.  Have you any reason to believe
these actions or behaviours are
continuing or are likely to happen
again?

Explain your reasons
in detail for this.

## 6 <u>CONTRIBUTORS TO THE RISK ASSESSMENT</u>

Who has been contacted?

How have they contributed? (e.g. by telephone, during a meeting, interview, written report, etc.)

Include any service users and state whether consent has been given to share information.

| NAME | DESIGNATION | EVIDENCE GIVEN |
|------|-------------|----------------|
| 1. | | |
| 2. | | |
| 3. | | |
| 4. | | |
| 5. | | |
| 6. | | |
| 7. | | |
| 8. | | |
| 9. | | |
| 10. | | |
| 11. | | |
| 12. | | |
| 13. | | |

## 7 DISAGREEMENTS OR CONFLICTING OPINIONS

To be used when a person disagrees with a decision or grading.

### NAME OF PERSON

### EXPLAIN WHAT S/HE DISAGREES WITH

---

## 8 LIKELIHOOD OF HARM OCCURRING IN THE FUTURE

☐ VERY LIKELY

☐ QUITE LIKELY

☐ NOT VERY LIKELY

☐ NOT AT ALL LIKELY

## 9  **AGREED ACTION·PLAN**

## 10  **DATE AND TIME SET FOR REVIEW**

## 11 SIGNATURES

| NAME | JOB TITLE/RELATIONSHIP | SIGNATURE | DATE |
|------|------------------------|-----------|------|
|  |  |  |  |
|  |  |  |  |
|  |  |  |  |
|  |  |  |  |
|  |  |  |  |
|  |  |  |  |
|  |  |  |  |
|  |  |  |  |
|  |  |  |  |
|  |  |  |  |
|  |  |  |  |

## APPENDIX 11.3: DEVELOPING PROTECTION PLANS

Protection plans must be *specific* and *detailed*. They should be developed and agreed in case conferences, but more detail can be added after the conference has taken place.

---

### SUGGESTED PRO FORMA

#### Objectives of the plan

What are you trying to achieve?

#### List of people involved

- Key worker, i.e. person who will coordinate the plan
- Primary worker, i.e. person who has most face-to-face contact with the victim
- Include professionals, volunteers, advocates, other important people (family, neighbours, friends), i.e. who is contributing

#### Responsibilities and tasks

(Remember to include work being done with victim and abuser.)

State for each person involved:

- Name, job/relationship with victim/abuser
- Objectives – what s/he is trying to achieve
- How s/he will do this (tasks)
- When this will be done – contact frequency/day/time/duration

#### Monitoring

- How each person is going to record what s/he is doing, what has been achieved, problems, etc.
- Specific tools to be used, e.g. bodycharts, checklists
- Where the record will be kept
- How the information will be presented for review

#### Review

Date must be set for review.

## NOTES

1   I shall use the term 'worker' in the generic sense to include anyone who may be working with a vulnerable adult in any sector, i.e. statutory, voluntary and independent.

2   I shall continue to use the term 'adult protection work' which will encompass the term 'safeguarding' throughout the chapter.

3   All names in the case studies have been changed to protect the anonymity of the victims and their location.

4   Capacity issues are discussed in full in Chapter 10 and will not be repeated here.

5   *The Needs of Vulnerable Adults: Services for Victims of Abuse* is a follow-on research project from the original project, *The Needs of Older Women: Services for Victims of Elder Abuse and Other Abuse* (Pritchard 2000; also see 2001 and 2003).

## REFERENCES

Association of Directors of Social Services (ADSS) (2005) *Safeguarding Adults: A National Framework of Standards for Good Practice and Outcomes in Adult Protection.* London: ADSS.

Brearley, C. P. (1982a) *Risk and Ageing.* London: Routledge and Kegan Paul.

Brearley, C. P. (1982b) *Risk in Social Work.* London: Routledge and Kegan Paul.

Department of Health (DH) (2005) *Independence, Well-Being and Choice: Our Vision for the Future of Social Care in England.* London: DH.

Department of Health (DH) (2007) *Independence, Choice and Risk: A Guide to Best Practice in Supported Decision Making.* London: DH.

Department of Health (DH) and Home Office (2000) *No Secrets: Guidance on Developing and Implementing Multi-Agency Policies and Procedures to Protect Vulnerable Adults from Abuse.* London: DH.

Kemshall, H. (1997) *Management and Assessment of Risk in the Probation Service.* London: Home Office/Association of Chief Probation Officers.

Kemshall, H. (1998) *Risk in Probation Practice.* London: Ashgate.

Lord Chancellor's Department (1997) *Who Decides? Making Decisions on Behalf of Mentally Incapacitated Adults.* London: The Stationery Office.

North Wales Vulnerable Adults Forum (2005) *North Wales Policy and Procedure for the Protection of Vulnerable Adults.* North Wales: North Wales Vulnerable Adults Forum.

Pritchard, J. (2000) *The Needs of Older Women: Services for Victims of Elder Abuse and Other Abuse.* Bristol: The Policy Press.

Pritchard, J. (2001) *Male Victims of Elder Abuse: Their Experiences and Needs.* London: Jessica Kingsley Publishers.

Pritchard, J. (2003) *Support Groups for Older People Who Have Been Abused: Beyond Existing.* London: Jessica Kingsley Publishers.

# CHAPTER 12

# SURVIVORS EXPLAIN HEALING THROUGH GROUP WORK

## MEMBERS OF BEYOND EXISTING

### PREFACE

### *Jacki Pritchard*

Very often books focusing on abuse give attention to theory, policy and practice – quite rightly so. However, not enough attention is given to survivors of abuse. It is imperative that victims are given a voice so policy makers and practitioners can learn to help them in the best way possible. In order to promote good practice with victims of abuse it is very necessary to give them the opportunity to tell their stories so practitioners can learn more about their needs and how they can be helped. In the following chapter survivors explain how they have progressed through the healing process through attending therapeutic support groups run by an organisation called Beyond Existing.

Members of Beyond Existing were asked if they would like to contribute a chapter to this book so they could speak to a wide audience. The members who wanted to do this have contributed in different ways. Some have participated in group discussions which were audio-taped, transcribed and then edited by the members themselves. Some members wanted to say things by writing rather than speaking verbally; others agreed to contribute pieces of work they have produced in the past whilst attending Beyond Existing groups.[1] What this chapter will demonstrate is that practitioners must not just be focused on crisis intervention and deal with practical matters, they need to be able to assess the best way of working therapeutically with victims in the long-term so that they can progress through the healing process. This chapter will show how survivors can be helped by using different methods; every survivor is an individual and it is necessary to find the best method of working for each one of them. The long-term work with victims is often forgotten or neglected. This chapter will illustrate how vital it is to plan long-term work, so that victims do not go on experiencing emotional pain for longer than they need to do so. A brief explanation regarding how Beyond Existing came in to being may be helpful to the reader.

Between 1997 and 2000 a research project entitled *The Needs of Older Women: Services for Victims of Elder and Other Abuse* was funded by the Joseph Rowntree Foundation (Pritchard 2000). The project was undertaken in three social services departments in the North of England and its main aims were to:

1.    identify women who were victims of elder abuse

2.    carry out a small study to identify the extent to which victims of elder abuse have also experienced abuse earlier in their lives

3.    identify the types of abuse experienced (in childhood and adulthood)

4.    identify the needs of victims

5.    consider what resources or services should be provided for victims.

The focus of inquiry was broadened during the project to include male victims because men also approached the researcher to tell their stories (Pritchard 2001). A key finding of the project was that both men and women survivors wanted to meet other older people who had experienced abuse. In 2000 a pilot study was set up to test out whether such groups would meet the needs of survivors; support groups were run for older people who had been abused either in childhood or adulthood. The pilot ran for a year and was extremely successful and so the organisation of Beyond Existing was founded. The groups were run primarily for older people until 2003, when the organisation's remit expanded to run groups for anyone over 18 years of age (Pritchard 2003).

During the past eight years Beyond Existing has run a variety of groups – some have been for men or women; others have been mixed. Different people have come together – people with mental health problems, people with learning disabilities and physically disabled people. The age range has been vast – the youngest person being 19 years old and the oldest, 93 years. What is made very clear to anyone who wants to attend a group is that they must want to go through the healing process; Beyond Existing is not offering 'tea and sympathy chat groups'. The groups meet once a month for two-hour sessions. This would not be ideal for all survivors as some need to meet more regularly; but most members who have attended the Beyond Existing groups feel it is 'enough'. They say that to deal with the abuse so intensely more frequently would be 'too much'. Telephone support is offered in between meetings; and other help is given when particular pieces of work are being undertaken – as will be shown by Debra's account later in the chapter.

What follows comes from the survivors themselves – they talk about the types of abuse experienced, give accounts of what work has been undertaken and present examples of the creative writing which has helped the healing process. This chapter gives them a voice to which all practitioners should listen.

## REFERENCES

Pritchard, J. (2000) *The Needs of Older Women: Services for Victims of Elder Abuse and Other Abuse.* Bristol: The Policy Press.

Pritchard, J. (2001) *Male Victims of Elder Abuse: Their Experiences and Needs.* London: Jessica Kingsley Publishers.

Pritchard, J. (2003) *Support Groups for Older People Who Have Been Abused: Beyond Existing.* London: Jessica Kingsley Publishers.

## CONTACT DETAILS

**Beyond Existing**
PO Box 1779
Sheffield
S6 3YB

## SHARON (Age 39)

### Abuse experienced

Started off with my Mum – neglect really. Then my Dad – sexual abuse. Grandmother – that's my Dad's mother – physical abuse. Steve who is my son's father – physical abuse. Five relationships after that were all abusive; one of them – Derek – anally raped me – sexually abused me. My ex-husband started off as emotional abuse – he was mentally ill – and before we split up he raped me. In between all that were partners that were abusing and also abused my two sons which is why it is a such a big step for me to be able to give Bethany and Amy my daughters that little bit of freedom as well so not only am I dealing with my own abuse but I also need to deal with my son's abuse as well.

I just remember always being at my Nana's; my Mum saying things – my sister being called the princess I'm my Mum's wicked witch. I just assumed her boyfriend that she was having the affair with abused me and I was about 7 then so I just assumed because of my memories it was just then. But talking to my grandmother – my Nana which is my Mum's mum – from the day I was born really she [Mum] didn't want me and what I have talked about in bereavement counselling and to Yvonne [Community Psychiatric Nurse] it is quite obvious my Mum was ill. We have tried to have a relationship. It always leads to her telling me bigger lies basically and me being pushed away again. The last time I had a relationship with my Mum was just after my Dad died she said she only had ten months to live and that's eight years ago. She's still alive now and she's a lot healthier than me. It's just rejection and neglect.

She knew her boyfriend was abusing me. She locked me in her bedroom while she had sex with him and it was a big secret you know 'Don't tell your Dad'. When I did try talking to my Dad he said I was a liar.

To a certain extent I can see that she was probably mentally ill; I know that is no excuse to how I was treated as a kid. I think a lot of issues that are there now are anger and letting go of that anger because the way I can explain it is that I am fighting everyday not to be like her. Not to bring my children up the way I was brought up. I am never going to be like her so what have I got to prove? I know that now.

More and more people are recognising that abuse happens and I want to be part of that – that part that says we have got a point. We don't have to be shut away in a corner and forgotten about. That's what I want to be able to do. I want more and more people to sit down and listen to what we've got to say rather than them saying 'we can't help because we don't know anything about it'. I think that's what brought me to Beyond Existing – it's like a safe place for me to be able to disclose what happened to me rather than me carrying on alone without help because there is nobody there.

**Being referred**

I had a review meeting with a psychiatrist and a community psychiatric nurse (CPN) who said try Beyond Existing. She contacted Beyond Existing but she did go into detail about everything she knew about it. I knew what I was going into and when I first spoke to one of the facilitators on the phone I then said to Yvonne that's where I want to be.

**Getting to the meetings**[2]

It is nice seeing regular faces in the taxi. The first time I was quite looking forward to the meeting but when I actually got here it was a bit daunting. I did not know Carol and Debra [who were in the taxi]. Had not met the facilitators. I could not get through the door. I did not want to get out of the taxi.

**Not being listened to**

I never had childhood counselling and mention the abuse well it was 'I'm going to stop you there because I'm not qualified to talk to you about that' – that's all they [professionals] kept saying to me. It's like I can't talk to my youngest brother – he was living with me at the time when I was raped. He can't talk to me about that he still is still hurting about that and that's why we are not close anymore he feels guilty for what happened. He feels he should have been in a position to stop what was happening. He was in the next bedroom he knew what was happening but with his age and everything he couldn't do anything but we are not as close now as we were and he's my baby I brought him up I was his Mum. We are not as close now and that's not because I've pushed him away he feels so guilty about what happened.

**The progress so far**

Fair enough when I first came to Beyond Existing I was very confused about who to talk to about what because there were a lot of other things going on. I had recently had an abortion. But as I am now I can honestly say coming here I am a changed person. Combined with coming here and bereavement counselling I am a different person.

I am no longer over-protective of my girls, which is a big step for me. Because of everything that has happened to me – especially Bethany she is 12 going on 13 she's developing, noticing boys and things like that – it was really freaking me out. She's going to be wanting to do this and going to be wanting to meet boys. It was really getting me down but I would say the last 6 to 8 weeks I have felt able to turn things around. She can go out she can meet her friends. I am always going to be protective because of what happened to me but I am more able to give her that little bit of freedom. That is a big step for me.

I know I have not talked a lot about my abuse but by being here it has let me go home and think more clearly about things. I have let go of a lot of things through bereavement counselling and I know I have got a long way to go. I feel stronger by coming here to be able to deal with that and know that I am in a safe environment to be able to do that.

The last bereavement counselling session I realised I had got as far I could...the person I need to grieve for is my Dad but I don't feel I can do that just yet. I need to deal with the abuse. The way that I explain it there are two parts to my Dad – the good Dad and the bad Dad. I can't let go of the good Dad until I have let go of the bad Dad. I know I have got a long way to go but by letting go of all the other stuff I feel stronger in myself.

*Editor's comment: Sharon finds writing poetry helpful. Examples of her work are given below.*

### *A new beginning...I am a survivor*

Why did you hurt me?
I just don't understand.
Why did you deny me
and never hold my hand?

Why couldn't you say you loved me,
What did I do wrong?
And why did you hit so hard,
Didn't you know you were so strong?

Why did you mock me,
when you knew that I would cry?
And why did you force me to do those things to you?
You knew I didn't want to, it made me want to die.

Something inside me
Said 'STOP! I've had enough,
I can't take this any longer'
and I started to get tough.

Can you see how weak you were?
I'm no longer afraid,
You really were pathetic
Just look at the life for yourselves, you've made.

I am the survivor, now I'm the strongest one,
I know it's not been easy but I'm feeling really strong.
I have grown to realise that I was not to blame,
I was your victim, and YOU were in the wrong.

### Untitled

Sick perverted people
Left to roam the streets,
Murderers, abductors
Paedophiles and creeps.

Bodies left to decompose
In places hard to find,
Shock, heartbreak and devastation
Is all that's left behind.

Abductors taking children
And brainwashing their minds,
Then killing or releasing them
To a life of a different kind.

The world is such an unsafe place
not knowing who to trust,
our children are our future
so their safety is a must.

### Difficult emotions

Sitting under a dark heavy cloud
Alone, feeling totally misunderstood.
I feel the blade of the scissors slicing through my flesh
Punishing myself through pain,
Watching the badness flow out with each drop of blood.

My emotions are numbed, I feel nothing,
No guilt, no anger, no sadness,
Just the strong urge to be punished
To rid my body of the badness.

Later when the blood stops flowing
I sit crying and wondering WHY???
So many unanswered questions,
The guilt making me want to die.

> Why do I hurt them, the ones I love the most?
> I make them feel so helpless not knowing what to say or do.
> Why do I feel so angry? They are not to blame,
> While the ones that really hurt me, well they haven't got a clue.
>
> All I want is to be happy
> Rid my mind of all this pain,
> I want to let go of the past,
> And find myself again.

## SAM (Age 22)

### Abuse experienced

Dad first – 90 per cent psychological damage with about 10 per cent physical. If you really wound him up too much he would hit you – if you pushed him too far. Next was Chris – sexual and psychological. It felt kind of like a family member even though he was never family. He was my teacher. He never hit me but he would manipulate me mentally and obviously the sexual side and then after him there was Shane – he was a partner he was physically and mentally abusive but his was temper based.

One thing I question – my Mum – the position she was in. A lot of people say she neglected me by not doing anything by allowing Chris to live in our home and do what he did and for Dad to do what he did. It always felt like she wasn't neglecting me because she was always crying with me and holding my hand – when the bad things would happen but she would never actually act on it. Yes sometimes I do feel she did neglect and let me down – she wasn't there.

### Finding Beyond Existing

At that particular time my life was on a rollercoaster type thing – one month I am high everything is going well it's all good and then a couple of months later the realisation of all that has happened kicks me and I get me into a really bad low funk. And at that time I was in a very bad position – I had been to the doctor who pushed me onto psychological services who pushed me away and everyone was just saying 'we can't help you' or 'we can help you but only offer you stuff that is going to be of no use to you'. They offered me a 12-week intensive counselling service which was basically for people who have lost their job and they feel really distraught so they need someone there to talk to and help them find their way back in life whereas they felt my case was a bit too severe for 12 weeks' worth of counselling and they recommended the Well Woman's Centre. When I spoke to the Centre they said they had an extensive waiting list so I had nowhere to go.

And one of the books I read said support groups could be helpful and so I thought OK I'll see if there is one. I checked everywhere and couldn't find one, so I went to the local government website and in the groups thing I put the word 'abuse' in and Beyond Existing came up so then I wrote to the PO box.

It was a big helping hand at that time I felt like everything and everyone had totally abandoned me. My life has been very much like that whenever I have called out for help there's been nothing there's been no-one and then at that time I realised I was an adult I needed to do something and the fact that Beyond Existing did respond – 'cos they weren't the only people I wrote to. I wrote to other places – mental health places to see if they knew of any groups and I got no replies. I got a response from Beyond Existing – that was good to actually know that there was somebody willing to help if I asked for it.

Then I came and I realised that there are people who have been through as bad if not sometimes worse things than I have and it's good to know that there are other people who have asked for help and are getting help. They are getting somewhere and not letting the bad things consume them. They are actually standing up and saying 'I'm not going to let this person win anymore'. Coming here has been a huge help especially when I come here I know I can let go. I can say things which I wouldn't normally say to people because they would be very shocked and horrified and they'd look at you or they'd put their arms around and say 'Oh that's so sad'. You don't want to be patronised. You want people to be on a level with you; not make you feel like the victim all the time. So being here is a big help.

**Being brought in a taxi**

It feels good to know we are all coming together. First time[3] – that was worrying yes but not that bit that was exciting but when I got in [the taxi] I didn't know where I was going so I am sat there thinking 'God what if I am going ten miles away and if I need to go how I am going to go.' It was daunting not knowing where I was going; I was putting my life in the driver's hands sort of thing. It didn't give me a chance to think about it and get scared and think 'ooh maybe – maybe not'.

*Editor's comment: Sam also finds writing poetry helpful and like Sharon is prolific. Some of her work is presented below.*

### Ignorance is bliss

The softest touch like electric, sparking my skin,
Flames burn inside, torching my heart,
Knowing this is the end, the last time,
The burning tears rise, clamping my throat,
You ask if I'm OK, tears still pushing their way to the surface,
But I daren't show it, I smile, say it's all fine,
You know better, you know the truth,
But we both act ignorant, for the truth is too scary to say.

Behind closed doors I weep for the past, for another chance,
Lord I wish this wasn't happening,
That this isn't the end, that, that,
That you knew, God only if you knew,
How much I care, how much I need you, you know,
But you daren't show it, you smile, you say it's all fine,
I know better, I know the truth,
But we both act ignorant, for the truth is too scary to say.

### In the corner you'll stay

For all those names you threw at me,
And all those sorrows I bore,
For all those times you broke me down,
This to my heart you tore.

For all those times I wanted it differently
And all those times I gave
For all those times it wasn't enough
I tried so hard to be brave.

For all those times you laughed at me
And all those times I was blamed
For all those times you did me wrong
For this I shouldn't feel ashamed.

For all those times I prayed for the end
For all those times I cried
For all those times you let me down
Something inside me died.

Now all these times I look back
And speak to you for a while
Know that I'm here fighting strong
And all those times I smile.

You'll have no hold on me soon
Your words will mean nothing at all
Because here I am, fighting strong
Here I am standing tall.

## CAROL (Age 45)

### Abuse experienced

Sexual, physical, emotional abuse by my brother
Mum and Dad – neglect – they were at work all the time
Son's Dad – physical, emotional, sexual – emotional blackmail
Bullying – siblings, classmates.

### The journey

My journey started here at Beyond Existing. I went to one group [run by another organisation] and they didn't listen. I felt very lonely. I had nobody else to talk to about abuse. My family – well my sister didn't want to hear any details of things and I needed to get them out. Even your closest friends don't want to listen. My twin sister she just says that she didn't want to hear it because it would make her upset – and feel awful because she knew what was going off and it would make her feel worse than she already does.

I can remember ringing Beyond Existing. I discussed it with my counsellor and she said it was fine. So I decided to take the first steps.

I just wanted to get the abuse out and to know that I was not on my own. I just thought I was on my own – nobody else had been abused. When I came to the group I realised there were other people and it was nice to talk to people that had been abused. It made me think I was not on my own.

It's like Sharon was saying about her daughters – I am still like that with my son even though he is 27 years old. I am even a bit like that with my grandchildren. I am really worried – I still have that. I know I should let go but it's very hard when I have felt like that for a long time.

I've got a lot out of this group. The facilitators have got me to talk. For years I never talked. That large group[4] you didn't have time to talk. Too many folk to go round and people would jump in sometimes. In a small group no-one jumps in and you can all have your time to talk without being interrupted. In that big group everybody had different issues; people would walk out. I felt a bit unsettled. There was a certain group of people who would all sit together and chit chat; they stuck together as a group.

I know I have come a long way. I read into the chair and I've got a lot of confidence and I am getting a bit more confident by myself. I am not feeling as low. I discuss things that need discussing.

*Editor's comment: Carol was very shy when she first attended Beyond Existing but has benefited from using a variety of methods including assertiveness training. Throughout childhood and into adulthood she has experienced literacy problems and wanted to do something about this. With the help of Beyond Existing she started attending literacy classes. She was found to have dyslexia. With the correct help she has made excellent progress. She now reads well and uses a journal to help give accounts of the abuse she experienced. Two short examples are given below.*

---

### Carol's writing

**Example 1**

When I was 11–12 years I was in the bathroom getting washed for bed. It was about 8.30 p.m. My sister was away from home. My younger brother was downstairs watching television and my mum and dad had gone out leaving him in charge. He came in the bathroom and started touching all over my body. I just froze. I asked him to stop. He said 'When I have finished'. Then he pulled my pants down and started to rub me down there then he put his finger inside me. It was hurting me. I started to cry and he said 'Shut up' and hit me and said 'It will hurt more in a minute'. He took down his trousers and his pants and then pushed his dick inside of me. He kept pushing it harder and harder inside of me. My stomach was hitting the sink. It was hurting. I was frightened. Then he pulled his dick out. I was wet and sticky. This glue stuff and blood was there between my legs. I started to cry and clean myself.

**Example 2**

I was 15 I remember walking up the stairs. I got near my mum and dad's bedroom and he came out of his bedroom and pushed me into my mum and dad's bedroom. He was violent and pushed me on the bed face down and pulled down my trousers and pants. I was crying. Soon he started to hit me and told me to shut up. Then he started to put his finger inside my vagina and then he pulled down his own trousers and pants and started rubbing his dick in my bum and pushed it up. It was so painful but he kept pushing it up when it came hard he put it in my mouth. I felt choked and feeling sick then the white stuff started to come in my mouth. When he finished I went to the bathroom and washed my mouth and cleaned my teeth. Then he came in and started to rub me down there with his hands and he said 'That was nice' and left the bathroom.

I feel horrible inside. People think I am getting better but I don't think so. My insides are full of knots. I wish I could go to sleep without one nightmare and feel relaxed in bed. The nightmares are about me putting his hand all over my body touching my breast and vagina and my legs. I feel hurt and dirty. Then he lays on top of me and starts rubbing his dick between my legs then he puts it up me.

## DEBRA (Age 44)

**Abuse experienced**

Uncle – physical and sexual
Mum and Dad had abusive relationship
Ex-husband – physical, emotional and sexual.

*Editor's comment: Debra has written two accounts especially for this chapter. In the first she explains about Beyond Existing. In the second – 'Kirk's Tree' – she describes a major piece of work, which was undertaken with the support of Beyond Existing, to find out the truth about her first-born son.*

I was quite ill at the time I joined Beyond Existing. It was my social worker who arranged things as I was receiving ECT [electro-convulsive therapy].

I believe Beyond Existing has given me a voice. I didn't think there was anyone out there who I could speak to. I felt and I was told that bad things would happen to me if ever I voiced the abuse that I had suffered. From an early age I carried with me a most terrible secret that my uncle was physically and sexually abusing me, which at the time I didn't have the words to say what was going on.

I witnessed my father abusing my mother constantly as a young child but he tried to reassure me that all mums and dads fought and acted in that way. That was frightening.

My ex-husband turned into a monster. Confusingly he would never recall anything bad that he had done. I was completely alone with this daily horror.

At Beyond Existing I see that these things are not right and I am trying to cope and acknowledge the terrible abuse I have suffered from an early age.

I want to scream that I would love to kill myself and put an end to all the torture. I feel abandoned and forsaken that there is no future for me and I simply want to go to sleep. I couldn't talk to anyone about my feelings. This is when Beyond Existing stepped in and gave me lots of support.

My cries at night go unheard. Nobody rescues me. But at Beyond Existing it was the first safe place for me to whom I am able to open up and discuss my real feelings. Though some things are still taboo. But even I could never have guessed how truly horrible my life was to become. When at last I built up the courage to leave my ex-husband (code name Dick) only for him later to take my son away from me and I am still suffering the heartache.

Beside the bad things in life Beyond Existing has helped with acknowledging my past in which my first son, Kirk, who was born asleep, has now been recognised and finally got a resting place where there is a wonderful tree and memorial stone. This gives me amazing comfort and I think this is a huge step towards my recovery.

---

### Kirk's tree

During a meeting at Beyond Existing in July of 2006 I expressed my wish to find out where my first-born son, Kirk, was buried to enable me to say my goodbyes properly.

I became pregnant at the early age of 15 hiding the fact until I was confronted by my mother at nearly six months pregnant. During my pregnancy I became very ill with severe pre-eclampsia and toxaemia and was rushed into hospital. I recall very little after my admission but I have always had flashbacks of my baby being put into a silver bucket with medical staff around me. These were to be rebuked. After several days I woke up in intensive care with tubes all around me and my arms were fixed to wooden planks.

I knew instinctively my baby had gone. But where? I asked my parents and nursing staff as to the whereabouts of my baby. I was told my baby had died. When I asked to see him or a picture I was sternly told he had been buried in a communal grave in the grounds of the hospital.

Neither the birth nor the baby was ever mentioned again. I so much wanted to find the grave and so my journey began.

Firstly the hospital was contacted and an administration assistant was extremely helpful in going through the archived records of the communal graves where I found out that ten babies are buried in each plot in the hospital grounds. Terror went through me: 'Was my baby squashed?' There was no record of my baby in any of the graves.

The next task was to contact the local Register Office to get copies of his birth certificate. When the record could not be found it was concluded that a stillbirth must have taken place and therefore there must be a stillbirth certificate instead.

The General Register Office in Southport was then contacted. They spent an enormous amount of time going through the still-birth records. Both two years before and two years after the date my baby was born. There was no record!

By this time I had reached a low ebb. I felt lost. Abandoned. Cut adrift. I had been programmed adept at keeping this incredible personal information to myself. There weren't any answers just more questions. These piling up inside me.

All I saw was more failure, more hopelessness. I didn't dare to expect anything other. I only wished I didn't have this confusing part of my life where I could never recall events properly. It was a huge wrench and I felt absolutely gutted. These findings were desperately bad times and for these I can never forget the blanking of my baby's birth by my family. I felt like instantly recoiling but they brought back all my insecurities and negativity during that period of my life.

The only thing left for me to do was to ask to see my medical records. These records should have been destroyed after 26 years. One of the officers in the Medical Records went down himself into the archives and hunted for the records. He found these during October 2006. So it was arranged that I would come into read the truth about my baby son.

The baby had not been stillborn. When I collapsed and was unconscious my mother had given permission for the medical team to carry out a therapeutic abortion. This is where the silver bucket came in. I now know I wasn't imagining it. It had been true. I was well advanced into my pregnancy (30 weeks) and I would have had to have gone through a proper birth to abort my baby.

I could not believe my eyes. What had these people done to me? The truth was in writing. My baby had existed. Even the proper birth date was different to the one I thought I knew (I think my parents and elders deluded themselves into thinking their ways were the best) – producing strong emotions. I'm upset and it makes me question their actions. It brought back bad memories for me.

This was a nervous time but the wave of relief washing over me was so overwhelming I could feel a huge release as the pain and wondering started seeping out of my body and a lot of my insecurities and negativity I had carried for so long could be answered.

The next big step was to mark my baby's birth somehow. Planting a tree that would thrive seemed a good way to achieve this.

A letter was sent to the Parks and Gardens Department of the local council. I was invited in to discuss what sort of tree I wanted. This being in January 2007 and where I would like it to be planted. Within two months the tree had been planted (March 2007). Planted at the end of March before spring came in. The man who was helping with the tree made a suggestion for a plaque. He liaised with a local stonemason who carved out a huge piece of Yorkshire stone and made a memorial which now stands two and half feet high in front of his tree. I wrote the following inscription for the stone:

> In Loving Memory of
> A Dear Son
> Kirk Wain Lyman
> Born Asleep
> 28th June 1980
> Always in My Thoughts
> Eternally Loved Mum

All through this period I was supported by members of Beyond Existing who were eager to hear all about the developments through the 'Journey of Truth' which lasted from July 2006 to March 2007.

Once Kirk's tree and memorial stone were planted I eventually decided that I would like 'A Celebration' of Kirk's proper birthday. So on the 28th June 2007 on my son's 27th birthday members of Beyond Existing, family and close friends were invited to gather under the tree. A eulogy was given which will stay with me forever. Blue and pearl balloons which I had tied to his tree were released into the sky and flowers laid.

My family only talked to each other and didn't have the courage to invite my father (my mother is dead). As my sister reminded me I had no right to talk about family matters with other people. My sister said people would laugh at the thought of a memorial from so long ago. My brother did not attend. They still did not want to acknowledge that Kirk had existed but I have lived with this myself for 27 years.

I visit his tree often and leave flowers which the gardeners of the park take in each night and place them back in the morning. They have taken a personal pride in Kirk's tree and memorial stone and attend to it like it was their own. They always take time out to talk to me on my visits and have said that the tree and stone have moved so many visitors to the park. Strangers have laid flowers and I have met one lady who takes comfort from sitting under the tree regularly.

Now for the first time in my life the work of others during my 'Journey of Truth' has somehow been restored. I feel free. It has taken too many years for this to evolve. I feel strange about it all but instinctively feel that I have done the right thing and finally put my precious baby son to rest.

## LOUISE (Age 39)

**Abuse experienced**

Father – sexual abuse
Mother – emotional abuse
Stepfather – sexual abuse
Rape – husband of work colleague.

*Editor's comment: Louise has completed the healing process and now helps to facilitate the current women's group. Whilst going through the healing process she did a lot of writing in a journal and art therapy was also used to help her. At the time when she was dealing with really difficult memories and flashbacks she was offered one-to-one sessions for a short time (which took place immediately before the group meeting). She has written an account for this chapter but also agreed the letter she sent to her mother (she kept a photocopy) could be printed.*

I was in my late twenties before I felt ready to try and recover from the abuse I suffered as a child. I was helped by various professionals and even wrote a letter to one of my abusers telling him exactly what I thought of him but nothing really seemed to really make me feel any better.

I began attending Beyond Existing meetings and through listening to others and after a gentle push in the right direction I realised I had unresolved feelings towards my mother. I began to write her a letter at first just to work through those feelings without actually meaning to send it.

I wrote about specific events and of how I felt she had known about the abuse and had failed to protect me. I sent the letter. I was able to do this because I felt the support and encouragement of the group. I had always felt responsible for my mother but now because these were people I knew understood and believed me I could cope with any repercussions.

Shortly afterwards I had the most vivid flashback. I was standing in the kitchen about eight years old. I approached her telling of how my stepfather had been coming into my room at night, how he was making me feel. For a brief moment I felt total relief a massive weight had gone from me but then I noticed she had not looked up from her magazine still casually flicking through the pages and I knew I had told her before and had just made things worse again. But once the memory lifted I was left with a total sense of peace. I did my best. I am not to blame and now I can finally move on.

---

### Louise's letter to her mother

16.9.06

Mum

I want you to stop telephoning us because every time you do it reminds me of how you and Mandy [sister] have not stood by me and are never going to and for that reason I can never forgive either of you. In your opinion I have lied about Fred [stepfather] so I really wonder why you would want to keep in touch at all.

Fred repeatedly raped me and while he did this he told me he could do anything he wanted. The worst and last attack happened the day before I broke my ribs. You had gone shopping Mum. I had gone to lie down because I felt ill. That night I was too afraid to go upstairs alone. I asked you to go with me. I know you remember this. I was 13 years old. His actions had completely devastated me. I am now 38 years old and just beginning to recover. The memories of that day were so terrible I have struggled with life.

The abuse started when I was about 7 years old. He had tried to touch me. I had run home and told you 'Fred is a nasty man'. I was sent to my room for interrupting. He then came to our door and accused me of stealing and then you came to confront me and I pointed to the place he had tried to touch and you just backed out of the room and told me not to be so silly.

Had you acted on that first occasion I would not have had to go through any more. It was years later when I was laid in bed having broken my ribs that you wanted to know who had been in the spare room. You tried to blame it on Gail [stepsister]. You had to change the sheets on the bed. It was then that I tried to tell you again about Fred about what he had done to me and you looked at me and you said 'Are you trying to break up my marriage?' That is what you said to me Elsie. I did not think about your marriage at all I simply wanted to be safe and allowed a childhood that every child is entitled to. No, I did not tempt anyone. So now you do the decent thing and let me go.

Louise.

## PETER *(Age 36)*
### Abuse experienced
Child sexual abuse by headmaster from the age of eight.

*Editor's comments: Peter gets very emotional and finds it difficult to express himself verbally; during childhood and into adulthood he has written about his abusive experiences but not shared them. The writings have been kept hidden. He stopped writing but has now started again. He has written an account for this chapter but in addition a special piece – 'My Landscape' – about a place he goes to when he feels suicidal.*

Twenty-seven years – still seems strange to be able to identify a period of time that long at just 36. Some may get elated or proud. They may say 'I've been married 27 years' or 'I've been at the same company for 27 years'. For me, it signifies a period of time devoted to hiding a secret and appearing to be anything but what I am. I can't say I'm ashamed. I can't say I'm proud. Only that I hope I've learned from that time.

But change in this life, like evolution, is inevitable, and so came a twist of fate. To this day, looking back, my mouth still gapes slightly when I think how a simple surgical procedure began a series of events which not only changed the entire course of my life, but led to the end of my 27-year silence and ultimately to Beyond Existing.

After consulting the usual avenues in mental health care, while being treated for depression, anxiety and insomnia, I found my secret became a blaming tool for the loss of home, business, financial security, relationships and almost my children. I was despairing at the lack of confidence and trust I felt with the 'professionals' dealing with my secret. And then came a call to change my faith – Beyond Existing.

When I first sat down with Jacki, Janice and the guys in that room I was scared, but something I couldn't explain and still can't if I'm honest, made me think 'This is OK. This may be of some help.'

I've survived to some degree by being objective and logical. It's kind of like 'I don't like me' *BUT* 'I understand why I don't like me – my secret made me that way'. It's a work in progress.

It sounds crazy, but it allowed me to accept and to some degree trust in those who have a wealth of experience in a field I am only an amateur at in my own life. And after only three sessions, I quit, or rather put off while I fooled myself into believing I needed to re-build my shattered life first.

That's where Emma comes in. My closest and most trusted friend of over ten years at that time and until recently the only person outside of the professional ranks who knew my secret. But as a good friend, slowly and surely she led me back to where, in my heart, I knew I should be. In Jacki and Janice I have two guides on a road I am scared and unsure of; both different in their professional approach, yet both strong, compassionate and dedicated in their efforts. They have shown and allowed me to trust, if only a little for now, in a system that allows me to express, question, learn and hopefully, in time, begin to heal.

Fortunately for me, I have a little proof! A guy I met over three years ago in one of the first meetings I attended. A man who sat with his eyes to the ground reciting a poem, a sad but beautiful poem which he'd committed to memory through his own pain and suffering. I will never forget that image, those words and the emotion and empathy I felt as he nervously tore a tissue and touches a place in me I thought I'd buried forever.

When I came back three years later I was the first into the meeting room. That same man entered, or at least to the rest of the world he may be the same, but not to me. He met me with a confident gaze, a broad and welcoming smile lit his face. He held out his hand and we shook hands like old friends – 'Great to see you again' he said. Those few minutes, three years apart, gave me hope. If I have hope, no matter how small, I am alive and maybe just maybe I have a future beyond existing.

---

### *My landscape 5.8.07*

High above the City, away from the cars, sheltered from the noise and pollution of this life and appearance of caring, is my field, my landscape.

Fenced off and invisible to those who fleet an awkward glance at my 'quirks' and persona. Formed by the lust and perversion of one trusted by those same narrow minds.

But hey! – up here is my place, my dream and my goal. Only those who see individuality, truth of character and of course those who love without gain or question are welcome.

The air is clean and warm and always a fresh breeze to cleanse the ever clinging dirt this life would sorely drown me in, if not for this place and my solitude.

A carpet of lush, swaying green velvet wraps my tired feet and gently strokes my ills, my fears as I move lazily under a pure sky, ever changing colours to suit my every mood.

Time holds no control nor meaning. Up here I wonder free, at peace and there is no care for when I return.

There is but one feature in need in my high up escape – a rock, my rock. Chosen by chance in a vain attempt to escape a life I never asked nor cared for. I need no trees to shade or shelter, no paths to guide or trace, no instruments or buildings to distract or entertain – only my rock. And when my field has refreshed my aching soul and shaken free some debris from battle, I sit. A peaceful recline, a warm soothing sun on my back with the only noise, a constant shh and hush as my velvet sways lazily back and forth. I know no pain will consume or overcome me here.

As I look to the east I see the roots of my life. To the south, the forming of my being. Dead ahead is another rock – but not for solitude – 20 miles away, a giant. Proud and strong, a place I conquered in my youth. And below, the race, the river of all we've achieved and as the same, failed as mankind. A reminder of why I am here.

Take my hand please. I insist. Sit a while and enjoy my solitude. For you are here as my guest – welcome to my landscape.

## RON (Age 64)

### Abuse experienced

Child sexual abuse from the age of five by two men who were deaf and mute. Gross physical and emotional neglect by parents, who were alcoholics. Father was a paedophile. Mother had mental health problems and was often institutionalised.

Well I was introduced to Beyond Existing by my support worker Carol and she said it in a way that it was either nothing or something. I was absolutely frightened to death to do anything like this at all but I thought go on then

I'll give it one go and see what happens. First time I ever come I was that nervous if I could have run home I would have done. There is no doubt about it. But as time went on it were helping me and I know it was helping me. Not only to relieve myself but I thought I was helping other people by talking about something they went through like myself when I was a child and it's like a trouble shared is a trouble halved. When I listen to everybody else's versions of their lifetimes it helps me with mine. Then I know for a fact that I am not on my own like I was the first 50 years before coming to Beyond Existing. Now I feel (although I am shaking at the moment) I feel absolutely great about it because it has helped me to move on with my life because I have been able to talk to people, tell them about what happened in my life but what was stopping me going out before looking at people as if they knew everything that was written all over me – all my past and all that. It has helped me to cope with that.

I have had nightmares for 50 years or more and it's always been the same. There have been two what runs into one. Nightmare about my sexual abuse and nightmare about a cave. I think I have come to know when I have linked both of them – they have exactly the same outcome. The cave – i.e. being my mouth – and noises, i.e. what Roy and Harold used to make when they were having sex with me. Cave being my mouth when Roy were coming – he used to pull my head onto his penis and make these noises. Harold used to make noises when he was having sex with me. Of course they did not know they were making noises but I remember them noises. I have come to the conclusion that the cave is my mouth. It was just before I was passing out – I used to pass out – after the second time I passed out with Roy, Harold got rid of him. Roy was not a big part of my life – he was a very important part as to why I had nightmares in the first place because if I thought it was just Harold I might not have had nightmares – I don't know. It is always with Roy never Harold.

Beyond Existing it is a like a life saver to me. I get a lot out of being able to vent me spleen. Knowing that when I go home that I can come back again and people will not look down on me. It has helped me to cope in the outside world a bit better like going to the centre for physiotherapy because I would not have let anyone touch me in the past. It has helped me to unwind my mind with poetry. I can sit and diagnose a situation and put a better face on it. When I am doing a poem – the majority of the poems are about me, so when I say I am venting my spleen I am putting them down. I have been able to put them since I became a member of Beyond Existing a lot better. I feel a lot more freer.

I feel able to go on better. Although I get spinny things and things do happen to me I sit down and look at my wife and think well that's not real. After a while it settles down. I am beginning to put my thoughts and my dreams in context. I am hoping I am going to come to a conclusion and everything I can cope with in the future.

*Editor's comment: Beyond Existing keeps a separate file of all the poems Ron brings to meetings. He often recites from memory which other men have found fascinating. I have read out 'Stigma' (with Ron's permission) at many conferences when I have been lecturing and people have asked for copies of it to use with their own service users. I felt it should be published in this book so more people can make use of it but also it seemed a powerful message with which to end this chapter.*

---

### My pen pal the nib

This tale is told by my pen pal the nib,
Famous for telling the most fabulous fibs,
Although unlikely to be true,
My pal, will pen, what my nib can do.
Cross over oceans, as if they were streams,
Give full vent to your wildest dreams
Travel to a star and back again,
Take the hardest of knocks, feel no pain.
Tickle the belly of a rainbow trout,
Make raging rivers from snuff-dry drought.
Shower the poor with gold and riches,
Create heavenly angels,
From black-hearted witches.
Take you everywhere no-one's ever seen,
Go anywhere no-one's ever been.
But they are only words, at the end of the day,
No matter what my nib may say.
Hugs, kisses, they cannot replace,
Or that tender look on a loved one's face.

---

### Stigma

Please listen you, that think you are sane
Well think, think again.
Think of the plight of such as we,
Who suffer the pain of stigma, indignity.
For misery is the price we must pay
When our minds, with their thoughts, go astray.
Think of the distress caused by a passing remark,
That you dismiss, as just a lark,
Being totally ignored, when we try to speak.
Treat us like some kind of freak.
Then point a finger, laugh out loud.
Should we mutter to ourselves,
While under a dark cloud.
But what really does hurt, makes us cry
When we are not believed, that we are living a lie,
Let us remind you of a fact we know to be true,
Our illness can strike anyone from out of the blue.
So before you put us down with that knowing stare,
Or turn your back as if not to care,
Just think how different life could be,
If we were you, and you were we.

## NOTE

1   All the writings presented in this chapter are the original work of the survivors; they have not been edited in any way at all. The editor's comments are shown in italics.

2   Taxis are booked for some members to transport them to the group meetings. A small taxi firm is used so the same drivers – who understand the work of Beyond Existing – can be used and trusting relationships are developed.

3   Sam spoke on the telephone to a facilitator one hour before a meeting was due to start. After a brief discussion about Beyond Existing Sam decided she wanted to attend that meeting rather than having to wait another month.

4   Carol has been a member of Beyond Existing for four years. She has attended different groups run by Beyond Existing during that time. The first group she ever attended was the largest group ever run – having ten members. This did not work well and has never been repeated.

# LIST OF CONTRIBUTORS

**Ghizala Avan** has a background in psychology and equality and discrimination issues and was a research fellow on the project discussed in the chapter. She has been involved on a number of other research projects with various academic institutions, voluntary organisations and public authorities such as Strathclyde University, (Scottish Institute for Residential Child Care), Save the Children and Glasgow City Council (on topics such as staff morale in Scottish residential child care, experiences of children and families of asylum seeker communities in Glasgow, self-harm and young women, and domestic abuse and forced marriage issues).

**Alison Bowes** is Professor of Sociology in the Department of Applied Social Science at the University of Stirling. Her research areas have covered minority ethnic groups and their access to housing, health and social care services, as well as older people's quality of life and social care and support. She publishes extensively in these areas.

**Seena Fazel** is Clinical Senior Lecturer in Forensic Psychiatry at the University of Oxford, and Honorary Consultant Forensic Psychiatrist with Oxfordshire and Buckinghamshire Partnership Mental Health NHS Trust. His research interests include the mental health of prisoners, the epidemiology of mental illness and violent crime and older offenders.

**Gary Fitzgerald** has been with Action on Elder Abuse since 2001, having previously worked for over 20 years within Local Government Social Care provision for older people. He holds strong views on the rights of people to maintain control and influence over their lives, regardless of age or disability. He is from an Irish background and has a special interest in equality and social inclusion issues, particularly in relation to aspects of abuse and societal prejudices. He has spoken in the United Kingdom and Ireland on elder abuse and regularly contributes to radio and television programmes on the subject.

**Adrian Hayes** is a researcher at the Prison Health Research Network, at the University of Manchester. He has worked in research on forensic psychiatry and prison health for the last few years after a first degree in psychology and a master's in research methods. His interests have focused on suicide and self-harm in prisons, and transitions between prison, secure psychiatric services and the community. He is currently completing a PhD into the health and social needs of older adults in North West prisons. Adrian is also chair of trustees for a charity sending volunteer teachers to rural projects in Asia.

**Adrian J. Hughes** is a qualified social worker and is registered with the General Social Care Council. He has worked in social care settings for over 30 years and since 1993 has been involved in the regulation of care services. At the creation of the Commission for Social Care Inspection he was appointed as a Business Relationship Manager in the south of England. He has worked as a provider and purchaser of care services and as a training officer working in both the public and independent sectors. These roles have enabled him to value the unique contribution training has on quality and safe services for people whose circumstances sometimes increase their vulnerability.

**Deborah Kitson** was a social worker with children and adults with learning disabilities before being appointed as Implementation Officer for Nottinghamshire Protection Procedures. She assisted in the production of the guidelines and is now a consultant for other agencies developing policies and guidelines on sexuality and the protection of people with learning disabilities. Deborah was the coordinator of the Ann Craft Trust and was appointed as the Trust's Director in February 2002. She is author and editor of a number of publications including *Facing the Possibility*, *Child Protection Handbook*, *Training to Protect* and *The Age of Inquiry*. She was also a member of the Steering Group of *No Secrets* and is the external representative on a number of Adult Protection Committees.

**Simon Leslie** is a solicitor with the Joint Legal Team in Berkshire. Based in Reading, the Team provide legal advice and representation to children's and adult social care in a consortium of local authorities in Berkshire. Professional interests include mental health and mental capacity, consent to treatment, and information-sharing. Simon has taken a particular interest in the legal aspects of adult protection for a number of years and contributed a chapter to *Elder Abuse Work: Best Practice in Britain and Canada* (Jessica Kingsley Publishers 1999). Simon spends his leisure time ferrying two children to birthday parties and standing on rugby touch lines in the rain.

**Sherry Bien Macintosh** is a research fellow in the Department of Applied Social Science, University of Stirling. She has a wide experience of working with older black and minority ethnic people, the wider community and people with disabilities. She consults with them on a wide range of community care, housing and health service issues focused on service development, provision and delivery to users and their carers in Central Scotland, Glasgow and Edinburgh.

**Jamieson Mornington** was educated at Merchant Taylors' School in Crosby, Liverpool, and it was here that he first developed a keen interest in politics after being taught General Studies GCSE lessons by the now Liberal Democrat MP for Southport, John Pugh. However, it was whilst reading Economics and Politics at the University of Manchester that his fascination with the post-war political environment in Britain really matured under the guidance of Professor Andrew Russell. After a year out, he returned to Manchester to complete a Masters in Governance and Public Policy, during which time he wrote extensively on the record of the New Labour Government in respect of the promotion of good governance within Britain. Away from academia, from a very early age Jamieson has had a passion for sport, particularly both codes of rugby and Gaelic games.

**Marilyn Mornington** LLB (HONS) SHEFF; FWAAS; FRSA: as well as working as a District Judge in Barnsley, Marilyn is a member of ACPO Domestic Violence and Honour-Based Violence Steering Groups; member of the Family Justice Council and Chair of the Domestic Violence Working Group; Founder and Chair of the Inter-Jurisdictional Governmental Domestic Violence Initiative 'Raising the Standards'; and Patron of the Community District Nurses' Association. She is a lecturer and writer on Family Law and, in particular, domestic violence and elder abuse – nationally and internationally. During 2007 Marilyn lectured at the London School of Economics, the Commonwealth Institute, Sheffield University, Punjab Law School and Cranfield Defence College.

**Lucy Naven** is a Senior Case Manager at J.S. Parker and Associates, Sheffield office. She is an advanced member of the British Association of Brain Injury Case Managers (BABICM). She qualified as a Chartered Occupational Psychologist in 2001 having worked as a Practitioner in Training since 1998. Her professional background is working with people with a variety of disabilities, specialising fully in traumatic brain injury in 2000. Lucy has experience of working with adults in the community and in residential rehabilitation settings.

**Arwel Wyn Owen** is Principal Officer with the Isle of Anglesey County Council and has specific responsibility for Planning and Commissioning Services. He has 17 years' experience of working within the public and voluntary sectors and is currently involved in reorganising and devolving day services from a traditional day centre to new community-based resources and also has responsibility for developing an integrated community equipment store in North West Wales. Married with two small children, Arwel has a wide range of interests and contributes to Welsh language publications on local history and collecting. He is a self-confessed hoarder, who has a passion for car boot and antique fairs.

**Jackie Parker** is a registered social worker, specialising in the field of brain injury. Since 1995 she has worked independently as a brain injury case manager. She is a past chair of the British Association of Brain Injury Case Managers (BABICM) and is a partner of J.S. Parker and Associates and a Director of JSP Manchester and JSP Training, companies providing case management, community rehabilitation and support worker training. Jackie regularly speaks at conferences and workshops on brain injury case management and is the editor of *Good Practice in Brain Injury Case Management* (Jessica Kingsley Publishers 2006).

**Jacki Pritchard** practises as an independent social worker and is registered with the General Social Care Council. She is Director of the company Jacki Pritchard Ltd which provides training, consultancy, research in social care and also produces training materials. Jacki specialises in working with victims of abuse and was the founder of the organisation Beyond Existing, Support Groups for Adults Who Have Been Abused. She is currently working on the research project: 'The Abuse of Vulnerable Adults: Services for Victims of Abuse'. Jacki has written widely on the subject of adult protection and been Series Editor of the Good Practice Series, Jessica Kingsley Publishers, for the past 15 years.

**Peter Sadler** qualified as a registered nurse in the field of Learning Disability in November 1982. He has worked both within National Health and Social Services settings; working with vulnerable adults in residential services, day services and community support services. Peter has a wide range of experience within operational management, strategic planning and development. He has been interested in the adult protection/safeguarding agenda from the early 1990s and has been directly involved in the safeguarding agenda within Lincolnshire and regional forums since 2001, when he was the first project manager supporting the Lincolnshire Adult Protection Committee in developing Lincolnshire's first multi-agency policy post *No Secrets*. Peter presents at workshops and conferences within Lincolnshire and also enjoys leading training and development workshops. From March 2008 Lincolnshire County Council have separated the safeguarding manager post into two parts, one being responsible for the operational delivery of the safeguarding team and the other to lead on the safeguarding strategic agenda. Peter was asked to lead on the strategic agenda which includes supporting the development of a new Safeguarding Board for Lincolnshire, the creation of a strategy for raising awareness of abuse, and quality monitoring of the safeguarding team/service.

# SUBJECT INDEX

# Author Index

Action on Elder Abuse
    16–17, 18, 23
Aday, R.H. 141
Allison, E. 140
Ann Craft Trust (ACT)
    133
Association of Chief Police
    Officers 60, 101
Association of Directors of
    Social Services 9, 18,
    45, 48, 60, 101, 122,
    193
Avan, G. 83

Baker, A. 13
Barron, J. 72
Biggs, S. 85
Blair, Tony 65
Bowes, A. 83, 85
Brearley, C.P. 193
Brown, H. 13
Burgner, T. 126
Butt, J. 85

Campbell, D. 140
Care Services Improvement
    Partnership 128
Challis, D. 104
Clark-Wilson, J. 152
Commission for Social
    Care Inspection
    (CSCI) 18, 60, 101,
    108, 113, 124
Community and District
    Nursing Association
    (CDNA) 73
Corbett, A. 125
Criminal Justice System
    10, 57

Dar, N.S. 85
Department of
    Constitutional Affairs
    69, 158, 163
Department of Health 9,
    10, 18, 20, 24, 28, 45,
    57, 60, 104, 121, 122,
    125, 139, 140, 144,
    145, 146, 151, 154,
    157, 193, 197
Department of Health
    (Social Services
    Inspectorate) 14

Eade, J. 85
Eastman, M. 13
Evans, S. 121

Fazel, S. 141, 143
Fielding, S. 67
Frazer, L. 144, 145
Fyson, R. 125

Garner, J. 121

Hall, T. 69, 72, 74
Harper, S. 85
Harvie, L. 91
Hayes, A.J. 141
Healthcare Commission
    124, 129, 130, 132
Her Majesty's Inspectorate
    of Prisons 139, 140,
    142, 143
Hildrew, M.A. 13
Home Office 9, 10, 20, 24,
    45, 66, 121, 125, 139,

140, 144, 145, 154,
    193, 197
House of Commons 135
House of Commons/Health
    Committee 20
House of Commons/House
    of Lords 20, 24

Jacoby, R. 141
Joint Committee on Human
    Rights 24
Joint Prison Service and
    NHS Executive
    Working Group 147

Katz, I. 140
Keating, F. 24
Kingston, P. 85
Kitson, D. 9, 125
Kosberg, J.I. 85

Law Commission 14
Lincolnshire Adult
    Protection Committee
    45, 49
Livingstone, Ken 69

Macintosh, S. B. 83
McMillan, J. 143
McPherson of Cluny, W.
    68
Mencap 132–3
Mirza, K. 85
MissDorothy.com 74
Mornington, J. 9–10
Mornington, M. 9–10

For enquiries or renewal at
Quarles LRC
**Tel: 01708 455011 – Extension 4009**